LIFE IN
MR. LINCOLN'S
NAVY

LIFE IN
MR. LINCOLN'S
NAVY

Dennis J. Ringle

Naval Institute Press
Annapolis, Maryland

Library of Congress Cataloging-in-Publication Data
Ringle, Dennis J., 1954–
     Life in Mr. Lincoln's navy / Dennis J. Ringle.
          p.   cm.
          Includes bibliographical references and index.
          ISBN 1-55750-736-8 (alk. paper)
          1. United States. Navy—Sea life. 2. United
     States. Navy—History—Civil War, 1861–1865.
     3. United States. Navy—Recruiting, enlistment,
     etc.—Civil War, 1861–1865. 4. United States—
     History—Civil War, 1861–1865—Naval operations.
     5. United States—History—Civil War,
     1861–1865—Social aspects. I. Title.
     V736.R55   1998
     973.7'5—dc21   98-15352

497 7076

Printed in the United States of America on acid-free
paper ∞

05 04 03 02 01 00 99 98   9 8 7 6 5 4 3 2
First printing

Unless otherwise noted, all photographs are from the U.S. Naval Historical Center.

To the enlisted engineers, and in particular to the former rating of Boiler Technician (BT). Although their rating, like that of the coal heavers before them, is no more, their contributions to the success of our Navy and freedom on the high seas will not be forgotten.

Contents

Acknowledgments

I am deeply indebted to a number of people whose assistance and support made *Life in Mr. Lincoln's Navy* possible. First I extend a sincere, heartfelt thanks to my sister, Diane Potts, whose moral support and encouragement over the years made this work possible. Additionally, her twenty-plus years as a registered nurse specializing in disease control proved to be invaluable in my research on the chapter dealing with nautical medicine.

I would like to thank Dr. Richard H. Abbott for his guidance, outstanding knowledge of the Civil War period, and willingness to support me in such an ambitious project. I am also grateful to Dr. H. Roger King, consummate social historian, who continued to provide encouragement and critical analyses of my work, and Dr. Richard Goff, whose knowledge of Civil War logistics and research methodology aided me in my in-depth analyses of a wealth of material. In addition, I would like to thank Dr. George H. Cassar, who encouraged me to pursue an avenue of historical research that would eventually lead to this book, and Dr. L. Gimelli, superb nineteenth-century historian.

A continual source of guidance and assistance was Dr. Craig L. Symonds, longtime mentor and friend. Not only was his editing of Alvah Hunter's journal informative, his work spawned many additional ideas concerning the life of the common sailor. I am also grateful to several other professional historians for their assistance. Dr. Joseph Reidy's review of this book and work on the black sailor in the Civil War was invaluable to me in constructing a major portion of chapter 2 on recruiting. Dr. Edward Frugal from the Naval Historical Center allowed me access to a number of original sailors' artifacts and documents. Ms. Rebecca Livingston, National Archives military reference branch, helped me navigate through the plethora of primary source material.

The University of Michigan is fortunate to have one of the finest library staffs in the nation, and in particular Ms. Denise Schoene of the government documents section. Her knowledge, research acumen, and logic in working with government documents were vital in my research, particularly in exploring the interface between government policy and its actual application aboard ship. Additional support from the University of Michigan includes the professional staff of the William L. Clements Library, Dr. John Dann, Arlene Shy, and John Harriman.

A number of individuals and research institutes helped make this book possible, including Jeff Johnston of the National Oceanic and Atmospheric Administration, Monitor National Marine Sanctuary Division; the research library and archives staff at the Mariners Museum, Newport News, Virginia; Jason Tomberlin of the Special Collections Library, Duke University; Barbara Mann Wall, Saint Mary's College, Department of Nursing, Notre Dame; Dr. Dale Smith, Uniformed Services University of Health Sciences; the staff of the U.S. Naval Historical Center, Photograph Department; and the staff of the Civil War Library and Museum, Philadelphia.

I also received enormous support from my former commanding officer of the University of Michigan's Navy ROTC unit, Capt. Michael Riordan. His timely critique and my access to his personal library of rare primary source material were critical to the development of the manuscript. Additional military personnel who variously contributed to my work include my former commanding officer from the USS *Cook* (FF 1083)—Captain Larry Penix—and the Honorable Wade Sanders, Deputy Assistant for the Secretary of the Navy, both of whom provided logistical and research support; and Maj. Mark Snell, USA (Ret.), Director of the Shepherd College George Tyler Moore Center for the Study of the Civil War; Lt. Cdr. Asa Morton, M.D.; Capt. Robert Johnston, Commanding Officer at the University of Michigan, NROTC; Lt. Wanda Gunderson; CPO Robert Bowmen; and CPO Gregory Bonner.

A special thanks is also in order for many friends who assisted me in my endeavors, including Dr. Penny Pierce, R.N., Ph.D.; Dr. Gerald Linderman and Dr. Paul Forage from the University of Michigan; Dr. Hal Friedman from Henry Ford Community College; Tom Nanzig, author, historian, and archivist who provided a series of timely recommendations and access to numerous historical documents; Frank Mansfield, former member of the Royal Navy, who aided me in my research of the common British tar during our Civil War period; William Lowe, colleague, friend, classmate, and historian; and Ens. Kevin Branson, who provided me with research assistance at the Navy Historical Center. Finally, I had the honor to have Ms. Patricia Boyd as the editor of this book. Her professionalism was greatly appreciated. Thank you.

Introduction

In 1943, noted Civil War historian Bell Irvin Wiley published his land-mark book *The Life of Johnny Reb: The Common Soldier of the Confederacy.* For the first time since the guns had fallen silent almost eighty years earlier, an author and historian had finally written a book dedicated exclusively to the men who bore the brunt of the war, the common soldiers. Nine years later, Wiley published a study of Johnny Reb's adversary, *The Life of Billy Yank.* These two superb books dealing with the social history of the enlisted soldier opened up new areas for future research. Since the initial publications of his two books, many distinguished historians and authors have published volumes of articles and books dealing with the various aspects of the life of the common soldier, both North and South. Unfortunately, historians have all but ignored the life of the common sailors and the vital role they played during the war.

Life in Mr. Lincoln's Navy is the first in-depth study covering all aspects of the common sailor's life in the Union navy, including recruiting, clothing, training, daily shipboard routine, diet, wages, entertainment, health, and combat experiences. The book also provides the first glance into the life of the fledgling world of steam engineering. The contributions of the men assigned to the engineering division proved critical to the success of the wartime ironclad monitors and the development of the powerful pre-dreadnought ships two decades later.

This study of the life of the common sailor provides a fresh look at the social history of the nineteenth century. In addition, the book clearly illustrates the enormous contributions that the common sailor made toward the development of the U.S. Navy at the end of the century by successfully providing the transition from wood and sail to steam and iron. Without the sailors' hard work, sacrifice, dedication, and professionalism, the emergence of the United States as a world power would not have been possible at such an early period.

In *Life in Mr. Lincoln's Navy* I have focused on the enlisted men assigned to the navy vessels operating on the western rivers, running along the coast enforcing the blockade, and dispatched elsewhere to destroy the Confederate commerce raiders. In addition, as a result of the plethora of books about the life of the common soldier during the Civil War, I sometimes found it challenging and informative to compare the lifestyles of the two rival services. I have also made several comparisons regarding pay, food, and discipline between the Union sailor and his foreign counterpart serving in the British Royal Navy. My twenty-one years of active naval service, including four steam engineering assignments and one executive officer tour, allowed me the unique opportunity to compare our modern navy with the Civil War Union navy. I have remarked on these comparisons in several footnotes throughout the book. Amazingly, I discovered many similarities between the two periods.

I drew upon numerous published and unpublished letters, diaries, journals, laws, and regulations to reconstruct the life of the common Union sailor. In addition, I extracted a wealth of information from several ships' logs. These documents provided a daily history of ships and contained important information about the daily life of the men serving on them. Today the navy continues to use these unique and valuable logbooks (which are legal records in a court of law) to document the various activities aboard ship.

The interpretation of several excellent photographs taken during the Civil War provided another vital source of information in constructing the life of the sailor. The cliché "One picture is worth a thousand words" was true in supporting several passages in my manuscript. The images of the various sailors' uniforms and how the men personalized their clothing were only a few of many images that reinforce the text and provide information about the unique way of life at sea.

Life in Mr. Lincoln's Navy covers every aspect of the common sailor's life at sea. The first chapter surveys the major social reform movements in the navy during the antebellum period. The development of professional enlisted cadre required the navy to improve the daily life of the sailor by abolishing flogging and by increasing pay so that the naval service could compete with the nation's expanding merchant fleet for skilled seafaring men. In addition, the development and growth of steam engineering required the navy to increase its recruiting efforts to meet the challenges of the new technical world of marine engineering. On the eve of the Civil War, some of the naval reform movements had enabled the navy to recruit and retain a small but professional force of sailors capable of meeting the demands of a rapidly expanding service brought on by the necessity of war.

The next nine chapters deal with the various aspects of the common sailor's life, from recruiting to combat. Chapter 2 looks at the different ways that the navy recruited, including its integration of runaway slaves into the service. The navy's ability to recruit runaway slaves not only helped it fill its ships' manifests, but also influenced the government's, and in particular the army's, policy toward the use of this new labor force. The chapter also covers the sometimes humorous attempts to recruit foreigners, and the influence of the draft on the navy's efforts to recruit American citizens.

Chapters 3 and 4 follow the transformation of a civilian recruit into a sailor. Chapter 4 also introduces the reader to the claustrophobic world of the new ironclad monitors and the life of the rapidly expanding steam engineering division. The fifth chapter covers in great detail the daily training received by the tars in seamanship, firefighting, and general quarters (combat training).

Chapter 6 analyzes the quality, variety, and quantity of food consumed by the tar at sea. The navy's dedicated efforts to provide an efficient logistical system ensured that the Union sailor was the best-fed warrior in the world. Chapter 7 describes what the sailor did with his precious few hours of free time and some of the mischief he got into while on liberty.

Although the navy attempted to provide a more humane atmosphere for the enlisted man throughout the decades before the Civil War, naval wages still lagged behind the civilian sector's and discipline remained harsh for the common sailor. Chapter 8 first addresses the changes in the sailor's wages, from the first recognition of arduous sea duty to the increase in pay for serving aboard the *Monitor*-class ships. Later the chapter deals with navy discipline and how the system worked aboard ship.

Chapter 9 compares the navy's amazingly low morbidity and illness rate due to disease with those of the army throughout the war. The navy's remarkable medical record was due to foresight, astute observations, increased education of its surgeons, and the use of new technology. Also discussed are various diseases common at sea and how the navy treated them.

In chapter 10, I compare how the men in the army and navy endured the terrible ordeal of combat. The final chapter, "Legacy," discusses the enormous contributions the Union sailor made in influencing the outcome of the war. Perhaps most important, the chapter shows the common sailor's influence on the development of the pre-dreadnought navy, an important precursor to the emergence of the United States as a world power.

I hope that, as Bell Wiley's books did for the army, *Life in Mr. Lincoln's Navy* inspires an interest in the daily life of the common sailor. This book is only the "tip of the iceberg." Considering the wealth of information available to the dedicated historian, each chapter has the potential to develop into an independent work. In addition, since this book deals only with the Union enlisted sailor, future naval studies could expand to include the life of the Confederate sailor.

1

The Antebellum Navy

When the American Civil War ended in 1865, at a cost of over six hundred thousand lives and untold human suffering,[1] officers, politicians, and historians substituted the pen for the sword and the rifled musket and embarked on a campaign to inform society of the heroic actions of the war's participants. Most books published over the next 130 years concentrated on the exploits of the army, its officers, and the political leaders who directed the nation during the conflict. Unfortunately, these writers ignored the contributions of the Union navy, and in particular the life and contributions of the enlisted sailor.

President Abraham Lincoln's call for a blockade of the Confederate coastline and the accumulation of additional wartime duties required the U.S. Navy to expand rapidly. The navy's ability to recruit men from all walks of life, with the majority of the recruits possessing little or no maritime background, filled the manifest of the proliferating fleet. What is more important, however, was the navy's ability to weld this heterogeneous group of men into an efficient fighting force that helped defeat the South. In addition, these men successfully ushered in the age of iron ships and laid the foundation for America's emergence as a global power by the end of the century.

During the Civil War, approximately 118,000 men served in the Union navy, blockading over 3,500 miles of southern coastline, convoying merchant ships, pursuing Confederate commerce raiders, and conducting combined operations with the Union army.[2] This rapid expansion of forces and missions was the product of necessity, opportunity, the vision of a few, and most importantly the sweat and ingenuity of the enlisted sailors. Every aspect of the sailor's background and life—from his recruitment, clothing, and training to his wages, daily shipboard routine, entertainment, diet, medical treatment, and combat experience—influenced his performance at sea and helped pave the way to final victory.

The common sailor who served in Mr. Lincoln's navy during the war enjoyed a better quality of life than did his predecessor in the antebellum navy. The technological advances in steam engineering and the development of ironclad ships substantially enhanced shipboard life. Of greater importance during the decades preceding the Civil War, a handful of dedicated men and women embarked on a reform campaign to improve the living conditions of the common sailor.

The impetus for this campaign came from Congress's concern about the increasing number of foreign sailors serving in the U.S. Navy during the War of 1812. To alleviate this reliance on foreign sailors, Congress enacted legislation in March 1813 permitting only American citizens, blacks, and natives of the United States to serve on board navy ships and private vessels.[3] To replace the foreigners, the navy appealed to the patriotism of the American citizens and offered sailors prize money for enemy vessels captured.

When the Treaty of Ghent, which ended the war with Great Britain, removed the lure of prize money, hundreds of enlisted men returned to their civilian communities. Other able-bodied tars opted for the better pay and living conditions on privately owned merchant vessels. The navy soon realized that if it was to compete with the merchant service for recruits, it would have to improve the living conditions aboard its own ships. In the decades following the war, some navy officers, with the critical assistance of several political activists and congressmen, embarked on an ambitious naval reform program dedicated to improving the living conditions aboard navy ships.[4]

In this effort, naval reformers drew inspiration and assistance from the proliferation of reform movements that swept civilian society in the United States during the first half of the nineteenth century. Naval reformers solicited the services and assets of the religious, temperance, prison, and abolitionist civilian reform movements to improve the quality of life for the sailors. To improve the sailor's life aboard ship, the reformers had to attack simultaneously several perceived vices that they believed discouraged men from joining the navy. Naval reformers believed that the key to success lay in their ability to improve the sailor's religious awareness, to increase his pay, to abolish flogging, and to eliminate the "spirit" ration aboard ship.[5]

Ironically, the first naval reformers concentrated their efforts on improving the sailor's life on shore and not aboard ship. The early reformers mainly consisted of chaplains and other clergy and women. These individuals believed that spiritual salvation was beyond the sailor's realm unless they removed the sinful temptations of prostitutes, alcohol, and "con men" from the sailor's life in port because the sailor's transgressions were most visible when he was ashore.[6] Initially, the religious reformers lacked a medium for spreading their message. In 1825, a group of prominent citizens, influenced by the work of the religious naval reformers, founded the American Seaman's Friend Society, dedicated to improving the living conditions of sailors. Within two years of its founding, the organization produced the influential *Sailor's Magazine and Naval Journal*. The magazine grew in popularity among the tars and became the primary propaganda tool for the religious reformers and the American Seaman's Friend Society.[7]

Besides the publication of the *Sailor's Magazine and Naval Journal*, the Seaman's Society provided respectable lodging for sailors while they waited for their ship's arrival in port. Funded by the society, these new boardinghouses contained small libraries consisting of bibles and religious tracts. The homes also operated small banks and provided nonalcoholic beverages.[8] For a sailor away from his home, the boardinghouses provided a comfortable and safe alternative to most of the vices available to the sailor in seaport towns. Although the religious naval reform took years to gain momentum, it did not lose energy as did the civilian evangelical crusade in the late 1830s.[9] The naval movement continued to carry the social reform banner for the sailor throughout the antebellum period.

In the 1830s, the religious movement prepared to expand its reform platform and tackled a more sensitive political issue, the abolishment of flogging on board ship. Since the navy's inception in 1775, its officers had relied on flogging as the primary means of punishing a sailor. The navy permitted its commanding officers to "award" a sailor a maximum of twelve lashes on his bare back for violating a variety of rules and regulations.[10] Among other things, a sailor received a whipping for indulging in profanity, becoming drunk, fighting, beating a black sailor, smoking after taps, or not washing.[11] The civilian community also liberally used the whip on slaves and in prisons during the antebellum period.[12]

As early as 1820, however, the naval reformers, with the support of several Northern legislators, tried to eliminate flogging from the navy as an inhumane and immoral practice.[13] In that year, naval reformers failed in their first attempt to influence Congress to approve a law abolishing flogging in the navy. The majority of the votes sustaining the practice of flogging came from Southern legislators, who were logically concerned that the abolishment of flogging in the navy would raise questions about the use of whips to discipline slaves.[14]

Opponents of flogging welcomed the support in the 1840s from the growing antislavery movement. Naval reformers drew similarities between the terrible life of a slave and a sailor, and as the abolitionist movement gained momentum, so did the naval reform movement in its effort to abolish flogging.[15] In 1848, the navy reported to Congress that it had awarded 5,936 floggings during the period 1846–47. Several members of Congress, shocked by the alarming number of floggings, renewed their efforts to abolish flogging in the navy. As the months passed, the number of individuals supporting the reform grew.[16]

Finally, in the late summer of 1850, the House of Representatives approved the abolishment of flogging by a wide margin.[17] In the Senate, the vote was much closer, with the measure passing by a narrow two-vote margin. Northern congressmen cast all twenty-six votes supporting the abolishment of flogging. The final victory of naval reformers was due to the increased awareness of the abolitionist movement and the "spirit of compromise" in the air after the recent passage of the Missouri Compromise.[18] Naval reformers had achieved a major victory in the battle to improve the quality of life for the sailor on board ships.

Naval reformers received even stiffer opposition from Congress when they attempted to abolish the "spirit" ration issued to the sailors aboard ship. In 1740, Adm. Edward Vernon of the Royal Navy introduced to the British navy a beverage consisting of a half-pint of rum and one quart of water. Admiral Vernon believed that the mixture would reduce the inebriating effects because the larger amount of liquid prevented the sailor from consuming the alcohol in one swallow. The tars, pleased with their new alcoholic drink, called it "grog" in honor of Admiral Vernon, who frequently wore a cape made of grogram cloth.[19]

At its inception during the American Revolution, the fledgling U.S. Navy adopted this traditional beverage. In 1806, in a move to purchase items made in the United States, the navy substituted American-made whiskey for rum. Although the type of alcohol changed, U.S. sailors still referred to their spirit ration as grog. The American tar, like his British counterpart, received a total daily ration of eight ounces: four ounces in the morning and four additional ounces in the afternoon. Initially the navy placed no age limit on who received the grog ration.[20]

The first person to advocate the removal of grog on board ship was Dr. Benjamin Rush, a distinguished physician and early leader of the civilian temperance movement.[21] Rush enlightened the public through lectures and published articles about the negative influence of alcohol on the health of an individual. In 1828, the *Sailor's Magazine* published temperance articles calling for the end of grog in the navy.[22]

A year later, several members of Congress, influenced by the naval and civilian temperance movement, proposed legislation calling for an increase in the sailors' pay in lieu of their coveted grog ration. Congress defeated the bill, and again the voting was regional. The Southern congressmen opposed the bill, believing the government did not have the right to legislate moral values. Farm lobbyists from the west also opposed the reform. For years western farmers had sold their surplus grain to distilleries, which in turn sold a portion of their spirits to the navy.[23] Congress continued to defeat the abolishment of grog throughout the 1830s. In 1842, partly because of the continued effort of the naval reformers and the civilian temperance movement, Congress passed a bill reducing the amount of whiskey from eight ounces to four. The legislators also stipulated that only enlisted men twenty-one years or older could draw the grog ration.[24]

In 1848, when the navy published the number of floggings awarded to sailors, Congress noted that almost 80 percent of the floggings were due to alcohol-related abuses.[25] The number of congressmen in favor of the grog ration, however, remained large enough to defeat any legislation recommending the elimination of the ration. Naval reformers would have to wait until the outbreak of the Civil War and the abdication of the Southern congressmen before they could muster enough votes to abolish grog in the navy.

Despite the improvements in the sailor's lifestyle in the early nineteenth century, low wages remained the principle obstacle inhibiting enlistments in the navy. This issue also drew the attention of the naval reform movement. This time the reformers had to influence not only Congress, but the president of the United States. Although the navy periodically issued small bonuses to sailors from its annual operating budget, the president controlled the tar's annual salary. In 1820, an able seaman received only $12.00 a month, an ordinary seaman $10.00, and a boy $7.00. To compete with the merchant marine for sailors the navy routinely authorized bonuses ranging from $2.00 to $3.00 for enlisting, but the small bonuses failed to provide enough incentive to ensure a constant flow of recruits.

In 1854, following years of aggressive lobbying by naval reformers, President Franklin Pierce authorized wages comparable to those in the merchant service. After thirty-four years without a wage increase, the tars enjoyed a substantial pay raise. Able seamen now received $18.00 a month, ordinary seaman $14.00, and even the boy rating pay increased a dollar a month.[26] To create a career naval force, the navy also continued the practice of awarding bonuses to sailors. In 1855, as a reenlistment incentive, the navy authorized a payment of three months' wages to a sailor if he reenlisted within three months of his discharge.[27]

The battle for increased pay was not the only naval monetary reform movement of this period. In 1842, Congress passed a law that eliminated the profits accrued by the ship's purser for merchandise sold to sailors on board naval vessels.[28] Before passage of this law, pursers procured their merchandise from civilian merchants. Acting as a retail agent, the purser resold the items to the tars. This practice allowed the purser to pocket all profits from his sales. Since the ship's purser operated the only store on board ship, he enjoyed a unique monopoly and usually sold items to the sailors at inflated prices. In view of the paltry wages earned by the sailor, it was not unusual for a sailor to return from a deployment in debt to the price-gouging purser. The passage of this new law stipulated that the purser procure his merchandise using public funds. As a result, the purser could no longer pocket his profits. As compensation for the lost revenue, the navy increased the purser's salary from $480 a year to a handsome $1,500 to $3,500 a year.[29]

From 1816 through 1850, the efforts of naval reformers greatly enhanced the quality of life for the common sailor and improved the navy's ability to meet its manning requirements. The sum of these reforms was essential to develop the navy as a career option for proven sailors. The abolishment of flogging, increased pay, fixed prices for items bought at sea, respectable boardinghouses, and a reduction in the grog ration and the age limitation on the ration all contributed to increased enlistments and the establishment of a career-oriented enlisted force in the navy. Many men, finding the navy of the 1850s a more humane place to apply their nautical skills, reenlisted in the navy instead of joining the merchant force. These career men provided an important nucleus for the navy as the service rapidly expanded during the Civil War.

Although naval reformers achieved most of their goals during the antebellum period, the parallel achievements of scientists and engineers were equally critical to improving the life of the common sailor. In the summer of 1815, the navy commissioned the world's first sail- and steam-powered warship, USS *Fulton*. Although *Fulton* successfully passed her sea trials, the navy placed her in ordinary in 1816.[30] The brief success of *Fulton* provided the foundation for future navy ships powered by sail and steam. In 1837, the navy commissioned its second sail- and steam-powered warship, USS *Fulton II*. The vessel enjoyed relative success during her twenty-five year career. Included in her laurels was her defeat of the British steamer *Great Western* in a race off the New York coast.[31]

When Capt. Matthew C. Perry assumed command of *Fulton II* in 1837, he recommended to the navy that the crew on a steam warship include a complement of engineers. He established as a minimum complement, five engineering officers, twelve firemen, and ten coal heavers. Foreseeing the potential professional friction between the fledgling engineering division and the well-established deck divisions, Perry recommended that the engineering division remain autonomous from the deck divisions. He even went so far as to provide equal status to the engineering officers and allowed them to live in the officers' quarters.[32] Under Perry's tutelage, *Fulton II*'s engineering performance inspired enough confidence in the navy's hierarchy to lead the navy to embark on an even more ambitious combined sail- and steam-powered shipbuilding program.

Although *Fulton II*'s engineering performance was successful, the navy believed that sail, not steam, was the primary motive force for a vessel. Senior navy officials viewed steam as an auxiliary propulsion system used only to assist ships during difficult maneuvering situations. The navy's shipbuilding program throughout the next twenty years reflected this uneasy marriage between sail and steam. In 1842, the navy commissioned the side-wheel sail and steam warships *Missouri* and *Mississippi*. Following closely on the heels of these two impressive ships, the navy built the first propeller-driven warship, *Princeton*. By 1847, *Susquehanna, Powhatan, Saranac*, and *San Jacinto* joined the fleet of combined sail- and steam-powered ships.[33]

On 6 April 1854, Congress approved the funds for the navy to build six first-class combined sail and steam frigates. The first ship commissioned was USS *Merrimac*. USS *Wabash, Minnesota, Roanoke, Colorado*, and *Niagara* followed *Merrimac* down the ways between 1856 and 1857. At the time of these ships' commissioning, naval authorities at home and abroad rated them the most dominant in the world.[34] The aggressive shipbuilding program of the navy during the 1840s and 1850s demonstrated to the world the navy's commitment to steam-powered warships.

The expansion of steam engineering required the navy to shift a portion of its recruiting efforts from enlisting deck sailors to skilled engineers. This was no easy task, considering the shortages of skilled engineers in the merchant marine and civilian industry. To obtain the requisite skilled engineers, in 1847 the president authorized a substantially higher annual wage for enlisted engineers. As a result of this pay raise, a first-class fireman received a very competitive $30.00 dollars a month. The first-class fireman's equivalent deck rating, able seaman, only received $12.00 a month. Even the unskilled but labor-intensive billet of coal heaver received $15.00 dollars a month for this dirty, backbreaking work.[35] The substantial pay raise for the engineering ratings enabled the navy to meet its manning goals in the engineering division and to expand considerably its steam-powered fleet in the 1850s.

Adoption of steam propulsion provided significant technological advances to shipboard life. Steam-powered ships distilled freshwater for drinking, thus eliminating water shortages and harmful bacteria-infested water. Steam propulsion also allowed ships to complete their assigned schedules on time despite the presence of fog or the lack of wind.

The advantages of these antebellum steam-powered warships, however, had only been realized under peacetime conditions. The question remained: How would the engineers and equipment withstand the rigors of combat?

On the eve of the Civil War, the navy possessed a strong nucleus of competent career engineers and deck sailors. These men were capable of training recruits and merchant marine transfers during the navy's rapid expansion during the first year of the Civil War. As one Southern state after another seceded from the Union during the first quarter of 1861, the navy's handful of ships continued on deployment around the globe.

When President Abraham Lincoln took the oath of office during the first week of March 1861, 70 percent of the navy's ships were on deployment; only twelve ships were in home waters. The navy had six ships in the East Indies, three in the Mediterranean, three off the coast of South America, eight patrolling the African coast, and seven in the Pacific Ocean.[36] On 12 April 1861, the Civil War began when Southerners fired upon Fort Sumter, located in the harbor of Charleston, South Carolina. One week later, President Lincoln ordered a blockade of the rebellious Southern states and directed the navy to conduct the blockade by a competent force large enough to execute his proclamation.[37] This presidential order required the navy to initiate an effective blockade of 185 harbors and approximately 3,500 miles of southern coastline. To accomplish this task, the secretary of the navy, Gideon Welles, had at his disposal only forty-two ships and 7,600 men. To make matters worse, 322 naval officers resigned their commissions and offered their services to the South.[38]

The president soon realized that the current naval force of 7,600 men was insufficient to execute a competent blockade. On 3 May 1861 he authorized the navy to increase its ranks by 18,000 men for one to three years.[39] Three months later Congress authorized the navy to enlist as many men as it deemed necessary to operate its ships efficiently.[40] By the end of the war four years later, 118,000 wore the Union blue of the U.S. Navy.

2

Manning the Fleet

The rapid expansion of the navy in the months ahead required an intense and sometimes innovative recruiting program. Unlike the army, which had numerous state militia from which it could draw its forces, the navy had no such reserve contingency. To fill the manifest of the expanding inventory of ships, the navy had to solicit the services of the skilled merchant marine force and competed with the army for services of the civilian population, former slaves, foreigners, and even Confederate prisoners of war.

When the war broke out on 12 April 1861, the navy had a surplus manpower of only two hundred men to call upon for reassignment.[1] Throughout the conflict, the navy experienced periods of stability and deficits in manning its ships. Northern morale, competition with the army for available civilian manpower, the rewarding of bonus money, and the vagueness of congressional legislation all influenced the navy's recruiting efforts.

The navy achieved its manning requirements during the first six months of the war, largely because of the patriotic fervor that gripped the nation and because of the merchant marine transfers lured by the prospect of prize money. By 4 July 1861, the secretary of the navy reported that the department was able to "recruit a sufficient number of seamen to man vessels added to the service with almost as much rapidity as they could be prepared, armed and equipped."[2] By the end of October 1861, however, Capt. Andrew Foote, Commander Naval Forces, Western Rivers, notified Secretary of the Navy Gideon Welles of the acute shortage of manpower stemming from competition with the lucrative civilian shipping industry plying its trade on the Great Lakes. In his correspondence with Welles, Captain Foote requested that 500 men be sent from the east to man the new ironclad boats currently under construction.[3]

In mid-November, the Navy Department dispatched to Captain Foote the 500 men requested. During the first week in December, however, Foote requested an additional 1,100 men. Secretary Welles turned to the army for help, and by the third week in December the army offered as many as 1,200 soldiers to Foote. Throughout January, despite the concerted efforts of the army and navy to man the western river vessels, Foote still experienced manpower shortages that required desperate action. To support the combined operations against Fort Henry, Foote transferred sailors from several vessels in order to fully man those ships required for the operation. Finally, by the middle of February, the navy's recruiting efforts and the transfer of men from the army helped alleviate the manpower shortages on the western rivers.[4]

By the summer of 1862, although the navy was averaging 1,529 recruits a month, Gideon Welles notified one of his squadron commanders that the navy had a 3,000-man shortfall.[5] Some of the shortfall was a consequence of the navy's success; when a navy ship captured an enemy vessel, it required a prize crew to sail the vessel north for sale or commissioning into the Union navy. By the fall of that year, the South Atlantic Blockading Squadron was experiencing a shortage of engineers because of the number of men required to sail the steam vessels north for adjudication.[6] These manpower shortages led the naval leaders to increase their civilian recruiting efforts and to solicit the services of runaway slaves, who were then reaching the southern coastal areas occupied jointly by the army and navy.

As early as the colonial period, many blacks, both free men and those serving in bondage, had developed maritime skills while working on fishing boats and coastal and river commercial vessels. During the American Revolutionary War, naval recruiters enlisted black sailors to serve in the fledgling Continental Navy. Numerous skilled black mariners also served aboard state-sponsored navies, privateers, and merchant ships. Unfortunately for the black sailor, American independence in 1783 brought with it the demise of the Continental Navy.[7] By 1785, the Continental Navy ceased to exist and most of the black sailors returned to the bondage of slavery. Only a few free blacks remained at sea, applying their nautical skills in the merchant marine.[8] Despite the demise of the Continental Navy, the black sailors had established a precedent as being highly skilled seafaring men. When hostilities with Great Britain erupted in 1812, many African Americans again volunteered their services in the American Navy.

After the war, several free blacks remained in the service of the navy. During the antebellum period, the navy provided for free black men a professional opportunity not normally associated with the civilian community. Navy recruiting regulations allowed free blacks to enlist in the naval service with the permission of the commanding officer. Unfortunately, in 1839, several senior naval officials, fearing a proliferation of blacks in the navy, severely restricted African American recruiting. The acting secretary of the navy, Cdr. Isaac Chauncey, levied a 5 percent ceiling on the number of black recruits enlisting in the navy each month.[9] The navy's self-imposed quota system, which continued for the remainder of the antebellum period, denied the navy the potential service of skilled mariners. On the eve of the Civil War, black sailors comprised approximately 2 1/2 percent of the naval enlisted force. The wartime requirement for additional manpower, however, forced the navy to abolish the 5 percent quota, and its officers actively recruited free black men.[10]

With the shackles of the 5 percent quota system removed and the Union army's concurrent refusal to enlist blacks, the navy experienced a rapid rise in the number of African American volunteers. Hundreds of free blacks enlisted in the navy in 1861, and another potential source of recruits soon emerged as hundreds of escaped slaves in the South sought refuge with the Union army and navy. On 18 July 1861, Cdr. Silas Stringham wrote Secretary of the Navy Welles regarding the possible employment of these escaped slaves. Secretary Welles directed Commodore Stringham to employ the contraband already on board the navy ships.[11] Later that summer, the secretary expanded the use of the runaway slaves in the navy when he issued a directive authorizing the navy to actively recruit runaway slaves. The new directive limited the contraband's wages, however, to only ten dollars a month, regardless of his previous job skills and shipboard duties.[12] Welles's landmark directive provided employment opportunities for these destitute runaway slaves and simultaneously increased the naval ranks.

During the fall of 1861, some ships operating close to the Southern coast and within easy reach of the contrabands enlisted these runaways to fill their ship's muster roles. One of the first senior officers to realize the potential value of the runaways was Flag Officer Louis Goldsborough, commanding officer of the North Atlantic Blockading Squadron. As the first winter of the war gave way to spring, Flag Officer Goldsborough encouraged his commanding officers to enlist contraband as an additional source of labor during the approaching "hot and sickly" season.[13] At the same time, the navy's decision to enlist contraband enabled numerous ships to remain on blockading station and conduct combined operations on the western rivers, despite a decline in enlistments in 1862. Secretary Welles notified Flag Officers James Lardner and David Farragut of the East Gulf Blockading Squadron to expedite the enlistment of contrabands since "enlistments do not keep pace with the wants of the service."[14]

As patriotism gave way to skepticism during the spring and summer of 1862, the army was also looking for a new labor pool. On 17 July, Congress authorized the president to employ "persons of African descent" as he saw fit to help defeat the rebellion. The army immediately began hiring contraband to perform various manual labor functions. The former slaves received wages exceeding those currently offered by the navy.[15] By the end of the year, the navy found itself engaged in a bidding war with the army for the services of the contrabands, forcing Secretary Welles to modify his contraband enlistment policy. On 18 December, Welles established a new policy set forth in the following circular:

> Persons known as "contraband" will not be shipped or enlisted in the Naval service with any higher rating than landsman, but if found qualified after being shipped, may be advanced by the commanding officer of the vessel in which they served to the rating of seaman, fireman, or coal heaver, if their services are needed in such ratings, and will be entitled to the corresponding pay. They will not be transferred from one vessel to another with a higher rating than that of landsman, but if discharged on termination of enlistment, or from a vessel going out of commission, will retain their advanced rating in the discharge.[16]

The new departmental policy aided the navy in its quest for additional manpower. Throughout the war, the navy actively continued to solicit the services of former slaves. In 1863, the navy even contracted civilian recruiting agents to enlist blacks for the navy. It offered an agent from New York the going rate of three dollars for every black man enlisted.[17] Free black volunteers, merchant marine transfers, and Navy Department efforts to recruit contrabands contributed to the large number of African Americans who served in the Union navy. By the end of the war, twenty-three thousand black sailors made up approximately 20 percent of the crews in Mr. Lincoln's navy (photo 1).[18]

Both the navy and the African American sailors benefited from the navy's progressive stance toward their employment. Although black sailors fared significantly better concerning integration and equality than did their army counterparts, racism existed in various forms aboard several naval ships. Many white tars resented the black sailors and blamed the war on them as a group. In addition, the white sailor reflected the racial attitudes of the society from which he came. Racial prejudices and discriminatory practices often led to disharmony aboard ship.

Ship-sponsored plays provided one example of the racial discrimination that periodically occurred afloat. One vessel, USS *Brazileire,* hosted numerous derogatory plays that portrayed blacks as inferior. Plays such as "Nigger in the Daguerreotype Saloon," "Ethiopians," "Virginia Mommy," and "Nigger Serenade" increased racial dissension and drove a wedge between the black and white sailors. Racial tension grew to such proportions aboard *Brazileira* that the commanding officer transferred the black sailors to another ship to prevent possible violence.[19] This unfortunate consequence of *Brazileira*'s racial tension, although rare, demonstrated the sinister side of society from which the white sailors came and the poor judgment and leadership of *Brazileira*'s commanding officer.

Additional examples of racism aboard naval vessels included isolated cases of forced segregation, verbal abuse, and fighting. In a general order to the Mississippi Squadron in 1863, Acting Rear Adm. David Porter prevented contrabands from becoming petty officers. In addition, he directed his officers to have them live and drill separately from the white tars.[20] One sailor aboard USS *Silver Lake* reported that his ship required blacks to cook and eat their food in separate areas of the ship. Alcohol also contributed to racial disharmony. The crew of one ship erupted into fisticuffs when inebriated black and white sailors fought with one another.[21] Although the navy did not condone discriminatory practices, the racial climate aboard ship remained a reflection of the attitudes and policies of the ship's commanding officer.

Despite this evidence of discrimination, the navy provided the African American numerous opportunities not normally available to him in the civilian society. Free black sailors and, eventually, former slaves received the same pay as that of their white shipmates. African American tars applied their merchant marine skills or civilian trade in the various enlisted ratings. They normally received the same uniform, provisions, medical care, quarters, and weapons as did the white sailor. They also shared the same boredom, dangers, and adventures that their fellow shipmates experienced.

The navy provided the black sailor the opportunity to succeed. Blacks served in every enlisted billet and on every type of ship in the navy's inventory. In an era when racial prejudices were common practice, and the African American merchant sailors were seeing a decline in opportunities aboard civilian ships,[22] the navy made a concerted effort to provide integration and upward mobility for the black sailor. Serving in every theater of the naval war and fighting heroically next to his white shipmate, the African American greatly enhanced the navy's ability to conduct successful operations.

The African Americans' superb performance, however, could not solve all the navy's manning problems. As the war dragged on and the nation became war weary, the manpower pool steadily evaporated. The navy then resorted to legal and illegal recruiting methods to fill its ranks. Men enlisted in the navy for a variety of reasons. Merchant seamen, who possessed valuable years of maritime experience, joined primarily for the financial opportunities associated with prize money. Without a reserve force to draw upon, the navy relied heavily on the services of the merchant marine transfers. These professional tars augmented the navy during the critical first year of the war, when the rapid proliferation of the navy required a professional force capable of training a large volume of raw recruits. In his annual report the secretary of the navy attributed much of the navy's early success to the transfer of these professional merchant sailors into the navy.[23] One naval officer eloquently praised these professional mariners:

> As the white wings of our commerce in these days were seen on every sea, the nation availed itself of this resource from which to draw many skilled officers and men to its service. . . . A number of these gentlemen

were appointed to the *Potomac.* They were good and experienced sailors and ready to learn the drill, discipline and routine of the navy. They served with distinction until the war ended, when they returned to their former calling in the merchant service.[24]

African Americans and merchant marine transfers did not keep pace, however, with the navy's expanding manpower needs. So after a hiatus of almost half a century, the navy again looked to Europe as a potential source of manpower. The congressional legislation prohibiting foreigners from serving in the navy remained in effect during the first three years of the Civil War. Nevertheless, in an effort to fill the manifest of his ships and enforce an effective blockade, Secretary Welles ignored the law and condoned the enlisting of foreign sailors. He continued to violate the foreign service exclusion until Congress repealed the act in 1864.[25] As the war progressed, the navy steadily relied on foreigners to fill its ships' manifests.

The most interesting and humorous incident involving the procurement of foreign sailors began in February 1862, when the recruiting brokerage company of James R. MacDonald claimed that it could deliver one thousand quality sailors from Denmark, Sweden, and Germany to the Union navy for a fee of forty dollars a head. Secretary Welles accepted the brokerage company's offer and agreed to pay forty dollars for every sailor who passed a physical and basic seamanship exam. Welles also stipulated that the men must be able to speak English and enlist for three years.[26]

Numerous problems then arose. On 31 July 1862, the MacDonald firm informed Welles that it was experiencing some difficulty locating one thousand qualified sailors. Its officials also notified Secretary Welles that they required an additional eight dollars to cover the recent price increase for a trans-Atlantic crossing. Gideon Welles agreed to the new price increase and urgently requested the firm to send as many able men as was possible.[27]

Some days later, the MacDonald firm asked the American-based company of Austin and Baldwin to act as a liaison between itself and the Navy Department. On 18 August, the Austin and Baldwin Company notified Secretary Welles of the departure of the first shipment of men from Hamburg. The company also informed the secretary that he should reimburse each sailor for the two-dollar head tax levied on each man entering America. The firm further stipulated that future shipments of men could arrive in the United States quicker if they booked passage on faster but more expensive steamships. At this point in the transaction, Secretary Welles lost his composure. He wrote a scathing rebuttal to the Austin and Baldwin Company clearly stating his original terms and declaring that the navy would not pay an additional penny.[28]

In late September, the navy enlisted a paltry thirty-four qualified foreign sailors and paid the James R. MacDonald Company for its services. Navy recruiters rejected an additional forty-five sailors sponsored by the MacDonald firm because of deficiencies in either the English language or seamanship. Less than a year later, Secretary Welles notified the MacDonald firm that the navy no longer required its service, since the navy was not experiencing a manpower shortage. Fifteen months after the only shipment of men arrived in New York, the MacDonald company wrote Welles, trying to charge the navy for the forty-five rejected men. Unfortunately, Secretary Welles left no written response. What appeared to be a positive business venture for both sides turned out to be a total failure.[29]

Despite the navy's failure to procure skilled foreign sailors from the MacDonald firm, foreigners continued to swell the enlisted ranks of the navy as the war progressed. One ship's commanding officer, however, took offense at the nation's reliance on foreigners, especially when newspaper reporters attributed his ship's success to the actions of her foreign sailors. USS *Kearsarge*'s stunning victory over the Confederate raider CSS *Alabama* off the coast of France during the summer of 1864 brought accusations from the French newspapers that the Union victory was due to a number of French matelots serving the cannon of *Kearsarge*. Capt. John Winslow, commanding officer of *Kearsarge*, sought to set the record straight by displaying the demographic breakdown of his crew. Winslow reported that only 5 percent of *Kearsarge*'s enlisted crew of 141 were foreign sailors when *Alabama* slid beneath the waves.[30] Captain Winslow did not maintain his small foreign complement for long, however. The expiration of enlistments required him to increase his foreign recruiting efforts, so that by late November 1864, the muster reports showed 21 percent foreigners.[31]

Kearsarge was not the only Union warship manned by a significant complement of foreign sailors. Admiral Farragut's flagship, USS *Hartford*, listed 35 percent of its crew as foreigners in September 1864. The October 1862 muster role of USS *Cairo* reported 33 percent foreigners. USS *Louisiana* perhaps showed the largest increase of foreign sailors.

Her muster for 1 January 1863 reported only 3 percent foreigners. One year later 28 percent of the crew were foreigners.[32]

Most foreigners serving in the Union navy were from northern Europe and, in particular, Ireland. Forty percent of the foreigners on board *Hartford*, for example, hailed from the Emerald Isle.[33] Although the seafaring nations of northern Europe provided the bulk of foreign manpower, it was not unusual to have foreigners from all corners of the world serving aboard Union warships. One ship's foreign complement even contained former adversaries from the Crimean War who were now serving as shipmates aboard a navy vessel.[34] By 1864, the continued evaporation of manpower led Congress to repeal the foreign exclusion law of 1813 and enabled the navy to increase its foreign recruiting efforts.

Despite its increasing reliance on foreigners, the navy never stopped actively pursuing the services of American citizens. Competition with the army for eligible Americans required the navy to develop a variety of recruiting techniques to enlist sailors. The navy relied heavily on advertising as one means to increase enlistments of eligible Americans and periodically paid as much as twenty-seven dollars to advertise for six consecutive days in the *New York Times*. These advertisements informed potential recruits of the location of the various recruiting stations. At the close of the first year of hostilities, the navy operated induction or rendezvous stations at Portsmouth, New Hampshire; Boston and New Bedford, Massachusetts; New York City; Philadelphia and Erie, Pennsylvania; Baltimore, Maryland; and Washington, D.C.

Newspaper advertisements also notified the potential recruit that the navy paid three cents a mile for travel expenses to a rendezvous station, three months' advance wages for former seamen and ordinary seamen, and two months' advance wages for landsmen. Additional benefits provided the recruit with the opportunity to open an allotment for his family and to receive a uniform, although he had to pay $31.27 for the various articles of clothing.[35]

The navy also relied on recruiting posters strategically placed in various urban areas to encourage Americans to join the sea service (see photo gallery for examples). One poster, issued during the summer of 1863, proclaimed that the navy provided an alternative to conscription in the army. The poster listed the monthly pay of $18.00 for seamen, $14.00 for ordinary seamen, and $12.00 for landsmen. The monthly wages included an additional payment of $1.50 as grog money. Additional information contained in the recruiting posters mentioned the possibility of receiving thousands of dollars in prize money and the stellar opportunity for promotion, especially for men who performed heroic deeds in combat.[36]

The navy's use of newspapers and recruiting posters enabled the service to attract some recruits early in the war without expending manpower. Unfortunately, this passive recruiting method failed to enlist the required number of men. As the war progressed, the navy increasingly relied on civilian recruiting agents and its own sailors to enlist civilians. The critical manpower shortages early in 1864 prompted the navy periodically to send ships north with the express purpose of recruiting. In March 1864, the Navy Department directed the commanding officer of USS *Rhode Island* to sail north on a recruiting mission to the various ports in Maine.[37] The navy also used USS *Michigan* as a mobile recruiting and training platform on the Great Lakes to secure men for the western river vessels.[38] The operational use of some naval assets for recruiting during the apex of the navy's war effort clearly demonstrated its critical manpower deficiencies by the fourth year of the conflict.

Because of the war effort, however, the navy could not dedicate many assets to recruiting. As a result, the navy welcomed the services of the civilian recruiting agencies who helped fill the recruiting void. Based on the continuing shift in manpower requirements, the amounts paid to the civilian agents varied. In 1862, the navy paid recruiting agents top dollar for skilled recruits, although the shortages of unskilled labor the following year reversed this policy. Much of the unskilled labor force volunteered for the army because of the lucrative bonus money offered by the states. In 1863, the navy paid agents only three dollars for skilled men, including seamen, ordinary seamen, and firemen, but paid ten dollars a head for unskilled laborers who enlisted as landsmen and coal heavers.[39] The economics of war required the navy to remain flexible to the shifting tide of available labor throughout the conflict.

The demands placed on navy recruiters and civilian agencies sometimes led to unscrupulous actions. In one instance, an agency near Canada occasionally ventured across the border and reverted to the age-old seafaring custom of shanghaiing men into the naval service. One evening, a fifteen-year-old Canadian native fell victim to this ruthless practice. After he gave directions to a stranger on the streets of

Niagara Falls, Canada, the next thing the teenager remembered was waking up as a member of the U.S. Navy on board USS *Michigan!* The British consul in Buffalo, New York, eventually intervened and secured the freedom of the illegally impressed sailor. Although the exact number of men shanghaied into the navy is not available, this scene probably occurred more than once.[40]

Kidnapping civilians into the naval service was not the only unscrupulous act conducted by the civilian recruiting agencies. In at least one case, a recruiting firm conspired with a senior naval officer to defraud the government. The firm received false names from the commanding officer of the North Street Naval Rendezvous Station in New York City and submitted the names of these nonexistent men to the navy for payment. The navy, without checking to see if the men actually enlisted, paid the firm the going rate for their services. After receiving payment from the navy, the firm in turn paid the commanding officer 25 percent of its profits.[41] The navy became aware of this fraudulent practice a month after the war ended. Unfortunately, available records do not reveal how much money was embezzled or the results of actions taken against the firm or the commanding officer. Despite such evidence of fraud, civilian recruiting firms helped the navy by obtaining recruits and filling the recruiting billets normally occupied by officers or enlisted men, thus freeing the military men for service afloat.

During the four years of war, the navy enjoyed periods of manpower stability followed by months of shortages. Despite the use of runaway slaves, merchant marine transfers, and foreign enlistments, by the spring of 1864, the navy reached its low-water-mark in recruiting. The nation was war weary, and military service had lost its luster. The expiration of many three-year enlistments also handicapped the navy's ability to fill its ships' manifests. Thirty percent of the sailors serving aboard ships assigned to the North Atlantic Blockading Squadron were eligible for discharge by that time.[42]

In 1863, Congress placed an additional burden on the navy's recruiting when it passed a landmark piece of legislation to bolster army recruiting efforts. The Northern army experienced manpower shortages following the carnage of Antietam and Fredericksburg. On 3 March 1863, Congress anticipated a continued drop in army enlistments and authorized the president to draft all men between the ages of twenty and forty-five to serve in the army. This legislation initially stimulated enlistments in both services, but it was full of loopholes exempting individuals from serving. Under the National Forces Act, a person conscripted into the army could pay three hundred dollars to the government or provide a qualified substitute in order to escape the draft.[43] The National Forces Act soon became unpopular with the middle- and low-income families since they did not possess the financial means to "buy" their way out of military service.

The navy, and in particular the seaport towns of the Northeast, soon discovered that the act contained additional injustices. The act allowed the president to establish enlistment quotas for the various districts. If a district failed to meet the president's assigned quota, the government intervened and drafted the balance of the men. Furthermore, the districts received credit for those men already serving in the army but not the navy. The Northeast, with its rich seafaring tradition, provided men for the army and a majority of the navy's manpower during the war. When the president assigned the districts their individual quotas, most New England districts experienced difficulty in meeting their quota. They had simply run out of men eligible to serve.

In the fall of 1863, President Lincoln issued a call for three hundred thousand additional troops. The proclamation contained a provision permitting men who volunteered or reenlisted in the army to receive bonus money.[44] With the lucrative offer of bonus money, many men joined the army instead of the navy. The bonus money exasperated the navy's already difficult task of recruiting men, while the president's call for additional troops placed an unfair burden on numerous seafaring districts. The town of Gloucester, Massachusetts, immediately felt the strain of the new quota and appealed to the secretary of the navy, requesting assistance. Its citizens informed Welles that although the warship USS *Niagara* required sailors, the town could not provide the manpower, because Gloucester had already contributed thirteen hundred men to the army and six hundred men to the navy.[45] Fortunately for Gloucester and dozens of other seafaring towns, their requests did not go unheeded.

During the winter of 1863–64, Secretary Welles lobbied Congress, requesting an amendment to the National Forces Act that allowed districts to receive credit for men serving in the navy. Congress amended the act on 24 February 1864. The amended act granted retroactive credit to those towns providing men for the navy and allowed men volunteering in the navy to receive bonus money. In addition, a man possessing nautical skill, upon receiving his induction letter, had eight days to decide between the army or navy. Congress even allowed former sailors currently serving in the army to transfer into the navy, provided they could prove prior maritime experience.[46] Under the amended legislation, the navy finally sat on equal terms with the army in its effort to obtain recruits.

The navy eventually benefited from these amendments, but the process of transferring men to the navy and enlisting recruits took time. During the spring and early summer of 1864, the navy continued to experience critical manning shortages. On 30 March 1864, Secretary Welles notified Vice President Hannibal Hamlin that the navy desperately needed men and that thirty-five ships lacked sufficient crews to operate. In his closing paragraph he informed Hamlin that at a minimum, the army should transfer 12,000 men to the navy.[47] One of the first army commands to respond was the Army Headquarters, Department of the Gulf. It transferred 130 men to the navy during the first week in May.[48] In another incident, the army transferred the entire 30th U.S. Colored Regiment to the navy.[49] By the end of the war the army had transferred approximately 800 African American troops to the navy.[50] In May 1864, USS *Florida* received 54 replacements, most of whom were transfers from the army.[51]

Congressional approval of the transfer of soldiers to the navy was not a new idea in 1864. The war was less than a year old when the army transferred a handful of soldiers to the navy. In late January 1862, Gen. Ambrose E. Burnside sent ninety soldiers to Flag Officer Goldsborough for distribution among the ships operating near Pamlico Sound, North Carolina. Of the ninety men transferred, eight-five had been former sailors.[52] Later in the year Secretary Welles authorized Cdr. Charles Wilkes, commander of the James River Flotilla, to accept any soldiers that Gen. George B. McClellan was willing to transfer into the navy. Wilkes did not pursue Welles's recommendation, however, because he questioned the quality and moral character of the soldiers.[53]

For a few unfortunate soldiers, a visit—and not a transfer—to the navy proved fatal. During USS *Cumberland*'s ill-fated engagement with CSS *Virginia*, three soldiers visiting the Union warship found themselves caught up in the heated action. All three pitched in and helped the tars serve the great guns. Two of the soldiers perished during the battle.[54]

Throughout the remainder of 1864, thousands of soldiers traded in their muskets for a navy cutlass and joined the ranks of the sea service.

For many men, the ability to return to sea duty brought much rejoicing. One "old salt" had left behind his seafaring life and enlisted in the army because he thought it would improve his health. The army had assigned the man to the teamsters. To his dismay he quickly discovered that he lacked the unique skills required to drive mules pulling the wagons. The former sailor gruffly described his problems navigating the stubborn mules: "[I] didn't know how to steer anything that had a rudder in the front." The man rejoiced when he learned that he could return to the navy, where he could better apply his nautical skills as a sailor.[55]

Congressional action greatly alleviated the navy's critical manpower shortages of 1864. Welles believed that the draft indirectly benefited the navy: now that communities received credit for naval recruits, men could volunteer for the navy to escape army conscription.[56] In his annual report in December 1864, Secretary Welles claimed that the amended National Forces Act had reduced the navy's manpower shortages, especially in the critical rate of seaman. A man normally took six to ten years to acquire the requisite skills of this rate. By the end of 1864, the navy actually experienced a surplus in the landsman rating, although trained seamen were still in demand.[57]

While army transfers and regular enlistments in the navy continued to rise during the summer and fall of 1864, the navy experimented with a new source of manpower, Confederate prisoners of war. The navy required the men to swear an oath of allegiance to the Union before shipping them in the service. Skeptical of the loyalty of these "Galvanized Yankees," however, the navy limited the number of former rebels who could serve aboard ship to 16 percent of the crew complement for large ships and only 6 percent for ships with crews of less than one hundred.[58]

The navy continued to enlist Confederate prisoners even during the latter stages of the war. In May 1865, Acting Rear Adm. William Radford of the North Atlantic Blockading Squadron learned that his squadron would receive "Galvanized Yanks" from prisoner-of-war camps Douglas and Rock Island.[59] Although no sources specifically document the prisoners' performance, the navy must have thought highly enough of their services to continue to enlist their former adversaries until the end of the war.

Through relentless political action and dedicated recruiting efforts, the navy weathered periodic manpower shortages. The navy's ability to man its ships ebbed and flowed based on patriotic zeal, success and failure on the battlefields, and Congressional legislation. Numerous ships' muster reports and correspondence from senior naval officials demonstrated that the navy's personnel shortages were cyclic and not continuous. The successful use of American citizens representing many ethnic and racial backgrounds, merchant marine transfers, contrabands, foreigners, former soldiers, and Confederate prisoners enabled the navy to shift and expand its recruiting efforts to meet each new manpower crisis. This unique blend of naval recruits continued to press home the blockade, close Confederate ports, support joint operations with the army, and pursue Confederate commerce raiders.

Unlike the army, in which most soldiers in a regiment came from the same community with similar occupational backgrounds, the crew of a naval ship was a heterogeneous mix of men from all walks of life. The unique operational characteristics of a ship required a wide spectrum of labor skills. It was not uncommon to find a dozen different states and countries represented on board any naval vessel. This broad demographic representation provided a welcome relief for the crews during long periods of monotonous blockading duty and patrols along the western rivers.

Almost 78 percent of the sailors who served in the navy during the war hailed from states located along the Atlantic coast. New York provided the largest volume of tars. A total of 35,164 men shipped in the navy from the Empire State. This figure represented nearly 35 percent of the entire naval force, but only 1 percent of the population of New York. Massachusetts contributed the second largest number of men, providing 19,983 men, or 1.4 percent of the state's population. The District of Columbia offered the highest number of men per capita for the sea service. Although only 1,353 men enlisted, these men constituted 1.8 percent of the total population of the district.[60] Pennsylvania contributed 0.5 percent of its population to the navy, for a total of 14,307 men.[61] Ohio enlisted 3,274 men, the largest number from the Great Lakes region. This number represented less than 1 percent of the state's entire population. Michigan, the state with the longest shoreline, surprisingly provided only 598 men, or less than 0.1 percent of its total population.[62]

A review of several ships' muster roles places the average age of the sailor in his mid-twenties, although boys as young as twelve and men approaching sixty graced the muster roles of the various ships (photo

2). The average age of the common sailor was close to that of the soldier.[63] Civilian backgrounds varied greatly among the men. In contrast to the army, in which almost half of the soldiers listed farming as their principle civilian occupation,[64] navy muster roles showed a plethora of civilian skills, including baker, blacksmith, bricklayer, butcher, cobbler, cook, farmer, foreman, hatter, mason, molder, sailor, shoemaker, waiter, woodcarver, and upholsterer.

Throughout the war the navy spent countless hours and money procuring enough men to man their ships. The men whom the service eventually acquired represented every state in the Union and dozens of countries around the world. Their diverse cultures and work skills contributed to the unique demographic diversity of the navy. Regardless of their background, however, the men who shipped in the navy were usually nothing more than civilians. It was up to the navy to clothe, feed, and train these recruits in order to transform them into effective members of the crew.

❖**3**❖

Metamorphosis

Manning the ships of Mr. Lincoln's navy was only the beginning of the battle. Once the recruits enlisted, the navy had to clothe, train, and distribute the men to their respective commands. The conversion from civilian to sailor required an efficient administration and a logistical system capable of ensuring a smooth transition for the recruit. The first step in this important process began at the numerous rendezvous stations (recruiting stations) maintained by the navy throughout the North and occupied coastal regions.

The navy required a recruit, in the presence of a commissioned officer, to sign a contract commonly called a shipping article. The shipping article was a legal contract between the navy and the recruit and contained the following information: date of enlistment, signature of the recruit, rating, monthly wages, wages advanced, and bounty money. A commissioned officer's signature legalized the document. The recruit was now a member of Mr. Lincoln's navy.[1]

Following the signing of the shipping articles, the navy either paid for or provided government transportation for the recruit to one of several receiving ships operated by the navy during the war. Some of the more well known receiving ships included USS *Ohio* at Boston, USS *North Carolina* at Brooklyn, USS *Allegheny* at Baltimore, and USS *Maria Denning* at Cairo, Illinois. *Ohio* and *North Carolina* were former seventy-four-gun, old, wooden sailing ships capable of holding up to one thousand recruits. Substantially smaller, *Allegheny* was built in 1844 as a side-wheel steam sloop. *Maria Denning* was also a small, side-wheel, wooden vessel built in 1858.[2] The ships acted as collection points for the recruits. During his brief stay on a receiving ship, the recruit received a physical exam of dubious quality and traded in his civilian clothes for a navy uniform. He also received eating utensils and rudimentary naval training while he awaited assignment to his first ship.

Alvah Hunter experienced the same routine shared by thousands of other recruits during the war. In 1862, at the innocent age of sixteen, he enlisted in the navy for one year in the "boy" rating. Hunter shipped in Boston and immediately underwent a brief physical exam. Following his successful completion of the exam, Hunter received a navy uniform in a canvas bag. The uniform consisted of two blue flannel shirts, socks, a hammock with a hair mattress, and two blankets. After his uniform issue, Hunter and several other recruits then marched down to the waterfront, where they obtained passage to the receiving ship USS *Ohio* via a small boat. Hunter languished on board *Ohio* for three weeks awaiting assignment to his first ship, the newly commissioned ironclad USS *Nahant*. The young man described life aboard *Ohio* as "boring." Although he mentioned that the food was "abundant and good," the recruits had little to do from reveille at 6:00 A.M. until taps at 8:00 P.M. except maintain their personal belongings and clean the ship.[3]

Another recruit, seventeen-year-old Stephan Blanding, shipped in the navy at the recruiting station in Providence, Rhode Island. The navy paid for Blanding's transportation to Boston, where he immediately received a brief medical examination. Following the exam, Blanding received a metal cup, quart bucket, knife, spoon, and fork before reporting on board *Ohio*. Once aboard the ship, he received his first navy meal, which consisted of hardtack, salt beef, water, and pineapple cheese. After dinner, Blanding received a second, slightly more thorough physical exam. He had to stamp in place, run in place, jump, hop, and cough; the doctor then inspected his teeth. After the surgeon proclaimed Blanding fit for service, the recruit received his uniform.[4]

While awaiting assignment to his first ship, Blanding described the daily activities aboard *Ohio*:

> There is constant movement among the men; some are drilling at the guns, some reading, some sewing, others tying or learning to tie fancy

knots; gangs working at swabbing or drying up the berth and gun decks; some whitewashing overhead, or drying up the orlop deck by swinging pans filled with charcoal to and fro close to the deck. . . . Some of the men engage in mending their clothes, other fill up the tanks with water; everything is in motion.[5]

Finally, Blanding and half of the six hundred men aboard *Ohio* received orders to collect their belongings and prepare for transfer to the receiving ship USS *Allegheny,* moored in Baltimore harbor. Although Blanding did not know his final destination at the time, he eagerly awaited transportation south in anticipation of assignment to his first ship.

Blanding and three hundred fellow shipmates boarded *Allegheny* after an uneventful cruise to Baltimore harbor via a naval transport. After several days aboard the ship, he received notification that he and twenty-nine other men would proceed to their new command, the gunboat USS *Louisiana.* Within an hour the thirty men collected their personal belongings and departed Baltimore harbor aboard the screw steamship USS *Themes,* the first of five ships that eventually transported the men to *Louisiana,* anchored in the Tar River near Pamlico Sound, North Carolina.[6]

Hunter and Blanding both described life aboard a receiving ship as periods of boredom broken up by cleaning and some training. Unfortunately, the large number of men present aboard the receiving ships often led to thievery. One officer described a receiving ship as a "floating hell": "A constant thievery is going on all the time which is impossible for the officers to prevent or trace."

Because the sailors paid for their own uniforms, these items became a favorite target of many unscrupulous tars. The commanding officer of USS *Fernandina* wrote about a group of new sailors as "in debt," because they had to purchase a new set of uniforms to replace the ones stolen.[7] The uniforms bought by the sailors of *Fernandina* consisted of a dozen items that financially set each sailor back approximately thirty dollars.[8] It usually took the sailor three months to pay off his uniform debt to the government. The uniform issued to the sailors had changed little since the uniform regulations of 1852. Although the navy issued new uniform regulations in 1864, the uniform prescribed by the 1852 regulations remained unchanged for the enlisted person. The 1852 and 1864 navy uniform regulation described the enlisted uniform as follows:

Boatswain's mates, Gunner's mates, Carpenter's mates, Sailmaker's mates and Ship's cooks, will wear, embroidered in white silk, on the right sleeve of their blue jackets, above the elbow in front, of an eagle and anchor, of not more than three inches in length, with a star of one inch in diameter one inch above. The same device, embroidered in blue, to be worn on the sleeve of their white frocks in summer.

All other petty officers, except officer's stewards, will wear the same device on their left sleeve. The outside clothing for petty officers, fireman, and coal-heavers, seaman, ordinary seaman, landsmen, and boys, for muster, shall consist of blue cloth jackets and trousers, or blue woolen frocks; black hats, black silk neckerchiefs, and shoes, or boots in cold weather. In warm weather it shall consist of white frocks and trousers; black or white hats, as the commander may for the occasion direct, having proper regard for the comfort of the crew; black silk neckerchiefs, and shoes; the collars and cuffs to be lined with blue cotton cloth, and stitched round with thread. Thick blue cloth caps, without visors, may be worn by the crew at sea, except on holidays or muster.[9]

Although uniform regulations prescribed a set uniform for the sailor, what he received varied considerably throughout the war, based on the quantity of uniforms available for issue, the commanding officer's individual uniform policy, and the time of year.[10] One sailor, after successfully passing his physical exam, described his uniform issue:

Each man was furnished a black bag in which to put his clothes; one pair of white duck pants, one white shirt with blue collar, one pair of blue pants, one blue shirt with wide collar and white star worked on each corner; two pairs of woolen stockings, undershirts and drawers, one canvas hammock, two single or one double blanket for all of which we were obliged to sign a book; than a blank form was filled out and given to each man, being a plain statement of what he owed the ship, the same to be taken out of his pay at the end of service. Looking the paper over I found I was in debt to the ship three months' pay.[11]

The uniform issued by the Navy Department was practical and comfortable. The dress jacket for petty officers and crew was a dark blue double-breasted cloth shell jacket with wide lapels. It sported two rows of medium-sized navy buttons, nine per row and placed approximately one inch vertically apart. The sailor usually wore the jacket unbuttoned over his frock for inspections and liberty, but he rarely wore it as a working garment.[12]

The primary upper garment worn by the enlisted sailor was a loose-fitting, dark blue frock. The frock was practical, lightweight, and made of wool. Wool, "the fabric of history," was an excellent material for nautical clothing because it wicks away perspiration from the body and is the only fabric that maintains its insulating qualities when wet. Wool's unique fibers expand when moistened, thus preventing cold air from penetrating the garment.[13] This unique property inherent in wool was an important feature for sailors exposed to the harsh, wet elements of the sea. The frock had an open neck without buttons, a pocket on the left breast, cuffs closed with two small buttons, and a 6 1/2-inch "sailor's collar" in the back.[14]

The "sailor's collar," or jumper flap, first appeared on American navy uniforms in the early 1850s. The flap served as a cover to prevent the collar from being soiled. Sailors of the day used tar to shape a fashionable ponytail, which inevitably soiled the back of the uniform. A portable flap, attached by buttons, protected the frock and could be removed during personnel inspections. By the 1860s, clothing manufacturers permanently sewed the flap to the uniform.[15]

The sailor's pants, also made of a dark blue wool material, contained a broad front fly that attached to the pants with thirteen buttons. The fly provided the sailor with a snug fit around the waist and eliminated the use of suspenders to hold the pants up. The flared, or "bell," shape at the bottom of the pants allowed the tar to roll his pants up easily over his knees when scrubbing the decks or wading ashore.[16]

The navy issued the wool frock and pants for use in the winter or at the commanding officer's discretion. Unlike the army, whose men wore wool uniforms year-round, the navy issued a summer uniform made of white cotton duck. The summer uniform was similar in design to the wool uniform. The white frock had a blue collar only four inches wide and a one-inch blue trim extending down the front opening to the sternum. Three buttons closed the front of the frock if the sailor so desired. The cuff sported a two-inch-wide blue trim and a button for closing. The summer white pants were of the same design as the wool bell-bottom pants.[17]

On the eve of the Civil War, the enlisted man's dress hat was the black varnished straw hat with a low crown and broad brim. The hat was uncomfortably hot in the summer and, because of its delicate construction, did not store well. The navy slowly phased this impractical hat out of its inventory, replacing it with the dark blue wool flat hat.

Originally, the navy designed the flat hat with a broad, soft, circular crown as a working cover for use at sea. As the war progressed, the practical flat hat gained in popularity, and the navy allowed sailors to wear it for all occasions. Sailors often decorated the rim of the hat with a piece of black silk embroidered with the name of the man's ship. Uniform regulation did not prohibit the sailor from customizing his flat hat. Creative tars frequently embroidered fancy designs on the tops of their flat hats.[18] During the summer months, the sailor placed a white cotton cover that acted as a sun reflector over the wool hat. Although navy uniform regulation did not mention straw hats for enlisted men, in the southern latitudes, sailors occasionally constructed them out of palm leaves purchased ashore. The straw hats were cooler than the wool flat hat, and the broad brim provided greater protection from the sun for the neck and face.[19]

The navy issued the sailor a black silk neckerchief for use as a rag to wipe the dirt and sweat from his hands and face.[20] A pair of government-issued leather shoes rounded out the sailor's uniform. The shoes were of all-leather construction, rough side out, with soles stitched or pegged onto the upper part of the shoe. The square-toed, ankle-high shoes had a right and left lattice.[21]

The sailor kept his spare uniforms and a handful of personal items in a canvas or cloth bag, which was stored in a secured compartment of the ship. At prearranged times, under the supervision of the master-at-arms, the sailors had access to their bags. In an effort to prevent theft and provide identification, the service required the tars to stencil their clothing. The ship's master-at-arms placed into the "lucky bag" any article of clothing not stenciled and carelessly left out. Periodically the crew could augment their uniform allowance by purchasing, at auction, items from the lucky bag.[22]

Another opportunity for the crew to replace lost or worn-out articles of clothing was through the purchase of numerous clothing and toiletry articles sold on board ship by the paymaster. Once a month, the ship's paymaster sold fabric for mending or making clothes and personal items deemed essential for the health and comfort of the crew. The paymaster aboard USS *Monitor* described the process in a letter to his wife:

> The last two or three days of the month and the first two or three days of the next are rather busy ones for me, as at these times I deal out the clothing and small things the sailors need for the coming month. . . .

[T]wo or three days before the month expires I give my steward a blank for clothing and one for small stores (such as needles, thread, buttons, [shoe] blacking, soap and the numerous little things the sailor wants) for each mess. The ship's crew are divided into messes of ten or twelve men each—four in our case. Each of these messes as I have said are furnished by my steward with a blank for clothing and one for small stores. The name of each one in the mess is on the blanks and each one places opposite his name and in the appropriate column the number or amount of what he wants. These are then given to me by my steward and I have them to look over to see that no man is calling for more than he needs. . . . I then carry the copies to the Capt. and he approves them as being necessary for the health and comfort of the men. . . . The head man of each mess . . . comes up to me and get what the men in his mess put down on the blank. . . . The articles each one has had is then copied on the rec't book and he signs his name, an officer signing as witness. Nothing is dealt out at any other time (except for provisions which are served every day) so that if one gets out of tobacco in the middle of the month he must wait till the first of the next for a supply.[23]

USS *Hartford* received the follow items for sale by the ship's paymaster: 1,045 yards of flannel, 20 blankets, 99 pair of shoes, 24 seventy-five-pound boxes of soap, 50 scrub brushes, 48 shaving boxes, 84 whisk brooms, 48 shoe brushes, and 120 boxes of blacking.[24] Even the small *Monitor* carried many items for resale in the ship's storeroom: clothing, stationery, tobacco, soap, candles, thread, buttons, and small knives.[25]

To ensure that the men maintained their clothing in respectable condition, the commanding officer usually ordered one of his officers to inspect the crew's clothing on a weekly basis. The inspecting officer had those articles in poor condition thrown overboard, and he further identified items requiring mending by the sailor. Many sailors proved quite innovative in manufacturing and designing their clothes (photo 3). One creative sailor, using material purchased from the ship's store and aided by his "housewife," made a flannel shirt. He personalized the shirt by embroidering the collar with stars and adding a crowfoot to the area below the neck opening. Another young tar embroidered a heart on the front of his winter frock (photo 2).[26]

Some sailors mastered the fine art of tailoring during the long, isolated hours at sea. Their ability to keep their uniforms clean in a harsh environment offered additional challenges. One distinct advantage the sailor enjoyed over the army was an inexhaustible source of salt water. His ability to purchase soap on board ship enabled the sailor to wash his clothes at regular intervals.[27] Laundering clothes while in port or at anchor required little effort on the part of the crew. The sailors even dried their laundry by hanging the numerous articles of clothing throughout the ship's exposed weather decks (photo 4).

The melancholy appearance of a ship doing laundry in port, however, concealed the potential hazards of washing clothes at sea. One Sunday morning, the crew of USS *Sophronia* experienced firsthand the hazards of washing clothes while under way. As the men were washing their clothes on the forecastle, a wave broke over the bow. The resulting mass of water scattered the men and their clothes, buckets, and baskets. When the ship rose to the crest of the next wave, the men's clothes disappeared through the scuppers and into the sea.[28]

Despite the hot and dirty environment of the engineering world, the officers expected the men to look clean when not on watch or working. The standing orders of the chief engineer on board *Hartford* stressed the importance of maintaining personal appearance: "Firemen and coal heavers shall keep themselves sufficiently supplied with changes of clothing, and as soon after coming off watch as practical, shall wash and dress themselves."[29] For many sailors, the risk of personal injury and numerous hours consumed in maintaining their uniforms was better than failing the commanding officer's weekly personnel inspection.

Every Sunday before church service, the crew, in their best uniform prescribed for that day, mustered by division on one side of the vessel. When the paymaster called out a sailor's name, the sailor walked across the deck to the commanding officer, who inspected him and noted any deficiencies in his appearance before permitting him to continue his sojourn across the deck.[30] Personal pride and peer pressure explained why many sailors went to great lengths to ensure that their uniforms and personal hygiene met the command's standards. The recruit, wearing a new uniform and having survived the ordeal of the receiving ship, eagerly anticipated reporting to his new command.

For many recruits, however, their first impression of their new home numbed the senses and subdued their enthusiasm. Immediately upon reporting on board his new command, the sailor signed the ship's muster book. He then received a personal number that corresponded to various duty assignments listed on the station, quarter, and fire bill. The bills listed the ship's company by their personal number. Next to their number, the bills listed the various daily duties, watch assignments while under way and in port, watch sections, battle stations, and fire stations.[31] These bills enhanced the sailor's indoctrination aboard his new home and provided a valuable management tool for the senior enlisted and officer cadre.

After the brief administrative procedures, a shipmate escorted the new tar to the berth deck, where he received his hammock assignment. The hammock used by the Union sailor was 72 inches long and 30 inches wide. It was suspended from the overhead of the compartment by a rope that passed through twelve grommets on each end of the hammock. Sailors found the hammock ideally suited for ship life, since the bed minimized the roll of the ship and prevented the sleeper from being tossed about while he tried to catch a few hours of precious sleep.[32]

Within a few hours of reporting aboard, the new crew member's curiosity usually led him to explore his vessel. For sailors assigned to the wooden ships, the tour was simple. Several wooden decks contained cannon, provisions, and nautical equipment. The long, spacious decks did not require a great deal of exploration. For sailors assigned to a new ironclad, however, a tour through the ship was an educational experience.

The scene that greeted a new sailor assigned to the newly commissioned USS *Nahant,* an ironclad of the *Passaic* class, was quite different from what he experienced on the large, wooden receiving ship USS *Ohio.* The *Passaic*-class *Nahant* represented a slight improvement over the navy's first ironclad, USS *Monitor.* This class of ship was slightly larger than *Monitor,* and naval engineers moved the vulnerable pilothouse to a safer location on top of the turret. In addition, these ships' main battery consisted of one 15-inch and one 13-inch smooth-bore cannon.[33]

From one to four inches of iron plate encapsulated the entire living quarters and most working areas of the *Nahant.* The forward part of the ship contained the anchor machinery equipment. Directly behind the anchor compartment were the captain's quarters, behind which were the officers' individual staterooms and wardroom.[34]

The crew's berthing and messing compartment followed "officers' country." This compartment was 30 feet long and 40 feet wide and was home for approximately sixty enlisted persons. Hooks fastened into the overhead supported the men's hammocks and permitted each

LIFE IN MR. LINCOLN'S NAVY

man approximately 14 inches of space between hammocks. The cramped enlisted quarters received mechanical ventilation from one or two steam-operated forced-air blowers located in the engineering compartment.[35] Unfortunately for the poor tar, the air was of dubious quality by the time it reached the berthing compartment.

The forced-air supply followed an intricate passage forward through two air ducts located below the main deck. The air ducts terminated in the anchor windlass room, a distance of almost 100 feet. Rising in the anchor room, the air passed aft through small openings in the upper partitions of the officers' berthing. The air, now increasing in odor, temperature, and humidity, passed through an opening high in the bulkhead separating the officers' quarters from the crew's berthing compartment. From here the stale air continued aft through the crews' quarters and through a door leading into the turret chamber. Nearing the end of its tortuous route, the air rose through the turret, passed the great guns, and exited through a thick, perforated iron plate in the overhead of the turret.[36] Although advanced for its day, this new air supply system failed to produce the required volume of fresh air to the men, especially during operations in warm climates or combat situations.

During the summer of 1862, the engineering officer aboard the *Monitor* recorded temperatures as high as 128 degrees in the engine room, 164 degrees in the galley, and 120 degrees on the berth deck. One officer attributed the high temperatures in the crew's berthing compartment to the mechanical ventilation. He also felt that the officers' quarters were better ventilated than the crew's quarters.[37] The engineer placed the blame on the poor design of the mechanical ventilation system.[38] Often, the oppressive heat below deck forced the men to cook, eat, and relax on the main deck (photo 5).

Winter months aboard a *Monitor*-class vessel proved to be as uncomfortable as the hot, suffocating summer. During her initial sea trials in February 1862, the temperature inside USS *Monitor* was a shivering 35 degrees. The only fires permitted were in the fire room and galley stoves.[39] Condensation forming on the inside of the iron hull added to the dampness and overall miserable living conditions. Fortunately for the inhabitants of the ironclads, the navy made alterations to a number of the original *Monitor* designs. One such alteration was the installation of small steam radiators that eventually made the living conditions tolerable during the winter months.[40]

Below the crew's quarters a series of smaller spaces contained solid shot, shell, and canister for the great guns. Four tanks held fresh water condensed from the engine room for the crew. Alongside the berth deck numerous smaller compartments held provisions, small stores, powder for the cannon, and medical supplies; there was also a hammock storage facility and one room for storing personal clothing bags. Aft of the berthing compartment, three doors penetrated an iron bulkhead. The starboard door led to the ship's galley, where the cooks prepared all the meals for officers and crew. The center door opened into the turret machinery room. This space contained the steam-driven steering gear machinery and an engine for rotating the turret.[41]

The port-side door led into the boiler and engine room. Two 25-pounds-per-square-inch steam-generating boilers provided the main motive force for the ship's propeller and its auxiliary equipment. Next to each boiler were the great coal bunkers, capable of holding up to 100 tons of coal each. The bunkers stored fuel for the boilers and galley stove and periodically served as a brig or jail cell for sailors convicted of petty crimes.[42]

Aft of the coal bunkers a compartment 25 feet long provided storage for small boat equipment and perhaps the most important invention found on board the fledgling *Monitor*s, the first compressed-air flushing toilet![43] Before the commissioning of *Monitor*, enlisted men serving aboard wooden ships relieved themselves in the forward part of the ship commonly called the "head." A small wooden bench with one or two holes cut in it allowed the sailor to sit down in the open-air portion of the ship and pass effluent through the hole and into the sea. During inclement and cold weather the open-air heads proved to be a challenge and injurious to the men's health. When John Ericcson built *Monitor*, the main deck was only 18 inches above the water and at sea the deck was constantly awash, thus rendering a toilet facility external to the ship impossible. To make *Monitor* a functional craft at sea, Ericsson designed a flushing toilet located inside the ship.[44]

The crew of *Monitor* shared two toilets, located just aft of their berthing compartment on the starboard side of the ship. The officers shared one toilet situated opposite the enlisted head facility on the port side. The commanding officer had his own toilet in his cabin.[45] The new invention, however, required some mechanical knowledge to be used properly. If the sailor failed to open the overboard valve when he flushed the toilet, the effluent had only one direction to go: up and all over the beleaguered sailor. Another hazard was clogging as a result of the labyrinth of pipe and the reaction of seawater with urine, which coated the pipe and reduced its effective diameter.[46] When the toilet failed to operate correctly, the offensive odor soon permeated throughout the vessel. As a result, the ship's engineers designed portable outhouses for use in a harbor or an estuary.

The ship's engineers placed the portable outhouses on the main deck in the after portion of the ship. Two metal stations fitted into the main deck cantilevered over the side of the ship. Suspended from the metal frame hung a wooden bench with a footrest and backrest. In the middle of the wooden seat a hole allowed excrement to pass into the water. A canvas tarp covered the top and back of the outhouse (photo 6).[47] These portable marine outhouses reduced the use of the internal flushing toilet and helped eliminate one additional source of foul odor that frequented the inside of the stuffy *Monitor*s.

Sixteen small circular windows in the main deck provided some natural light for the occupants of the vessels.[48] Whale-oil lanterns lit the turret room, and candle lanterns provided additional shadowy light for the crew throughout the ship.[49] Although the living conditions on board the ironclads appeared oppressive, the technological advancements in artillery in the decades before the Civil War made the *Monitor*s the safest vessels afloat during combat. The inconveniences were but a small price to pay for the preservation of one's life and limb.[50]

The men assigned to the river ironclads found their living conditions as oppressive as those of their *Monitor* shipmates. With sloped armor and flat top, the iron-encased vessels allowed the sun to beat down unmercifully throughout the day. The still nights and radiant heat from the boilers made life aboard these vessels a "living hell." A member of the *Cairo*-class river ironclad USS *Cincinnati* described his warship as "not fit for a dog to live in."

Sailors assigned to wooden vessels experienced the same enlightening, and sometimes equally depressing, first impressions as did their counterparts assigned to the cramped, stuffy, and damp ironclad. Those serving aboard wooden vessels also suffered from heat and dampness. The surgeon from the gunboat USS *Delaware* requested the installation of stoves to combat the humidity and "preserve the health" of the men in the winter months.[51] The commanding officer of USS *General Putman* wrote to his superiors about the poor condition of his vessel:

I would respectfully report to you the very bad condition of the hurricane deck of this vessel. The canvas covering of which is entirely worn out in many places. The officers and men's quarters are very uncomfortable and unhealthy, being continually wet, in wet weather. I would respectfully request permission to call a survey on the above mentioned deck and covering.[52]

Prolonged presence of fog contributed to the dampness, misery, and declining physical and mental health of the crew of a sailing ship. Without wind to maneuver, a ship shrouded in fog was helpless and at the mercy of nature. A surgeon aboard a warship becalmed in fog over a period of several days described the declining state of affairs in his journal:

Everything in and about the ship is damp. Clothing, books, papers, instruments, accouterments, decks, and staterooms are not only damp but beginning to get moldy. Decayed teeth begin to ache. The chills-and-fever boys are commencing to complain. Some of my old cases of rheumatismus chronics are coming to me for some medicine to drive away, as they say "damn pains." In short, all are as grim as bears with sore heads. Nothing taste good; reading matter not interesting; and none feels like sleeping.[53]

Heat, cold, and dampness were not the only enemies of the men at sea. The warm weather ushered in the arrival of the pesky and sometimes deadly mosquito, as described by a member of the *Monitor*:

The past two days have been very hot and to add to our discomforts the bowels of our iron monster are already populated with flies and mosquitoes. You may imagine me writing this with a towel in one hand brushing off mosquitoes and wiping off perspiration, my brains in sort of mix with the buzzing of the mosquitoes, the hum of the flies, the trickling of sweat and the amount of mental labor necessary to express my thoughts on this sheet. . . .[54]

For the ships anchored off New Orleans during the summer of 1862, the oppressive heat forced the men to sleep on deck and at the mercy of the mosquitoes.[55] Another crew member referred to the weather as an "abominable climate and atmosphere down here. . . . We are scorched through the day by the sun and at night we are oppressed by a sullen atmosphere and annoyed almost to distraction by bugs of all descriptions, including mosquitoes."[56] One person called the mosquito the "enemy and the greatest torment to man possessing iron bills capable of penetrating the toughest hide as they drink the crimson stream of man and beast."[57]

The constant presence of mosquitoes frequently dominated the men's concentration and rest. A member of the river ironclad USS *Mound City* conveyed the sense of irritation: "I have nothing to write about unless it be mosquitoes for they and a few gnats claim all our attention. . . . I turn in at nine o'clock, but owing to the heat and insects . . . I did not have an hour's quiet sleep."[58]

Over time the new sailor became "acclimated" to the heat or the bone-chilling cold, damp weather. The increasing presence of steam radiators helped control the cold. The navy even occasionally claimed victory over the mosquito, fly, and heat when a ship put to sea well beyond the endurance of the pesky insects and entered an area of cool sea breezes. Unfortunately, one problem left a lasting first impression on a new sailor and was very difficult to defeat: the presence of rodents, insects, and other vermin. In an era before pesticides and rodent control, it was not unusual for vermin to overrun a ship. One crew member assigned to the timberclad USS *Tyler* disgustingly described his ship as being "alive with roaches and rats, mosquitoes and flies, gnats and bugs, of every description. I never saw a place like it. While I am writing, the roaches are running all over my patent desk."[59] Another sailor said that the cockroaches were "fearful in numbers—they are in every place about the vessel."[60]

Unfortunately, there was little the officers and men could do once the unwanted stowaways infested a ship. Rats gained passage aboard ship by crawling up the mooring lines, and roaches entered via the crates and sacks of food that the men carried on board when reprovisioning the ship. Other vermin practically walked aboard a vessel on the backs of the officers and crew. Lice on an individual's clothes or body multiplied and spread rapidly from sailor to sailor living in the close confines of a ship. The only cure for the lice was the frequent washing of clothes, bedding, and bodies.

Despite the early hardships endured by the new sailor, he quickly became accustomed to the ways of the seas. Thanks to an efficient and thorough routine consisting of work and training under the auspicious eye of the veteran petty officers, the new man rapidly learned the ropes for survival and even thriving at sea.

4

Shipboard Routine

When a sailor enlisted in the navy he signed on to serve in either the time-honored deck rating or the rapidly expanding engineering field. A handful of recruits under the age of seventeen shipped in the "boy" rating. These teenagers worked in the officers' area as servants assisting the officers' cook in preparing and serving meals and cleaning the officers' staterooms. During combat the boys (commonly called powder monkeys) hand-delivered 30-pound black powder cartridges to the great guns (photo 2). For ease of handling, the boys placed the cartridges in an oak bucket, which caught any grains of powder that escaped from the cartridge. After delivering the critical propellant, the boys inverted the bucket over a tub of water near the powder magazine to neutralize the loose grains of powder.[1]

The majority of unskilled recruits enlisted as "landsmen," who constituted approximately 50 percent of the crew on wooden ships. The navy expected these green recruits to learn their trade rapidly in order to contribute to the success and safety of the vessel. They required considerable supervision and accomplished the bulk of the menial, labor-intensive tasks such as holystoning the wooden decks and cleaning the ship.[2]

"Ordinary seaman" was the next higher rating in deck division and usually made up 25 percent of the deck force. These men normally had one deployment or significant at-sea time. They possessed basic naval skills and assisted the petty officers and seamen in training landsmen. After serving several years as an ordinary seaman, if the man displayed skill and promise, the commanding officer promoted him to the rate of seaman. The seaman rating was perhaps the most important deck rating on board ship. Under ideal manning conditions about another 25 percent of the deck division consisted of seamen. With between six and ten years' naval experience, the deck seamen understood all facets of a sailor's duties and responsibilities. The best seamen were promoted to petty officer by the commanding officer. The petty officers provided the vital communication link between the orders of the officers and the actions of the crew, and they supervised the training of the junior enlisted ranks. In addition, the petty officers were responsible for the timely execution of the ship's daily routine.[3]

Navy regulation did not specify a ship's daily routine for in port or under way, but allowed the individual commanding officers to establish their own ship's routine. Overall, most ships followed weekly at-sea schedules similar to that of the sailing vessel USS *Fernandina*:

Sunday
Morning—Wash decks, clean bright work, square yards, haul taut gear fore and aft, 9:00 A.M. general muster. 7:30 P.M. Quarters for muster and clear battery. [Strangely, Naval Surgeon Samuel Boyer's journal, from which this schedule is derived, makes no mention of religious services or personnel inspection.]

Monday
Morning—Wash clothes, scrub decks, clean bright work, square yards, haul taut gear fore and aft. At 9:30 A.M. Exercise at general quarters. 7:30 P.M. Quarters for muster and clear battery.

Tuesday
Morning—Wash decks, clean bright work, square yards, haul taut gear fore and aft, general overhauling ship's rigging. 7:30 P.M. Quarters for muster and clear battery.

Wednesday
Morning—Wash decks, clean bright work, square yards, general drill with small arms and single sticks. 7:30 P.M. Quarters for muster and clear battery.

Thursday

Morning—Wash decks, clean bright work, square yards, haul taut gear fore and aft. 9:00 A.M. Fire quarters. 7:30 P.M. Quarters for muster and clear battery.

Friday

Morning—Wash clothes, clean decks, clean bright work, square yards, haul taut gear. 8:00 A.M. Holystone berth deck. 7:30 P.M. Quarters for muster and clear battery.

Saturday

Morning—Holystone spar deck thoroughly, clean bright work, square yards, haul taut gear.

Afternoon—Make, mend, and mark clothes. 7:30 P.M. Quarters for muster and clear battery.[4]

Naval officer Uriah Levy followed a weekly schedule similar to that of *Fernandina*. Levy's routine at sea consisted of breakfast for the crew at 8:00 A.M. and dinner at noon. He permitted one hour for each meal (his manual failed to establish a time for supper). The crew washed the deck every morning, and daily work stopped at 4:00 P.M. Every evening before turning in for the night, the crew mustered for inspection. Levy required that all unnecessary lights, including galley fires, be extinguished by 8:00 P.M. in the winter and 9:00 P.M. in the summer. There was no work scheduled on Sundays except for watches and procedures required for setting the sails. The crew mustered at 10:30 A.M. in the proper uniform prescribed for the day for religious services.[5]

Levy also established a monthly schedule as a guideline for commanding officers to follow. Weekly routines included wash days for Mondays, Wednesdays, and Fridays. Tuesdays were air-the-bedding days, and on Fridays, some poor junior sailor cleaned the galley funnel. Saturdays the landsmen holystoned the deck. On a biweekly basis the crew washed hammocks on Monday and aired clothes on Saturday. Levy believed that once a month, usually on Monday, officers should inspect the crew's clothing to ensure that they were properly stenciled and to submit requisitions to the paymaster for issue of new articles of clothing if required. On the fifteenth of each month, the paymaster issued small stores to the crew. One Sunday a month, following religious services, a commissioned officer read "An Act for the Better Government of the Navy," commonly called "Articles of War" or "Navy Regulations."[6]

Sunday was the one day whose routine most ships followed with a degree of regularity. The typical Sunday consisted of reveille, breakfast, clean ship, mustering of the crew for religious services, followed by the commanding officer's personnel inspection (photo 7). The paymaster aboard USS *Florida* described in a letter to his wife a typical Sunday routine aboard his ship:

> At the beat of the drum, at about 10 o'clock, all the crew quietly take their places on the port side of the quarter deck dressed as the executive officer thinks the weather requires. Today each man is dressed in blue pants, white shirt with blue collar and cuffs embroidered with white and straw hats. . . . The captain then comes on deck accompanied by the executive officer, the officer and crew making the usual salute which [is] returned by the captain when the pair proceed to various portions of the vessel to see that all is neat, clean and everything in proper working order. On their return to the quarterdeck the Articles of War are read, all new orders received from the department and when the captain directs the Episcopal service is also read. After all this the muster role is called by the paymaster clerk, each man as his name is called crossing over the starboard side and taking off his hat passes in review before the captain and other officers and woe betide him if his shoes are not well brushed, his white shirt without a spot, his neckerchief properly tied and all his "rigging" without fault—the drum beats the retreat which ends the formalities of the day and the watch off duty is at liberty to pass the time as they please.[7]

George M. Ransom, commanding officer of the steam gunboat USS *Kineo,* wrote his articles for the internal regulations of his ship. Today the navy refers to these articles as the Commanding Officer's Standing Orders. Ransom, in great detail, described how he expected his vessel to operate on a daily basis. Various articles that governed Ransom's ship included the following:

> Article No. 1, Hammocks; When hammocks are piped up the men are to out and lash with alacrity. . . . The time allowed for getting up and stowing hammocks is 10 minutes, after which, none are to be received in the nettings, but excluded and report for action of the First Lieutenant.
> Article No. 2, Scrubbing and Hanging up Clothes to Dry; Scrubbing clothes is forbidden at all times except when the hands are piped up or permission is given by the Officer of the Deck or First Lieutenant. Clothing will be allowed to dry by regular lines when piped. Drying of

clothes never permitted at night. There will be two wash mornings in port, Monday and Friday. At sea, every day except Sunday.

Article No. 3, Morning Watch Duties Underway; Carpenter, will inspect small boats and spares daily. Sailmaker, will inspect sails daily. Boatswain, will inspect rigging daily.

Article No. 6, Meals, Meal Hours and Smoking; Breakfast at 8 bells [8:00 A.M.]. All duties will be avoided except watches and emergencies during meal hours. Boisterous behavior is forbidden. Smoking allowed during meal and up to fires extinguished in galley usually around 8:00 P.M. [Smoking permitted] for crew only on spare deck.

Article No. 7, Dressing of Crew; Crew will dress with uniformity. Working clothes are to be essentially clean. Uniform of the day will be according to card stating which article of clothes will be worn that day.

Article No. 8, Inspection at Quarters; Underway: In the morning [time not specified]. In Port: Morning and evening [time not specified]. Officers will muster and inspect the condition of their crew.

Article No. 9, Inspection, Exercise and Drill; At 9:50 A.M. Commanding Officers inspection [tour of ship which lasted only ten minutes]. 10:00–11:00 A.M. Exercise crew at guns. Afternoon and evening: drill and exercise men with small arms. Miscellaneous Items, [crew] not allowed to have hands in pockets while on watch, or being addressed by officer. No spitting overboard except at the head of ship or in spit boxes provided on deck.[8]

Asa Beethman, a seaman aboard a naval vessel in the summer of 1861, provides the most enlightening information regarding a ship's daily routine in a letter to his sister. What makes seaman Beethman's letter interesting is the time and amount of whiskey he received in the morning. Beethman wrote his letter a full year before the navy abolished the whiskey ration:

> 4 O'clock in the morning the gun fires, all hands are piped up and have to lash up hammocks and have them stowed in the nettings on deck by 1/2 past 4 O'clock. 5 O'clock we get coffee and hard bread, tho we get grog first 1/2 gill [2 ounces] of good whiskey and then coffee and bread. Six O'clock we wash decks. 9 O'clock all hands to muster roll call which generally takes more than an hour. 1/2 past 11 another 1/2 gill of whiskey and then dinner which generally consists of beef soup or rice and salt beef or pork and beans. 4 O'clock supper of coffee and bread again. 5 O'clock muster again. 7 O'clock hammocks piped down.[9]

Throughout the course of a day the crew performed a myriad of tasks. Every week, the junior ratings holystoned the wooden decks. Holystoning was an age-old practice first initiated by the English. One day English sailors obtained small pieces of broken monuments from St. Nicholas Church in Great Yarmouth, England. The ingenious sailors found the semisoft stones ideal for scrubbing the decks, and appropriately named them "holystones." During the Civil War, sailors used pumice or sandstone to scrub the wooden decks, but the term "holystoning" continued to describe the procedure of wetting the deck and pulling a stone back and forth across the deck until it was clean. Although holystoning was an effective way to clean the deck, the stone's extreme abrasiveness rapidly wore down the deck, requiring expensive and time-consuming work to replace it.[10] One recruit, while awaiting orders to his first ship, described in his memoirs the teamwork required in holystoning a deck:

> The decks were holy-stoned three times a week. . . . Holy-stoning the deck is accomplished by attaching a strong rope to both sides of a stone, usually a grind stone, of course grit, about twelve by sixteen inches, and about eight inches thick. Five or six men, or even more, then take hold of the rope at each end, and while one side pulls, the other slackens, then the opposite pulls while the other slackens, and so on. Canvas and sand are used to scrub where Holy-stoning cannot be used. Small hand stones are also made use of to scrub the hatches and the wood work; for the brass work, pumice stone is used.[11]

During the Vicksburg campaign the navy, at the request from the army, transferred an 8-inch cannon and gun crew ashore in support of army land movements. The sailors, not wanting to break from their shipboard lifestyle and routine, erected a large tent replete with hammocks, mess gear, and a wooden floor. Periodically the tars holystoned their makeshift deck, much to the amusement of the soldiers.[12]

Sailors assigned to steam vessels incurred additional cleaning duties after the coaling of their ships. They also had to remove the greasy soot from the soiled decks and sails caused by the boiler's smoke.[13] Painting the ship was another time-consuming activity conducted by the sailors. During the Civil War, the Union navy first experimented with gray paint, which aided in camouflaging a ship at sea (photo 8).[14] One officer wrote in his journal, "The boys are scraping the sides . . . working today on the starboard side . . . preparatory to giving her a coat of paint—not a coat of black, as heretofore, but a coat of lead so as not to be so prominent a mark for the Rebels."[15]

Cleaning and painting the ship and holystoning its decks were labor-intensive and tedious—but not dangerous—duties. Other duties were more hazardous, however. Sailors on sailing ships faced enormous hazards working 100 feet above the deck in the mast and spars. Day or night, under some of the most extreme weather conditions, sailors faithfully went aloft to set or reef sails, always conscious that one misplaced step could be their last. USS *Powhatan* experienced one such tragedy while conducting training for the men in the mast. A twenty-three-year-old seaman lost his footing and fell to his death on the wooden decks below.[16] An additional danger always present aboard a ship at sea was falling overboard. The poor maneuverability of the ships of that period and the lack of safety harnesses and life vests made falling overboard extremely hazardous, especially at night or during inclement weather. An accident on USS *Florida* typifies the constant danger. While the ship was sailing off the coast of North Carolina during heavy weather on 28 November 1863, Seaman John Crane fell overboard. Despite the immediate and heroic action of his shipmates, Seaman Crane slipped beneath the waves before a rescue boat could reach him.[17] Even the calm waters of the western rivers could prove fatal to the men working on the main deck. Seaman D. Bice of USS *Tyler* accidentally fell overboard, struck his head on the anchor, and drowned during what began as a routine anchor weighting.[18]

Although working aloft on a sailing ship, navigating a slippery deck during a storm, and conducting a routine evolution proved fatal to many sailors, the greatest noncombat fear shared by the crew was the constant threat of fire aboard ship. The officers and crew aboard a naval vessel closely monitored all open flames, including smoking. In the evening, sailors extinguished all lights in order to darken the ship. A darkened ship not only enhanced the watch stander's night vision but helped conceal the ship from the enemy. The "no open flame" policy also reduced the possibility of an accidental fire. The absence of fire at night, even in the galley stoves, denied the men the luxury of hot coffee during the long evening watches. Even smoking was a closely supervised and restricted activity. The commanding officers usually did not allow the men to carry lucifers (matches) and frequently restricted their smoking privileges to the forward weather deck on sailing ships during meal hours and before the men turned in for the evening.[19]

In addition to the deck sailors, a new breed of tars was rapidly carving a niche in the annals of naval history: the steam engineers. This unique breed of men required endurance, brawn, and intelligence to operate the massive engines, maintain the temperamental auxiliary machinery, and feed the enormous appetite of the boilers. These men laid the foundation for the American navy of the 1880s.

The engineering division consisted of three ratings: first-class firemen, second-class firemen, and coal heavers. The first-class firemen represented between 20 and 25 percent of the engineering manning. Their responsibilities included supervision of the various engineering watches; safe operation of the boilers, main engines, and auxiliary machinery; general maintenance of the equipment; and training of the subordinate engineering ratings. Occupying approximately 25 percent of the engineering billets, the second-class firemen had duties similar to those of a first-class fireman. Coal heavers were at the bottom of the engineering rating structure and filled the remaining engineering billets. The total number of engineers assigned to a river ironclad averaged 11 percent of the total crew, while engineers on the combined sail- and steam-powered ship varied from 11 to 20 percent of the ship's total complement. The engineering division aboard a *Monitor*-class vessel usually comprised 40 percent of the ship's crew. The higher percentage of engineers was due to the absence of sails and the presence of only two cannon, which eliminated the majority of the traditional deck billets.[20]

The typical fire room on board a first-class steam frigate carried four vertical water tube boilers approximately 35 feet long by 8 feet wide. The boilers operated at an average steam pressure of 26 pounds per square inch. Each boiler held four furnaces, and at a modest speed of 5 knots, without sails set, the four boilers consumed 3,400 pounds of anthracite coal per hour. Coal heavers laboriously shoveled each pound of coal into the boiler's furnace.[21]

The *Monitor* engineers, during a dockside experiment measuring the efficiency of the engines, fed almost 600 pounds of anthracite coal per hour into the boilers under ideal conditions.[22] The *Cairo*-class river ironclad consumed almost 2,000 pounds of coal per hour at 6 knots.[23] The steam generated in the boiler passed through a maze of iron pipe and proceeded to the main propulsion engine, located in the engine room, via the steam chest, main engine inlet valve, cylinder, piston, and condenser feed pump and then flowed back into the boiler. Auxiliary equipment siphoned off some of the steam generated in the boiler for use in the mechanical ventilation blowers, the de-watering pumps, and, in *Monitor*-class ships, the turret machinery gear.

The outlet temperature of the steam exiting the boiler was 240 degrees Fahrenheit. The iron pipes carrying the steam were not insulated and thus were an excellent conductor of heat because of the primitive metallurgy of the period. As a result, the external temperature of the iron pipe was approximately 230 degrees Fahrenheit. Not only did the uninsulated pipe radiate heat into the engineering spaces, but it was also a serious burn hazard for any unfortunate sailor who accidentally encountered the steam piping.[24]

An enlisted engineer serving on board the USS *Chicopee* described the hazards of boilers and associated equipment in a letter to a friend: "when we beat to quarters, my place is in the boiler room—hot steam pipes all around me and I know the gas inside would admire to get at me for the work I've made it do; it hisses out sometimes as if to say 'Look out young man, you got me in a tight place now, but it may be my turn some day.'"[25]

Although *Chicopee*'s boilers did not exact revenge on the engineers, for the crew of the USS *Hartford,* the boiler's day had come. Regardless of the amount of training received by the crew of a warship, nothing prepared them for the cataclysmic violence of a boiler explosion.[26] In February 1862, *Hartford* experienced one such explosion. Fortunately, the hatches leading to the fire room were open and the steam escaped directly through the hatches and into the atmosphere. Miraculously, only the men's pride and not their physical well-being suffered from the explosion. When the boiler exploded, the roar of the escaping steam so frightened the men on deck that they lost their composure and stampeded to the bow of the ship to escape injury.[27]

In the realm of boiler misfortunes, the crew of USS *Sonoma* appeared to be as lucky as the men aboard *Hartford.* During *Sonoma*'s pursuit of the Confederate raider CSS *Florida,* the commanding officer ordered the engineers to "crowd all steam." The engineering officer notified the captain that the requested pressure exceeded safe operating parameters and that the boiler could explode at any minute. The commanding officer ignored the recommendation of the engineer and told him, "Your duty is to obey orders, mine to capture or destroy the CSS *Florida* at any risk." The engineering officer continued to follow the captain's orders and fired the boilers beyond their rated steam pressure.[28] Fortunately for the men in the fire room, the boilers did not explode. The engineers had cheated the Grim Reaper again.

The USS *Wachusett* was not quite as fortunate as *Sonoma* during her pursuit of the CSS *Florida*. On 12 December 1862, *Wachusett* experienced an internal explosion when one of its boiler tubes failed. The boiler tube rupture did not pose an immediate threat to the engineers, since the rupture was internal to the boiler. The damage, however, did place the boiler out of service until the engineers repaired the tube. Under normal circumstances, the engineers would extinguish fires in the other boilers to prevent the scalding of the men repairing the inoperative boiler in case the boiler isolation valves leaked. Operational commitments did not allow such safety measures, however, and the engineers courageously repaired the tube while the other boilers remained steaming. Fortunately, the isolation valves held, thus preventing possible injury to the men.[29]

Boiler explosions and ruptured tubes were not the only hazards faced by the men of the engineering division. Water gauge glasses designed to measure the amount of water in the boiler often failed and sent a lethal combination of hot water and steam throughout the boiler front area. The few moments required to close the isolation valve to the gauge glass provided enough time to scald a coal heaver and watchstander.[30]

The constant threats of burns and scalding were only a part of the potential hazards lurking in the engineering spaces. Engineers also lived under the threat of asphyxiation if the mechanical ventilation providing combustion air for the boiler fires failed. The *Monitor* almost foundered on her maiden voyage from New York to Hampton Roads, Virginia, in March 1862. During her transit she experienced mechanical ventilation failure while the ship steamed through inclement weather and high seas.

The low silhouette design of the *Monitor*-class ships made them roll terribly in bad weather and ensured that the deck was always awash with water (photo 9). Periodically, water entered the ship through the turret seal on the main deck amidships and through the ventilation blower intakes. During *Monitor*'s maiden voyage, water leaked into the vessel and soaked the steam engine ventilation blower belts that provided combustion air for the boilers. The wet belts stretched and started to slip, thus preventing the blowers from providing the required volume of combustion air for the boiler. Despite the herculean effort of the engineers, the fires in the boilers eventually went out. Without propulsion and ventilation, the ship floundered at the mercy of the waves and was in serious danger of sinking. To add to the engineers' mounting problems, the loss of steam pressure rendered the de-water pumps inoperative. The rising water level in the bilge eventually mixed with the coal ash and produced a toxic carbonic acid. The engineers, overcome by the fumes, evacuated the engineering space and sought refuge on top of the turret. Several courageous crew members eventually tightened the blower belts and reestablished the fires in the boiler. With steam pressure restored, *Monitor* proceeded on her course with destiny.[31] Despite the inherent dangers to the crews operating the marine engineering equipment during the Civil War, high ambient temperature, humidity, and offensive odors were the engineers' greatest nuisance.

Wooden steamships also contributed to the misery of the engineers. The wooden timbers throughout the ship, and in particular the bilges, provided a haven for dirt, excrement, food, oil, grease, and vomit. The odor intensified when exposed to the high heat and humidity that permeated the engineering spaces. As second engineer on board the screw steamer USS *Princeton,* the future engineering chief of the Union navy, Benjamin Isherwood, described the deplorable conditions in the engine room as "overpowering" because of the high temperatures and stench from the bilge water under their feet.[32]

A "hell on earth" best described the working and watch-standing conditions of the beleaguered sailors assigned to the engineering division. The third assistant engineer aboard the USS *Wachusett* called 7 August 1862 "the hottest day of the season, 128 degrees in the Engine room. . . ."[33] Another engineering officer recorded temperatures as high as 140 degrees in the engine room and a staggering 156 degrees in the fireroom.[34]

Conditions in the engineering spaces aboard a *Monitor* were just as bad as in the wooden steamships. During combat, the working conditions in an ironclad's engine room pushed the endurance of the human body to the extreme. When a *Monitor* prepared for battle, the engineers had to close the hatches that provided natural ventilation to the engineering spaces in order to prevent the possible penetration of an enemy shell. The men also briefly secured the mechanical ventilation every time the great guns fired to prevent damage to the machinery from the enormous concussion of the guns. To make matters worse, the acrid smoke from the cannon drifted throughout the ship and made the conditions an absolute nightmare. Constant exposure to these oppressive elements eventually took its physical toll on the engineers.

The *Monitor*-class USS *Nahant* could not get under way after the bombardment of Fort Wagner, near Charleston, South Carolina, because most of the engineers were heat casualties unfit for duty. The ship's surgeon transferred a number of these men to other vessels in the area to allow them to recuperate.[35] The coal heavers aboard *Nahant* averaged only two months on board before rotating off the ship to preserve their health.[36] *Nahant* was not the only *Monitor*-class ship to suffer heat casualties during the bombardment of Fort Wagner. USS *Catskill* lost two engineering officers and several firemen from the heat.[37] The engineering officer on one of the *Monitor*s that took part in the battle of Mobile Bay on 5 August 1864 periodically rotated his men out of the 150-degree engine room. In the turret chamber, the men enjoyed a brief respite from their self-imposed hell and assisted fellow crew members before returning to Dante's inferno.[38]

Despite the oppressive heat endured by the engineers, the navy expected the men to conduct logistical operations, perform maintenance, effect repairs, and stand watch. Of the multitude of evolution conducted by the engineers, the least favorite was the regular coaling of the ship (photo 10). Steam-powered vessels consumed vast amounts of coal. The screw sloop USS *Wachusett,* while patrolling the Caribbean and South Atlantic for the Confederate raider CSS *Florida,* steamed 4,582 miles from Port Royal, South Carolina, to the Brazilian port of Bahia. The ship, with sails set, averaged 176 miles a day and consumed 6,240 pounds of coal daily. Every pound of coal was monotonously shoveled into the boiler by the coal heavers.[39] At this rate of consumption, ships frequently had to replenish their coal bunkers.

It often required up to 12 hours to complete the coaling of a ship. Hundreds of man-hours were consumed transporting the coal in bags from the delivery ship to the steamship. In one case, USS *Lexington* took 19 hours to load 2,375 sacks of coal. Not only was this process labor intensive, it spread coal dust throughout the ship as the sailors emptied the individual bags of coal into a chute leading to the bunker. The additional hazard of breathing the coal dust only made conditions worse for the crew during this unpopular event. Upon completion of coaling, the crew substituted their brawn for a mop and bucket and cleaned the entire ship of the black dust.[40] During the coaling process, and while under way, coal heavers routinely entered the cavernous coal bunkers to reposition the coal or move it into the boiler furnace area. The lack of natural light and the presence of coal dust and methane gas added to the dangers for the men assigned to this task. The officers required the men to sign for each covered lantern used in the bunkers. The unique design of the covered lanterns prevented an exposed flame from igniting the potentially dangerous methane-rich atmosphere. When the coal heavers completed their assignment in the coal bunkers, they returned the lanterns or signed them over to the next group of men working there. This constant vigilance and personal responsibility for the accountability of the lanterns drove home the importance of safety among the men of the engineering division.[41]

Additional unpleasant jobs requiring the engineer's brawn included caulking boiler rivets, reframing boilers, removing ash from the boiler, scrubbing the decks, and cleaning the bilges, condensers, boiler tubes, boiler fronts, and main engines.[42] In addition, the new and often temperamental machinery required constant maintenance and repair. The engineer's ability to overhaul machinery and provide preventive maintenance on the equipment required intelligence, common sense, years of experience, and long hours. Although Sunday was typically a day set aside for personnel inspections, worship, and rest, the constant demands placed on the engineers seldom allowed them a day of reprieve. Often the engineers worked long hours, seven days a week, to repair equipment to ensure that their ship met its assigned operational duties.[43]

Despite the constant presence of personal injury, a hostile environment, and long, arduous working conditions, the steam engineers during the Civil War performed well. Unfortunately, the engineers' superiors occasionally believed that their performance was less than satisfactory. Rear Adm. Samuel Lee, commander of the North Atlantic Blockading Squadron, complained to Secretary Welles about the poor quality of the engineers serving on board USS *Britannia*. Rear Admiral

LIFE IN MR. LINCOLN'S NAVY

Lee believed that their poor maintenance record with saltwater boilers was due to deficient training and lack of experience in operating low-pressure engines. The admiral, a veteran of the traditional sailing navy, failed to appreciate the stress placed on the engineering equipment required to operate for long periods without maintenance. In addition, the constant steaming of the saltwater boilers led to severe scaling inside the boiler tubes, which eventually led to metal fatigue and tube failure.[44] One senior naval officer, in a letter to a friend, commented on the condition of the Gulf Coast Blockading Squadron ships: "People don't know how difficult it is to keep boilers in order as ours are when steam is kept up month after month without the opportunity being permitted for the necessary repairs and cleaning out. . . . Some of the vessels on the coast have not been in port for six months."[45] The complaint levied against *Britannia* was rare and in most cases unwarranted. Not only did the engineers perform superbly, but their accomplishments rivaled, and sometimes exceeded, today's engineering accomplishments.

Early in the war, the engineers assigned to USS *Niagara* established a standard of excellence for other engineering divisions to emulate. During the spring of 1861, the vessel steamed from Hong Kong to Boston via Cape Town, South Africa, a total distance of 6,731 nautical miles. Two weeks after arriving in Boston, *Niagara* proceeded to her assigned blockading station outside the harbor of Charleston, South Carolina. The ship accomplished this feat with the benefit of only minor engineering repairs during her brief stay in port.[46]

The *Niagara* was not the only ship with an excellent engineering crew. The engineers aboard USS *Kearsarge* performed admirably during her pursuit and subsequent victory over the Union nemesis, CSS *Alabama.* Even the secretary of the navy praised the ship's engineering accomplishments during his annual report in December 1864.[47] William Clark described the outstanding performance of the engineers aboard his ship in a letter to his mother: "The engine was never handled better since the ship had been in commission while under attack from 12 shore cannon while operating close to shore."[48]

Perhaps the engineers of the USS *Wachusett* produced the finest engineering performance during the war, maintaining constant steam pressure for six consecutive months during the spring and summer of 1862. The navy finally relieved *Wachusett* of her blockading station in the James River, and the warship steamed north to the Washington Navy yard for a much needed but brief material upkeep.[49] Her ability to maintain steam pressure for six months without a respite is an amazing accomplishment by today's standards. Two years later the engineers of *Wachusett* equaled this performance when their ship captured the CSS *Florida* in Bahia, Brazil.

The commanding officer of *Wachusett* sent a prize crew to sail *Florida* back to the United States for adjudication. The engineering complement consisted of two junior officers, one first-class fireman, one second-class fireman, and only two coal heavers. These six men successfully operated *Florida*'s engineering spaces throughout the entire five-week journey northward. Remarkably the two coal heavers shoveled an average of 2,600 pounds of coal per day without assistance from the *Florida* crew.[50] The commanding officer of *Wachusett*, fearing trouble from the Confederate prisoners, confined them in double irons for the entire voyage north.[51]

Throughout the Civil War, the men who comprised the fledgling engineering division performed magnificently while overcoming numerous obstacles new to maritime history. Their perseverance, hard work, and sacrifice proved to the maritime nations of the world that the application of steam engineering was practical aboard warships and, in particular, ironclad ships built without sails. The success of the engineering division depended not only on their professionalism but on the safe and continual vigilance of the entire crew functioning as a team while standing watch.

A navy ship never sleeps. Even during darkness a ship remains vigilant and alive with activity. The necessity of safely navigating a ship and operating the engineering machinery required the officers and men to stand several watches, which included lookout, roving security, helmsman, and quartermaster of the watch. In addition, a sailing vessel required a complement of tars capable of setting the numerous sails to meet the dynamic weather conditions and course changes. Steam-powered vessels maintained a 24-hour watch to ensure that the boilers received the requisite amount of coal and that the main engine and auxiliary equipment operated correctly.

Deck division stood a 4-hour watch followed by 4 hours off, then back on watch again. The engineer division stood a 4-hour watch followed by 8 hours off, because of the extreme heat in the engineering spaces.[52] The constant requirement to stand watch and perform general cleaning and maintenance duties quickly fatigued the men. The following passage written by a sailor faithfully described the methodical routine and demands placed upon the crew of a warship:

> After supper there is seldom any work done except in the case of coaling ship. At 7 hammocks are "piped down" every man slings his hammock on his own particular hook and skylarking reigns supreme till 9 o'clock at which time every man must be in his hammock except the "Watch on Deck." At some of the small hours you are called to relieve the watch on deck and if you don't make your appearance in five minutes from the time you are called, the Black list receives an addition to its members or you have (If it's a decent officer) a double watch to stand and you're done with it. A watch lasts two and a half and the first watch is set at 7 o'clock in Winter, and 8 in Summer. The watch that goes on at 7 is relieved at 10:30 and the watch that goes on then is relieved at 1 o'clock, the next watch is the last it goes on at 3:30 and stands till 5:30 when all hands are turned out. The watches are changed every night so that a man has the first watch on Monday night has the second watch on Tuesday night and so on.
>
> I can tell you it used to be rather tough having to turn out and carry a musket $2^1/_2$ hours last Winter when if you spit out on deck and counted 4 you would find said spit frozen perfectly hard. Sentries were very regular in walking as fast as he could or I believe he would have got frozen. If it were not my turn to go on sentry I had just to turn out and be there but if I could I might lie down and go to sleep so long as I did not go to my hammock. I used to on those occasions go into the "fire room" (where the boilers are kept) and lie down on a heap of coal and go to sleep opposite a roaring fire. These gunboats are obliged by government regulations always to have steam up. A coal bed, you will say, is a very dirty one, but a fellow thinks very little of that when it is a case of freezing or comfort and I found a coal bed with a big lump for a pillow very comfortable and had many a good sleep on said bed.[53]

The navy required ships operating on the western rivers and southern estuaries near the enemy's shore to maintain additional watches to prevent surprise night attacks. As a precaution against such attacks, the vessels posted armed guards about the deck and each ship provided one small boat to patrol the river. The small boat served as an early warning and signaled the ships by lantern in the event of an attack. One officer wrote, "The constant watchfulness both by night and day was fatiguing to the officers and crew, disturbed their rest and harassed them."[54] These additional watches contributed to the fatigue of the crew and sometimes required the reduction or suspension of certain drills and maintenance duties.[55]

The daily requirement to clean the ship, stand watches, and perform maintenance consumed most of the ship's daily schedule. The commanding officer, however, ensured that enough time remained in the busy day for training the crew in a variety of seafaring skills.

✥5✥

Shipboard Training

The frequency, duration, and type of drill scheduled by the captain varied from ship to ship, based on the proficiency of the crew, the ship's deployment schedule, and the demands of the ship's commanding officer. The rapid expansion of the navy required the service to "ship" many unskilled sailors. Only 16 percent of USS *Cairo*'s crew had nautical experience, and one sailor described the crew of his ship as "ignorant" with the exception of the "captain" and a few "eastern officers."[1] This scenario continued to repeat itself throughout the war as the navy proliferated and the number of skilled tars available for recruiting dwindled.

The commanding officer had the greatest influence on the morale, discipline, and training of the crew. The paymaster aboard USS *Miami* noted that "our new Commander has not been a week on board before a marked change was visible. . . . Everything about the ship was put in first class man-of-war order. Drills were more frequent and more exacting, and the rattle was sprung at any moment when least looked for."[2]

Uriah Levy, a senior naval officer, published his *Manual of Rules for Men-of-War* in 1862, which recommended that sailors receive training every Monday at general quarters and specialized training on Tuesday, Wednesday, and Friday. Thursday's schedule contained fire drills.[3] Although Levy's manual was only a guideline, many other officers also believed in the merits of a well-trained crew. Capt. William Ronckendorf, commanding officer of the USS *Powhatan,* ensured that his crew trained daily, and he periodically drilled them at night.[4] Captain Ronckendorf astutely realized the importance of night training since most Confederate blockade runners entered or left from Southern ports at night.

The commanding officer of USS *Portsmouth* demanded quickness from his men. When the rattle sounded signaling general quarters, sometime between taps and reveille, he allowed the men only 6 minutes to dress, trice up their hammocks, and stow them in the netting topside. The men then continued to their battle stations wondering if it was just another drill or if the enemy was actually within sight.[5] The sailors aboard USS *Forest Rose* could answer a fire alarm in less than 2 minutes, fully equipped with buckets and hoses.[6] The crew of USS *Fernandina* appeared ready to engage the enemy at any hour of the day. To test the crew's mettle, the executive officer sounded the general quarters alarm at 4:00 A.M. Much to the satisfaction of the executive officer, the men responded in kind and were ready to fire the ship's great guns within 2 minutes.[7]

A ship's proximity to the enemy and the inevitability of a battle increased the frequency of drill. As an anticipated battle with CSS *Alabama* approached, Capt. John Winslow, commanding officer of USS *Kearsarge,* increased the number of drills. On the eve of battle, the crew was capable of repelling boarders within a remarkable 15 seconds. Although the men of *Kearsarge* did not have to repel boarders in their famous engagement with the Confederate raider, their frequent drilling paid handsome dividends when they sank *Alabama.*[8] Without a doubt, training played a major part in *Kearsarge*'s victory.

Remarkably, another ship, even more famous than *Kearsarge,* did not drill at the great guns before their epic engagement. During its engagement with the CSS *Virginia,* the crew of USS *Monitor* fired the ship's guns for the first time! The urgency to complete the radical new ship on time and the poor weather during her transit to Hampton Roads had prevented the crew from drilling at the great guns. Fortunately for the Union, the men of *Monitor* were all seasoned veterans who volunteered for service aboard the new ship.[9]

Finding time to drill with small- and large-caliber weapons was not as big a problem as the navy's failure to equip the ships with an adequate number of standard, modern small arms. The small-arms weapons used by the tars in drill and combat included smooth and rifled muskets, breech-loading rifles, pistols, cutlasses, and boarding pikes. The standard small-arms weapon carried aboard the Union man-of-war varied greatly because of the navy's prewar failure to standardize its purchase of small arms. Halfway through the war, the navy's small-arms inventory was in such a state of chaos that the head of the navy's Ordnance Bureau reported a shortage of small arms and admitted that he relied on the army for weapons. The various calibers and models carried aboard ship exacerbated the ammunition supply problem and hindered the sailor's opportunity to train with small arms. During a drill, a sailor was never sure what weapon he would receive or if the appropriate ammunition was available.[10]

Throughout the Civil War, the nation witnessed the navy's rapid movement toward a technologically advanced service. The navy's successful application of steam, large-caliber rifled cannon, and ironclad ships with revolving turrets clearly demonstrated its commitment to building a world-class navy. Ironically, during this period, the navy continued to maintain a small-arms arsenal of antiquated weapons and outdated tactics. Throughout the war, the navy issued weapons used for boarding enemy ships, a tactic that the ironclad ships and rifled cannon had rendered obsolete.

The battle ax was one of several antique weapons issued to the sailors for use in hand-to-hand combat. The 20-inch-long weapon had a hickory handle and a metal head sporting a 4 1/4-inch blade and hammer head. The tar usually carried the weapon in a black leather frog suspended from his belt. Although the battle ax was designed for close combat, it also served a dual role as a damage-control tool to cut wooden debris and remove damaged rigging from the ship. The navy did not phase the weapon out of its inventory until the 1880s.[11]

The boarding pike was another antiquated close-combat weapon found in the navy's inventory throughout the war. Measuring 8 1/2 feet long, this simple weapon consisted of a metal point approximately 8 inches long attached to a wooden shaft. The boarding pike suffered the similar fate as the battle ax in the 1880s.[12]

The cutlass was also carried by boarding parties. The last edged weapon to be used in the navy, the cutlass remained in the navy inventory until 1949. The patterns 1841 and 1862 made up the bulk of the navy's cutlass inventory. The pattern 1841 had a straight, double-edged blade and was 26 1/4 inches long. A brass basket attached to the handle helped protect the user's hand. The pattern 1862 cutlass sported a curved, single-edged blade, was 32 inches long, and also had a brass hand guard. In order to train the men in the proper use of the cutlass, the navy substituted the lethal weapon with a round wooden stick measuring approximately 32 inches.[13]

One of several handguns used by the sailors was the model 1843, a single-shot, smooth-bore percussion pistol manufactured by the Ames Company of Massachusetts. The pistol measured $11^3/_4$ inches, weighed almost 2 pounds, and fired a .54-caliber round lead ball. Sailors normally tucked the pistol inside the top of their pants.[14] The primary revolver used by the navy was the Colt navy revolver, model 1851. The six-shot percussion pistol fired a .36-caliber lead bullet through a rifled barrel, was 13 inches long, and weighed 2 pounds, 10 ounces. Other revolvers used by the navy included the Colt navy revolver, model 1861, and the Remington navy revolver, models 1861 and 1863. Although these six-shot rifled pistols had a maximum range of 300 yards, their effective range was only 50 yards.[15]

The shoulder weapons employed by the navy during the Civil War were primarily variants of the U.S. musket, model 1842. The model 1842 used a percussion ignition system and fired a .69-caliber round lead ball through a smooth-bore barrel. The weapon measured $57^3/_4$ inches and used an 18-inch socket bayonet. During the decade preceding the Civil War, the army adopted the .58-caliber percussion rifled musket. The navy preferred larger-caliber muskets partly because of the influence of their leading weapons expert, John Dahlgren. In 1862, the navy ordered ten thousand new Whitney navy rifles, model 1861, a .69-caliber percussion weapon (sometimes called the "Plymouth" or "Dahlgren" rifle). The 50-inch-long weapon used a 22-inch saber bayonet. In 1863 the navy, pleased with the performance and durability of the Whitney rifled musket, ordered an additional ten thousand. This remarkable weapon saw service throughout the war and remained in navy warehouses as late as World War II, when the U.S. government issued the Whitney rifled musket to native Pacific islanders to fight the Japanese. The islanders preferred the rifled musket over the modern rifles of the period because of its simplicity. Additional rifles that saw service in the navy during the Civil War included the .52-caliber Sharps and Hankins breech-loading rifles, the Spencer seven-shot repeating rifle, the Springfield .58-caliber rifled muskets (models 1861 and 1863), and the British-made .58-caliber Enfield rifled musket.[16]

Despite the variation of small arms aboard Union warships, the men overcame the deficiencies and trained regularly with whatever weapons they found aboard ship. Frequent training with small arms instilled a degree of discipline and confidence in the men. The officers and men on USS *Florida* periodically honed their marksmanship by firing at a barrel placed in the water approximately 300 yards from the ship.[17] The crew of USS *Nahant* received regular training with small arms at general quarters and occasionally went ashore and conducted live small-arms target practice.[18]

Although the tars spent numerous hours improving their small-arms skills, the primary weapons aboard the Union warships were the large-caliber cannon, commonly called the great guns. At the commencement of hostilities, the navy's heavy ordnance inventory consisted of various large-caliber smooth-bore and rifled cannon. Early in the war a common weapon found aboard ship was the 32-pound smooth-bore cannon capable of firing solid shot and requiring a crew of seven men. The most numerous cannon found aboard Union warships were the 9-, 11-, and 15-inch Dahlgrens, all smooth-bore, muzzle-loading cannon.[19] The massive 15-inch Dahlgren cannon fired a 440-pound solid shot or a 330-pound fused exploding shell. This massive cannon used 30 pounds of black powder to propel the shell approximately 1 mile. The cannon required a crew of fourteen to sixteen men to operate, and at close range, a solid shot fired from the weapon penetrated the Confederate ironclad *Atlanta*'s 4 inches of iron plate.[20] The navy also used 8- and 10-inch rifled Parrot cannon on some ships.[21]

Because of the enormous size and weight of the cannon and its projectiles, under ideal manning conditions, the 9-inch Dahlgren cannon required sixteen men and a powder monkey to operate (photo 11). The cannon positions included one gun captain, two powder and shell loaders, two rammers, and two spongers. The rammers' and spongers' primary duties were to seat the powder and projectile in the base of the muzzle-loading cannon. After firing the weapon, the spongers extinguished any residual embers remaining in the barrel by swabbing it with a water-soaked sponge. Additional crew positions included four side tacklemen, who trained the cannon laterally, and five train tacklemen, who returned the cannon to its forward position after recoil and loading. One powder monkey rounded out the cannon team.[22]

The sheer size of the great guns and the number of men assigned to each cannon required rigorous training for the men to work in harmony. The numerous tasks required under the noisy, hot, and smoke-filled confines of a compartment is testimony to the men's dedication and skill in handling the great guns. Alvah Hunter described the clock-work precision required to fire a cannon aboard a *Monitor*-class ship:

> When a Gun was discharged, the recoil brought it well back within the turret, the port stopper was swung around to close the porthole and the turret was turned a third to half around so that the portholes were away from the enemy. The port stopper was then swung back and the sponge handle was passed out through the port hole until the sponge could be entered into the muzzle of the gun, then two men, standing one each side of the muzzle, pushed the sponge down inside the gun till the bottom of the bore was reached; a couple of turns of the sponge and then it was withdrawn. . . .
>
> Another cartridge-bag of powder had been passed up from below as soon as the gun was fired, and was now placed in the muzzle of the gun and rammed home. The rammer handle had to be passed out through the porthole before the rammer-head could be inserted in the gun, and the handle had to be passed out through the porthole again in withdraw-ing the rammer from the gun. Next, a shell was rolled along [the deck] to near the muzzle of the gun, where grappling-tongs was clasped on it and a tackle hoisted it to the muzzle; the men pushed it into the muzzle and the rammer was used a second time in ramming the shell home.
>
> There were three time fuses screwed into holes drilled into the top of the shell, each fuse being capped with a small bit of lead on which was stamped figures which told the number of seconds required for that fuse to burn down to the powder charge within the shell. If we were ten, twelve or fifteen seconds distant from the target, the fuse cap so stamped was torn off as the shell was passed into the gun. If we chanced to be within close range, so that the shortest-timed fuse failed to explode the exploding charge there were two more chances that the shell would explode.
>
> A sharp-pointed steel rod was passed down the touchhole of the gun till the cloth envelope of the cartridge was pierced, then it was with-drawn and a primer having a percussion-cap-head was set into the hole. The gun was run out [tars using block and tackle manually pulling on ropes to move the cannon] . . . then the turret was turned until the gun bore upon the target. The right elevation of the gun was obtained by turning a huge screw set in an extension of the breech. A lock, much like a small hammer, was fixed near the touchhole, the hammer being swung over and down on the primer by a sharp pull upon a lanyard attached to it, the gunner holding the lanyard and waiting the word, "all ready sir," and the officer in charge of the gun gave the order, "Fire!"[23]

This evolution repeated itself dozens of times during combat. The loading and firing of one 13- or 15-inch Dahlgren cannon aboard a *Monitor*-class ship took between 6 and 8 minutes. Despite the close confines of the turret, the gunners enjoyed the protection of the iron-enclosed turret.

Constant training with the great guns eventually enabled several ships to boast of excellent gunnery teams. The surgeon on board USS *Fernandina* commented about the positive impact the constant training at the guns was having on the men: "Some shots were splendid . . . the boys deserve great credit for their skill in handling the guns."[24]

Even fleet admirals became involved in gunnery practice. Before the invasion of Fort Fisher, at the mouth of the Cape Fear River leading to Wilmington, North Carolina, Admiral Porter ordered his warships to practice live firing daily in preparation for the naval bombardment of the Confederate stronghold.[25] The practice paid off; a number of well-placed Union rounds found their mark and disabled dozens of Confederate cannon during the battle.[26] The enormous naval bombardment enabled the invasion force to land and subsequently seize the Confederate bastion.

The number of drills conducted on board ship played an important part in training the men. The degree of realism and enthusiasm instilled into the drill greatly enhanced the sailors' motivation and learning ability. One sailor described a lively drill period that included training at the great guns and small arms simultaneously:

> Gun practice started with the rapid roll of the drum. Here, there, everywhere, men jumped to their feet and rushed to their battle stations fully equipped with cutlass and gun. "Pass nine inch shell and load!" roared the captain. "Now run out! Train her two points [twenty-five degrees] off port quarter; elevate for five hundred yards! Fire! Run her in. . . ." While the captain supervised the gunnery drill, the First Lieutenant called away boarders: "Boarders and pikemen at port quarter! First boarders advance! Second boarders advance! Repel boarders." The men then simulate slashing with cutlasses and firing with rifles and pistols at an imaginary enemy. After several minutes of repelling an imaginary foe the drill is secured and the crew continued on their daily assignments.[27]

Ultimately the constant drilling at the great guns and small arms slowly molded the crew into an efficient and cohesive fighting unit.

❖ **6** ❖

Pork and Beans

Food played a vital role in the navy throughout the Civil War. Not only did the provisions provide nourishment for the men exposed to long hours of fatiguing work and standing watch, but meals also broke the monotony of blockade duty and contributed to the morale of the crew. For many sailors the opportunity to eat three times a day became the highlight of the daily routine. As one sailor put it, "When breakfast is done, the next thing I look forward to is dinner, and when that's done, I look for supper time. . . ."[1]

The navy made a concerted effort to ensure that its men received a balanced diet that included fresh provisions. On 18 July 1861, Congress approved the following daily naval ration that incorporated a variety of foods rich in protein, carbohydrates, and vitamins:[2]

> One pound salt pork, with half a pint of beans or peas; or one pound salt beef, with half a pound of flour, and two ounces of dried apples or other fruit; or three quarters of preserved meat [canned], with half a pound of rice, two ounces of butter, and one ounce of desiccated mixed vegetables; or three quarters pound preserved meat, two ounces of butter, and two ounces of desiccated potato; together with fourteen ounces of biscuits [hardtack], one quarter of an ounce of tea, or one ounce of coffee or cocoa, two ounces of sugar, and a gill [four ounces] of spirits

[grog]; and a weekly allowance of a half a pound of pickles, half a pint of molasses, and half a pint of vinegar.[3]

The navy diet exceeded the army's daily ration by four ounces of salt pork, one-half ounce of desiccant potatoes, and one-half ounce of coffee. In addition, the navy provided butter, whereas the army did not.[4]

The Union sailor not only enjoyed a slightly larger bill of fare over his army counterpart, but he also benefited from a far superior system that ensured a steady diet of fresh meat and vegetables. Under the tutelage of Secretary Welles, the navy established a remarkable and unprecedented logistical system that contributed to the health and morale of the men. Early in the conflict, Welles expressed the importance of keeping the sailors well provisioned: "It is essential that the crews have frequent supplies of fresh provisions and other necessaries conducive to health . . . and it proposes to continue to supply the crews of the squadrons until the insurrection is suppressed."[5] The key element of this logistical system centered around a group of ships designated as supply vessels. Their primary mission was to provide fresh meat, vegetables, and ice to the blockading fleet. A typical supply ship assignment, originating from New York, took approximately three weeks to complete. During this period, the ships delivered their provisions to the various blockading squadrons located along the Atlantic seaboard and the Gulf of Mexico. As a result of this superior supply system, a blockading ship regularly received fresh provisions every two or three weeks.[6]

One ship that faithfully served the navy during the war was the USS *Massachusetts*. This steam-powered auxiliary ship carried only government-purchased supplies. On her southbound voyage she furnished the blockading squadrons with fresh food, ice, mail, spare parts, and replacement sailors. On her return trip north, she distributed the remainder of her cargo, provided transportation for the sick and wounded, and delivered mail to the postal service for distribution.[7] The sight of this supply-laden vessel immediately raised the spirits of the sailors. One tar described the anticipated rendezvous with *Massachusetts*: "We, too, soon come up, and hear that letters, papers, fresh meat and ice awaits us, on the good old Bay State steamer *Massachusetts*. We prepare to lower boat and get our goodies. . . . The boat returns well laden with barrels of potatoes, quarter of beef, and chunks of ice, but no mail."[8]

The men patrolling the western rivers not only relied on supply vessels but frequently augmented their food by liberally foraging along the river, bartering with contraband, and purchasing from agents and loyal unionists living in the South. In a letter to his sweetheart, a crew member of USS *Forest Rose* described the fruits of a foraging expedition: "We left Natchez yesterday . . . stopping at several plantations on our way up to procure forage. We succeeded admirably, obtaining a good supply of vegetables and some poultry."[9]

Contrabands also provided a steady supply of provisions for the river squadrons. One officer described one such encounter with the African Americans: "the boat thronged all day with negroes who brought various articles of food such as corn and apples, muscadines [grapes], sweet potatoes, quinces, &c. . . . The chief articles we give in exchange for provisions are tobacco, coffee & flour. . . ."[10] In a later encounter, the contrabands provided the men of *Forest Rose* with "sweet potatoes, butter, eggs, chickens, corn meal," in exchange for "coffee, tea, flour and spices."[11] The river squadrons also purchased meat from civilian supply agents or loyal unionists living along the rivers. On one occasion USS *Mississippi* purchased 1,268 pounds of fresh meat for $101.44 from Mr. Jose M. Vallejo Jr.[12]

Throughout the war, the navy continued to improve its logistical system. As the navy's inventory of warships steadily grew, so did the number of supply ships required to provision the ships on blockading duty.[13] In May 1864, as Admiral Farragut began collecting his fleet for the eventual attack on Mobile, Alabama, his ships continued to receive a constant supply of provisions. A typical delivery to his flagship, USS *Hartford,* included the following items: twenty barrels of beef, thirty barrels of pork, eight kegs of pickles, butter, two barrels of molasses, eighty boxes of beef, twenty barrels of flour, five kegs of apples, eighty-five barrels of bread, twenty-five barrels of beans, twenty boxes of mustard, twenty-five boxes of pepper, fifty barrels of potatoes, fifteen boxes of coffee, three boxes of tea, fifteen barrels of sugar, ten boxes of candles, thirty boxes of soap, and twenty-four spools of cotton.[14]

One of the more remarkable accomplishments of the navy's logistical system was its ability to provide fresh meat and ice to the ships operating in the southern latitudes during the summer months. Although the use of mechanical refrigeration was thirty years away, supply ships were able to maintain fresh meat in their cargo holds for up to three weeks. The standard method of preserving fresh meat was layering it with ice in a designated compartment below decks.[15] Throughout the first summer of the war, this type of preservation system worked well for the supply ships.

In the fall of 1861, the navy department decided to experiment with a new type of preservation. The service ordered the commanding officer of USS *Connecticut* to store his fresh meat in a new manner, which required hanging four hundred quarters of fresh beef in a large locker lined with ice. The naval service believed that this new method would preserve the meat longer. The unforeseen problem with this plan was the inability to circulate a sufficient amount of cold air in the compartment to maintain the meat. Foreseeing the weakness of the new method, the commanding officer astutely stored a portion of the meat in two smaller lockers using the proven method of layering the meat with ice.[16] *Connecticut* departed New York with 59,000 pounds of fresh beef and 125 tons (250,000 pounds) of ice in a ratio of 1 to 4. The cruise proved the commanding officer's theory correct. The meat suspended in the locker began to spoil midway through the deployment. By the time the ship reached the blockading squadron off Galveston, Texas, most of the hanged beef had spoiled. Fortunately for the ships in the various blockading squadrons, *Connecticut*'s commanding officer had the foresight to store some beef the old-fashioned way. On the vessel's northbound journey, the supply ship issued fresh meat from its two smaller lockers.[17] After *Connecticut*'s voyage, the navy abandoned further experimentation with suspended beef and returned to the proven practice of layering the meat with ice.

Although both the larger wooden vessels and the smaller *Monitor*-class vessels received fresh provisions, the *Monitor*s did not have sufficient stowage space below decks to store large quantities of fresh provisions. Engineers aboard these smaller vessels quickly overcame the stowage problem by constructing "ice" boxes on the main deck. Although the dimensions varied from ship to ship, the engineers on USS *Nahant* built an iron box 8 feet long, 4 feet wide, and 4 feet deep. The iron container held approximately half a ton of ice and 300 pounds of meat, which stayed fresh for about seven days.[18]

Despite the navy's dedicated efforts to provide provisions on a regular basis, periodically the supply system could not meet the squadrons' demand for food and other consumable items. By 1862, the four blockading squadrons consumed an average of 3,000 tons of coal a week, not to mention other essential items required by the ships.[19] In

February 1863, Adm. Samuel Du Pont notified Secretary Welles that his South Atlantic Blockading Squadron was experiencing shortages in engine lubricating oils, coal, sugar, coffee, flour, butter, beans, dried fruit, and clothing.[20] Ships that detached from their squadrons also experienced food shortages. When USS *Fernandina* received orders to proceed to her home port in New England for upkeep, the northern voyage took the sailing vessel longer than expected because of a lack of favorable winds. By the third week of the cruise, the men had consumed their supply of fresh meat and vegetables. Throughout the remainder of the voyage they dined on a steady diet of salt pork, salt beef, and pork and beans.[21]

When the fresh meat, fruit, and vegetables eventually ran out aboard ship, the crew occasionally had the luxury of dining upon the latest technology of the day: canned food. As early as 1804 the French navy, and later Napoleon's Grande Armée, had used food preserved in glass bottles developed by the French scientist Nicholas Appert.[22] By 1812, Englishman Brian Donkin had improved on Appert's invention and successfully preserved food in a more durable tin can.[23] American entrepreneurs picked up on this new technology, and in 1822 the William Underwood Company of Boston produced canned meat for sale to the public. In 1856 Gail Borden received a patent for condensed milk, and on the eve of the Civil War, the Gilbert Van Camp Company introduced canned pork and beans in a tomato sauce.[24] By 1861, the navy had a variety of canned products available for purchase.

The navy bought canned meat packaged in tin cans that weighed between 2 and 6 pounds.[25] The ability to purchase canned products that could withstand the rigors of transportation at sea and the various temperatures aboard ship contributed to the sailors' varied diet. Additional processed foods available to the navy on the eve of the war included desiccated (dehydrated) vegetables and fruits, including onions, carrots, potatoes, turnips, string beans, peas, asparagus, apples, and apricots. The mechanical process of removing water from these items kept them from spoiling and proved ideal for use aboard ships. When placed under hydraulic pressure, vegetables and fruits yielded their water content, which could be restored when these foods were soaked in water for at least one hour. Although the process of dehydration diminished a portion of the vegetables' and fruits' nutritional value, they did provide an important substitute when fresh provisions were not available.[26]

LIFE IN MR. LINCOLN'S NAVY

The new technology in food preservation greatly improved the sailor's diet. Despite the navy's capacity to provide fresh and mechanically processed food, however, the sailor continued to receive a fair amount of salt pork and salt beef. Although canning revolutionized the meat industry, the chemical process of salting meat continued to be the primary means of preserving meat during the war. The ship's cook usually soaked the meat in water for several hours to remove most of the salt before preparing the meat for consumption. He then either boiled the meat or added it to a soup or stew.

Hardtack served as the staple bread ration issued to the sailors aboard ship. A filling food, hardtack was the primary source of carbohydrate in the sailors' diet. The hardtack cracker, measuring 3 inches square and approximately 1 inch thick, consisted of plain flour and water. The manufacturer baked the dough at a low temperature for several hours. The dry, hard cracker was durable and easy to package and transport to the fleet. Unfortunately, over time, hardtack acquired an affinity for moisture, which encouraged mold. In addition, maggots and weevils often took up residence in the cracker.[27] One sailor likened the worms he found in hardtack to those of chestnut worms. He described the worms as having white bodies and black heads. His frequent encounter with worms enabled the tar to pen the following passage in his memoir: "Break open a hard-tack and perhaps two or three [worms] would lie imbedded in the—well, cracker. But after being on board some time I could munch them equal to any vet, without examining the interior."[28]

Periodically the cooks made a dish out of hardtack called dandy-funck. The cook soaked the hardtack in freshwater and then baked the cracker with salt pork and molasses. As a substitute for hardtack, the ship's cook occasionally baked fresh bread or used the flour ration to make a unique dish called duff. Duff was a flour pudding boiled in a bag. Another delicacy prepared with the flour ration was sea pie. This hearty meal consisted of pie crust alternately layered with meat and then baked.[29]

Fresh, piping-hot coffee was the tars' favorite nonalcoholic beverage. The ship's cook received the coffee bean either fresh or roasted. He prepared the coffee in large kettles, out of which the men ladled the contents into their cups for consumption. One advantage steam powered-vessels had over sailing ships was the constant source of heat available to boil coffee. Standard shipboard procedure required the extinguishing of galley stoves during combat and hours of darkness. During these periods the men went without hot coffee. For the men assigned to a steamship, however, fresh hot coffee was always available. The ingenious sailors heated their coffee over hot coals removed from the boiler. The sailors even drew scalding hot water directly from the main condenser to brew their beverage.[30] Unfortunately, not all the coffee served aboard ship met with the satisfaction of the crew. One sailor disgustedly wrote about the creatures that inhabited his coffee: "One thing I never got used to, and that was finding cockroaches in my coffee, although after picking a few out of my tin cup I would manage to worry the liquid down."[31]

The sailor's preferred beverage aboard ship was not coffee, but his daily grog ration. One sailor gave an excellent description of the daily ritual of receiving grog:

> Grog was served out twice a day, in the morning before breakfast and again at night before piping down for supper. When the Boatswain piped for grog time, the crew fell into line and marched in single file, before the ships steward, who dealt out each share as he came up. Each man received one gill [4 ounces] in a small round measure. The boys often tried to trick the steward by falling in line again and thereby getting a double ration, but they were not always successful in this, for the steward, master-at-arms, and a marine stood by to see that each man got his ration and that no man was served twice.[32]

The men not only received the alcoholic beverage daily, but the commanding officer sometimes issued whiskey during combat. Lt. John Worden, commanding officer of USS *Monitor*, ordered the paymaster to issue half a gill (two ounces) of whiskey to the crew during their epic naval engagement with CSS *Virginia*.[33]

Although several congressmen and civilians lobbied during the antebellum period for the abolishment of the grog ration, the drink survived until the summer of 1862. Then, with the defection of the Southern congressmen, both houses approved the abolishment of alcohol in the navy. Instead of their grog ration, the men received five cents a day.[34] To the dismay of the sailors, the law officially went into effect on 1 September 1862. One sailor recalled the reaction of his fellow shipmates upon hearing the news about the abolishment of grog:

> I well remember the day we received the news that grog was abolished. . . . Curses not so loud, but deep, were indulged in by old tars, some of

whom, had seen years of service, and who, by custom, had become habituated to their allowance of grog, that the very expectation of it was accompanied by a feeling of pleasure. It was a long time before the men forgot the actions of congress, and in fact, they never ceased to talk about it.[35]

One man assigned to USS *Portsmouth,* lamenting over the abolishment of grog, wrote the following song, "Farewell to Grog," in honor of the popular beverage's departure:

Oh! Messmates, pass the bottle around,
  Our time is short, remember;
For our grog must stop, our spirits drop,
  on the first day of September.

Farewell old rye! 'tis a sad, sad word,
  But alas it must be spoken;
The ruby cup must be given up,
  And the demijohn be broken!

Jack's happy days will soon be past,
  To return again, no, never
For they've raised his pay five cents a day
  And stopped his grog forever.

All hands to splice the main brace call,
  But splice it now in sorrow,
For the spirit-room key will be laid away
  Forever, on to-morrow.[36]

Even officers showed a touch of remorse over the parting of a time-honored custom. On 31 August 1862, the commanding officer of USS *Augusta* recorded in his journal for the last time, "at 6:15 P.M. all hands spliced the main brace."[37] Five hours and 45 minutes after his entry, the navy official closed the chapter on grog.

Although the navy believed that it was finally free of alcohol and its inherent problems, the Union sailors proved to be wily characters who frequently tried to smuggle various alcoholic drinks aboard ship. At Port Royal, Jamaica, sailors purchased liquor for ten dollars a bottle and regularly smuggled the bottles on board. In one incident, several petty officers stationed aboard USS *Powhatan* stole whiskey earmarked for medicinal purposes. The authorities aboard ship apprehended the men, and a court-martial followed.[38]

Although the men purchased a considerable volume of spirits ashore, the greatest source of alcohol available to the men was the government-licensed trade (sutler) schooners. The secretary of the treasury issued to civilian captains a sutler permit, which allowed the captain to sell merchandise to the sailors. Because the secretary limited the number of permits, the handful of licensed sutler ships secured a monopoly on their trade and sold items at inflated prices. Despite the inflated prices, these floating store ships maintained an impressive inventory of goods that enhanced the sailors' living conditions. In the spring of 1863, one sutler ship sold a pair of shoes for $5.00 (open-market price was $2.50). Tobacco sold for $1.00 a pound (open-market price $0.75), twelve bottles of ale went for $3.00, and envelopes sold for $1.00 per hundred.[39] Additional inventory included toiletry articles, pipes, playing cards, reading and writing material, foodstuffs, and, to the dismay of the commanding officers, alcoholic beverages. Cdr. Percival Drayton called the sutler ships "floating grog shops" and even complained to his superiors about the selling of spirits to the tars.[40]

The presence of a sutler schooner brought great rejoicing from the men, who looked forward to shopping aboard these ships, especially after the abolishment of grog. Although it was illegal for the sutler ships to sell spirits to sailors, they continually violated the law and sold whiskey at the going rate of $2.00 a bottle. On one occasion, sailors illegally bought liquor from a sutler ship and tried unsuccessfully to smuggle the spirits aboard in canned goods marked "oysters and milk."[41] The surgeon on USS *Fernandina* described in his journal some effects of a visit to the sutler ship: "Some of the boys feel lively, having imbibed rather freely while on board the sutler." He further elaborated on the drunken stupor of the men when he described their "sore heads" the next morning at "sick call." The doctor showed no mercy for the men suffering from hangovers and refused to place them on the sick list, declaring them fit for full duty.[42]

The enlisted men were not the only violators of the alcohol ban in the navy. On several occasions senior officers continued to issue spirits to the men. The officers believed the consumption of alcoholic beverages in battle contributed to the tar's courage and stamina. Rear Adm. John Dahlgren authorized the consumption of whiskey for the men in his squadron during combat. When Secretary Welles discovered that Dahlgren was violating the alcohol ban, he chastised the flag officer and cited a memo written by Surgeon William Whelan, chief of the

Bureau of Medicine and Surgery, regarding the adverse effects alcohol had on the body. Whelan correctly contended that alcoholic drinks provided a brief stimulant followed by a longer period of depression. He recommended that the men, as a stimulant for combat or other arduous duties, drink strong coffee or tea, preferably served with ice. Whelan recommended that after combat, the men receive a good meal, dry clothes, and rest. In addition, the medical chief encouraged the engineers who were exposed to extreme heat, to eat a mixture of water and oatmeal to help quench their thirst.[43]

One year after Welles chastised Rear Admiral Dahlgren for serving spirits to his men during battle, a subordinate officer in Admiral Farragut's squadron recommended to the admiral that he should issue a ration of grog to the men to bolster their courage before the fleet assaulted Fort Morgan. Farragut, after reviewing the request, remarked, "I . . . have seen a battle or two, but I have never found that I wanted rum to enable me to do my duty. I will order two cups of good coffee to each man, at two o'clock."[44] Several hours after the men received their coffee, they defeated the Confederate forces blocking the entrance to Mobile Bay. The Union sailors held courage in their hearts but not a drop of liquor on their breath.

The departure of grog in the navy removed a vice that many sailors looked forward to in order to break the monotony of blockading duty. The demise of their favorite beverage meant that the men placed an even greater emphasis on the quality of their meals. Fortunately for the tars, they frequently received three hot meals a day prepared by men assigned the professional rating of cook. Unlike the army, which did not have a special billet for a full-time cook, the navy stationed several cooks on each ship. The cook's express duty consisted of preparing, cooking, and supervising all the meals served to the officers and men. It was not uncommon to find cooks who were former civilian chefs. The senior cook aboard *Nahant,* for example, served as a civilian chef at a well-known Boston restaurant before applying his culinary talents at sea.[45]

Navy chefs did not do all the work of preparing, cooking, and serving the meals. The cooks received daily assistance from a handful of men chosen by their peers from their respective messes. A typical mess aboard a ship consisted of ten to fifteen men usually from the same rating or watch rotation. The number of individual messes varied with the ship's complement. The men shared a common chest full of cups, plates, knives, forks, and spoons. Periodically, each mess chose one member to serve as the cook's assistant, or "mess cook." The mess cook's duty involved spreading a large piece of canvas on the deck for the men to sit on while they ate. In addition, he drew from their assigned chest the various eating utensils for each member of the mess. Before the meal, he assisted the cook in drawing the daily rations from the storeroom. While the cook prepared the meal, the mess cook drew a pan of hardtack or soft bread and a bucket of boiling water. He added either coffee or tea, and sugar for sweetening. While the men drew their beverage of the day, the mess cook returned to the galley to draw the meal's main course. After the meal, the mess cook policed the area and returned the eating utensils and canvas. The mess cook routinely received a small stipend of approximately seventy-five cents a month, drawn from the pockets of his messmates.[46]

The professional preparation of food, three times a day, required teamwork, foresight, imagination, and work. Charles Poole, quartermaster aboard a cruiser, eloquently described the daily ritual of eating:

> We go down to breakfast which consists of a pan of potato scouse [potatoes and hardtack cooked together with butter], a pot of hot coffee, and plenty of hard bread [hardtack], and thus passes the most important hour in the day. . . . At 12 M we have dinner consisting of fresh bread and vegetable soup. . . . At 4 PM we get our supper, which consist of hot tea or coffee and hard bread.[47]

Although the navy occasionally failed to provide the authorized quantity and variety of food for its sailors, a review of numerous ships' logs, personal diaries, letters, and journals clearly illustrates the navy's commitment toward a balanced diet. When fresh meat was available, it was not unusual for the men to enjoy it twice a day. A standard bill of fare aboard the South Atlantic Blockading Squadron's USS *Nahant* was scouse for breakfast, hot stew for dinner, and boiled beef and potatoes for supper.[48] A passenger aboard USS *Delaware* referred to breakfast as "a hearty meal, consisting of canned meats, scouse, and good hot coffee."[49] The quality of food served aboard USS *Portsmouth* received mixed reviews from a twenty-one-year-old carpenters mate, who described a meal of soup with meat as "tasting good," although he thought a Christmas dinner of bean soup and "halt junk" (salted meat) was inappropriate for the holiday.[50] A crew member of USS *Tyler* sarcastically wrote about his New Year's Day meal: "A Happy New Year! . . .

I had some boiled pork and beans, nearly cold, and I had some cold peternicks [?] and I had some cold mashed potatoes and cold boiled cabbage and lots of other good things. . . ."[51] Another sailor referred to navy meals as themes that varied in quality:

> There was duff day, when flour was boiled in bags, and usually so hard that it could be thrown across the deck without breaking it. This was served with molasses. Then we had bean day, hardtack and cheese day, and soup day. And here let me say the soup was excellent; plenty of vegetables were put in to make it palatable, and each man had enough given to him.[52]

Even the admiral's flagship did not always dine on the finest cuisine. When the fresh provisions gave out, as they frequently did aboard the ships assigned to the distant Gulf Coast Blockading Squadron, the men received a steady diet of salted food. During a period of five months, the crew of USS *Hartford* ate pork and beans for dinner 34 percent of the time.[53]

Despite the periodic lack of fresh provisions, some ships managed to eat quite well. Although *Nahant* had not received fresh provisions for almost two weeks, its cooks were still impressive hosts. Following the defeat of the rebel ram CSS *Atlanta,* several prisoners from the Confederate ironclad transferred to *Nahant,* where they received a fine breakfast. One Confederate midshipman believed it was the best breakfast he had eaten in a long time, and he called the coffee "Sure enough coffee."[54] Eventually, however, the fresh provisions "played out" before the much-anticipated supply ship arrived with fresh stores.

As the men slowly tired of the never-ending supply of salted meat, they sometimes turned to the land and sea to augment the navy ration and satisfy their palates. Sailors frequently augmented their diets with items purchased ashore while on liberty. When the combined forces of the army and navy occupied several Southern coastal islands, escaped slaves established small communities under the protection of the American flag. The contrabands quickly learned the value of capitalism and established small businesses that sold a variety of amenities to the sailors. By the summer of 1862, both the officers and the men paid five cents for a quart of milk or a dozen ears of corn. Eggs sold for twelve cents a dozen, and one chicken went for the same price. Shrimp sold for a steep ten cents apiece, but fish were only two cents a pound. The men also had the opportunity to have a dozen pieces of clothing washed for fifty cents, and if the tar provided the material, the local inhabitants would make a new pair of pants or a shirt for fifty cents.[55] Perhaps the greatest irony associated with the navy's occupation of the Southern coastal regions occurred during the summer of 1863. While the women of Richmond, Virginia, protested food shortages, only 90 miles to the southeast the Union navy dined on an abundance of fresh fish, oysters, crabs, cucumbers, melons, and tomatoes.[56]

Onshore, the men also enjoyed superb dinners prepared by local inhabitants trying to establish a livelihood. One contraband, Harry, operated a small dining facility on St. Simons Island off the coast of Georgia. Harry charged the sailors only fifty cents for a meal consisting of fresh pork, chicken, rice, green vegetables, and potatoes. Another contraband couple, in competition with Harry, charged the men only twenty-five cents for fresh beef, fried fish, oysters, apple pie, and sassafras beer.[57] The new economic expansion along the Union-occupied Southern coastline enabled the contrabands to work the land and receive a modest income while the sailors enjoyed their liberty. An additional benefit of these small businesses was the added variety to their navy diet. The outer islands slowly developed into small, successful communities. Unfortunately, the end of the war meant the departure of the blockading fleets and an economic decline for the inhabitants of the outer islands.

Many sailors also applied their hunting and fishing skills on shore. The crew of USS *Fernandina,* operating off the northern coast of Florida, frequently landed parties in quest of food. One expedition netted over two hundred turtle eggs, and another foray brought in a hefty sum of one thousand oranges.[58] Crew members on a blockading ship at anchor off Key West caught seven sharks ranging from 7 to 10 feet long.[59] One sailor wrote his mother: "The fishing is very good and I can at any time feel certain of getting fish enough for a meal in a half hour."[60] The crew of another ship feasted on steamed mussels they had collected when their navy rations dwindled.[61]

Navy supply ships, sutler schooners, foraging, fishing, and liberty enabled the sailor to obtain a variety of foods. Although these sources provided the sailor with a balanced diet, nothing rivaled the shipment of food from the various civilian community organizations. In July 1864, the good citizens of New York sent a supply of fresh vegetables to the sailors of the North Atlantic Blockading Squadron.[62] The civilian committee from the same state also donated on Thanksgiving 18,841 pounds of turkey, 8,878 pounds of chicken, and 2,437 pounds of geese to the men of the squadron.[63] On board USS *Miami,* the men ate quite well for Thanksgiving. They dined on roasted turkey, chicken, and geese, each man receiving approximately 2 pounds of fresh meat.[64]

Although the Thanksgiving bill of fare for the sailors was impressive, Christmas dinner was the finest meal served to the men during the war. The crew of *Fernandina,* for example, ate fresh roasted pig for their 1862 Christmas dinner, and the officers purchased two additional pigs out of their own purses for the crew on New Year's Day.[65]

Although the men of *Fernandina* enjoyed a tasty Christmas meal in 1862, their cooks prepared a Yuletide dinner the following year that exceeded even today's lavish holiday meal. The men collected donations from the officers and crew in order to purchase additional food from the supply ship USS *Massachusetts* for their Christmas dinner. The bill of fare included roasted beef, pig, raccoon, rabbit, turkey, and ham; boiled duck; baked, roasted, and stewed chicken; raw, fried, and stewed oysters; baked, boiled, and fried fish; sweet potatoes; baked potatoes; tomatoes; corn; plum, apple, and orange pudding; apple, mincemeat, and pumpkin pies; and, finally, plain cake, fruitcake, and sponge cake! During the feast, the men toasted with water and coffee the president, the secretary of the navy, the army, the commodore, the captain, the ship, the flag, and the fair sex. The entire crew dressed in their finest uniforms and ate at specially prepared tables 40 feet long. Although the crew members would have rather spent the holidays with their loved ones at home, the bountiful meal contributed to the morale of the crew and helped alleviate potential homesickness.[66]

While the three meals a day kept the sailors healthy and helped break up the monotony of blockading duty, food alone could not eliminate the boredom. One sailor likened blockading duty to sitting on the roof of a house and drinking lukewarm water. Another sailor wrote home: "I have seen enough of the sea, I am not sea sick but I am sick of the sea." Distraught over his pitiful plight, another man penned a letter to Secretary Welles, requesting a discharge: "Give me my discharge and let me go home. I am poor, weak, miserable, nervous, half crazy boy . . . everything jars . . . upon my delicate nerves. . . ."[67] Another sailor also found blockading duty boring and less than desirable because the enemy was situated on one side of them and a "great waste of water" occupied the other side of the ship.[68]

Even in a foreign shipyard, prolonged periods of inactivity contributed to the monotony and the decline of morale of the sailors. The men of USS *Kearsarge* endured a terrible ordeal during the Christmas holidays in La Carraca, Spain, while the ship's engineering equipment underwent repairs. The daily grind of work coupled with only a view of the surrounding mudflats slowly sapped the moral strength from the men as desertions and incidents of fighting increased.[69] Despite the continued presence of palatable food, the only cure for boredom was entertainment, and sailors went to great efforts to obtain this.

7

Entertainment, Liberty, and the Lord's Day

The monotonous grind of the daily routine aboard a blockading vessel slowly eroded the sailors' spirit. It was not unusual for blockading ships to spend two months or more on station, and within the sight of land.[1] Although three meals a day, training, cleaning, maintenance of the equipment, and watch standing occupied a large portion of their day, the tars nevertheless experienced long periods of idleness. The sailors' ability to break the monotony of blockading duty became one of their greatest challenges during the war.

One ship that did not have to worry about the problem was the USS *Monitor.* After her naval engagement with CSS *Virginia,* the ironclad experienced an overabundance of visiting dignitaries and reporters. During the spring and summer of 1862, the president, the vice president, the secretary of the navy, the assistant secretary of the navy, senators, congressmen, admirals, generals, colonels, and foreign naval officers all provided a steady stream of inquisitive visitors seeking a glimpse of the famous little ironclad. The ship's fame soon began to wear out the officers and crew. The ship's paymaster described the ordeal:

> Of course with every fresh arrival of troops, and which are now almost continuous, we have fresh interruptions of visitors. We are hardly up from the breakfast table before they commence and do not cease until

after dark. I propose at supper tonight to get up a guide book for the MONITOR and hand a copy to each visitor as he arrives—to read after this fashion—This is the turret, gentlemen, and made to revolve on a central spindle by means of engines placed below the deck. . . . The above is a very small fraction of what we go over with 40 times a day—day after day.[2]

Overseas, USS *Kearsarge* was almost as popular as *Monitor.* While at anchor in the Azores, the warship hosted as many as five hundred Portuguese in one day, including the governor of the islands.[3] For the remainder of the fleet, however, the constant presence of tourists was not a problem. The crews' ability to create diverse recreational activities remained a challenge throughout the war.

A ship's routine usually allowed free time for the sailors between 6:00 P.M. and 8:00 P.M. Some of the more popular forms of recreational entertainment included boxing, card games, dominos, singing, dancing, and storytelling. At 8:00 P.M., the fun and games abruptly ended and the men turned in for the evening. The ship remained quiet, except for commands given to operate the ship, until reveille broke the silence again early the next morning.[4]

A favorite pastime enjoyed by the ship's crew was music, which provided a welcome relief from the daily routine of shipboard life. Many vessels carried their own musicians and minstrel groups. The USS *Forest Rose* had a six-piece band whose leader was a former member of a New York minstrel group. One officer was pleasantly surprised by the quality of the band's music, despite the dearth of practice time.[5] Ships enforcing the blockade close to shore relaxed occasionally to the sounds of a concert performed by an army band, and from time to time, foreign vessels also serenaded the men in blue.[6] In a letter to his wife, one officer described the daily concert given by a British band aboard one of Queen Victoria's warships at Hampton Roads:

> I have just been on deck listening to some very fine music from our English neighbor, ARIADNE—she carries a fine brass band. Every morning St. George's cross is hoisted to the tune of "God save the Queen" as I suppose they called it, we call it "America." After they are done saving the Queen they compliment the Yankees with the "Star Spangled Banner," "Hail Columbia," &c &c which being well played are duly appreciated. . . .[7]

It was not unusual then for larger warships to have musicians assigned to the ship as part of her complement. The USS *Brooklyn* reported nineteen musicians on her April 1863 muster report. The personnel shortages experienced by the navy during the first half of 1864 required the warship to reassign the musicians into the deck and engineering divisions. By the end of the year, however, with the manpower crisis subsiding, the muster role once again reported a number of musicians present for duty.[8] Even the smaller ships, unable to enjoy the luxury of a professional band, usually had several crew members capable of entertaining the crew with their gifted voices and their own musical instruments. The steam warship USS *Mattabesett* formed a glee club that entertained the crew nightly. While the men danced to the songs sung by the group, the vocalist received musical support from a handful of sailors playing their own instruments, including a violin, a tambourine, a guitar, and the bones.[9]

Periodically, spontaneous musical entertainment erupted. One evening, the black sailors assigned to *Mattabesett* gathered to sing spiritual songs. A group of white sailors, taking note of the black sing-along, started their own chorus of Irish drinking songs, sentimental ballads, and patriotic tunes. The noise grew to such a crescendo that both sides tried to out-sing the other, much to the amusement of the observing officers.[10]

The presence of music greatly aided the men in relieving their boredom. An officer described the positive atmosphere that prevailed over his ship during their evening's musical entertainment: "A gay and happy time the boys are having. The drum, fife, violin, and accordion are being played at the same time; besides that hubbub several are dancing and laughing, while others singing. In short, they all appear to be a merry set of tars."[11] Another sailor considered his ship fortunate just to have one shipmate skilled enough to play the violin so the rest of the crew could dance.[12]

Regardless of the size of the band, the number of members in a minstrel group or glee club, most tunes played aboard ship described the heroic exploits of a ship or her crew or famous naval engagements. In addition, patriotic tunes, sentimental ballads, and ethnic songs floated across the water every evening. Several popular tunes describing the life at sea included "The Banner of the Sea," some U.S. Navy quadrilles, "The Press Gang," "Sugar in the Hold," "Shallow Brown," and "Away Rio." Several sentimental favorites sung by the men were "Homeward Bound," "Shenandoah," and "The Gal I Left Behind Me." Music honoring naval engagements were quite numerous, including songs like "The Battle of Port Royal," "The Battle of Roanoke," "The Battle of New

Orleans," and "The Last of the *Alabama.*" This last piece was a stirring song dedicated to the crew of USS *Kearsarge* in celebration of her victory over the Confederate cruiser *Alabama.* The most moving song written to honor the exploits of men in combat was "The Last Broadside," which described the heroic deeds of valor performed by the men of USS *Cumberland* before she sank under the muzzle blast of the cannon from the Confederate ironclad CSS *Virginia.* The USS *Monitor* had the most songs written in her honor. All these songs—"*Monitor* Polka," "Ericsson Gallop," "*Monitor* Grand March," and "Oh Give Us a Navy of Iron"—described her engagement with CSS *Virginia.*[13]

Instrumental and vocal music were just two examples of the fine arts performed by the men assigned to the Union warships. In addition to her musicians, USS *Braziliera* had a theatrical group that performed plays, musicals, and operas. The commissioned officers even exhibited their thespian talents and now and then set aside their epaulettes long enough to entertain the crew. On one ship, the officers dressed up as American Indians, donning old coffee bags as costumes. During the play, with the hearty approval of the crew, the officers performed an Indian war dance.[14]

Although the fine arts were among the most numerous and enjoyable forms of entertainment on board ship, sailors frequently participated in other recreational endeavors. For tars who could read, their literary skills provided an alternative form of entertainment. Some ships, especially the larger vessels, maintained libraries on board. In 1864, the Navy Department purchased seventy-five Bibles, eighty Webster dictionaries, twenty-five atlases, and twenty copies of George Bancroft's *History of the United States* for distribution to the fleet. One warship, USS *Dictator,* possessed a superb library that contained over two hundred books of various titles.[15] The USS *Hartford* also had a fine library. Unfortunately, during the battle for New Orleans in 1862, a well-placed Confederate shell destroyed the warship's library. Later that year, an article in *Sailor's Magazine* solicited donations to help restock the library.[16]

Newspapers were another source of reading material available to the men. Because of their proximity to the major Northern cities, vessels of the North Atlantic Blockading Squadron frequently received daily mail and newspapers. For the sum of only two dollars, a sailor could purchase and have delivered a four-month subscription to the *Philadelphia Inquirer.*[17] The presence of newspapers aboard ship helped stimulate many lively discussions on the latest news about the war and political events that shaped the sailors' destiny. Although most Union sailors were at sea during the presidential election of 1864, the Bureau of Equipment and Recruiting ensured that the men received their absentee ballots. The bureau requested that every squadron submit, by state, the legal number of voters assigned to its command. Upon receiving the squadrons' list of authorized voters, the bureau submitted the number to the individual states, which in turn mailed the absentee ballots to the sailors by way of the Navy Bureau and squadron commander.[18]

Although the elections of 1862 and 1864 provided a temporary diversion for the men, nothing excited them more than the anticipation of receiving mail. The men of USS *Calypso* were so desperate for mail, even from strangers, that several crew members placed personal ads in the *Waverly Magazine* published in Boston. They hoped to correspond with anyone willing to write.[19] Throughout the war, the U.S. Post Office and the navy provided commendable mail service. The South Atlantic Blockading Squadron often received mail weekly.[20] Even the Gulf Coast Blockading Squadron received mail that was only ten days old, an amazing accomplishment considering the distance the mail had to travel by sea.[21]

The sailors benefited from a superb postal system under the tutelage of Postmaster General Montgomery Blair. Throughout the conflict, Blair streamlined the antiquated delivery service, thereby improving the efficiency and delivery time of the mail. A letter mailed to a sailor typically traveled overland to one of several major Northern ports. A local postal clerk collected the mail that was postmarked for the men of the fleet, and transferred it to the next U.S. flagged ship scheduled to rendezvous with the squadron commander's flagship. It was not unusual for the large supply steamers to carry as many as four hundred thousand letters and two thousand parcels to the men assigned to the blockading squadrons. When the individual ships in the squadron received notification that mail had arrived, they sent an officer with an armed escort to pick up and distribute the morale-enhancing letters to the men.[22]

The men greatly looked forward to the flagship's having mail for them. For some tars the mail would bring joy, to others despair. Regardless of the news from home, mail call was one of the men's great pleasures. With great excitement, a sailor described the anxiety-filled mail call: "At last the signals float [from the flagship] and read; 'letters for the —; come and get them.' At Last! The seals are broken and we read the news. One tells of a sick mother, dying, and longing to see her son. Another from M— 'a Lady love'. . . ."[23]

One of many disparities between the army and navy during the war included the method of payment for mailing a letter. On 22 July 1861, Congress authorized soldiers to mail letters collect on delivery (COD).[24] For some unexplained reason, sailors and marines did not receive the same COD opportunity for another six months.[25] Ironically, very few sailors, if any, took advantage of the postage due policy, as exemplified by the letter of a sailor on a *Monitor* in the summer of 1863: "After dinner was over, I sat at the wardroom table writing letters home. . . . I finished, sealed and stamped the letters. . . ." Moreover, many envelopes mailed by sailors in 1864 also had canceled stamps attached.[26]

Besides reading and letter writing, another popular pastime for many men was games of chance. Sailors frequently played various card games, including poker, rummy, and euchre. Other games of chance enjoyed by the men were chuck-or-luck and various other dice games. Although Article 7 of Navy Regulations made gambling an offense punishable by court-martial, sailors nonetheless played the games with a certain degree of regularity.[27] The volume of gambling on one warship so impressed a sailor that he described the berth deck in the evening as a "grand saloon." Additional games popular with the men included backgammon, chess, and checkers (photo 13).[28]

When the men were not participating in games of chance, they often enjoyed unique collections of animals living aboard ship as mascots and pets (photo 12). The USS *Fernandina* maintained a variety of pets, including an owl that had its wings clipped so it would not fly away. Another sailor returned from liberty with four black snakes, much to the dismay of his fellow crew members. After playing with the reptiles for a while, he placed the creatures in a bottle and tossed them overboard. During another liberty foray, several crew members returned with two raccoons, which they quickly added to the ship's growing list of pets.[29]

The USS *Wabash*, flagship for the South Atlantic Blockading Squadron, had the most unusual mascot in the navy. Enjoying free rein of the ship was a black bear, which the crew kept as their mascot. Unfortunately, the bear became too aggressive one evening and mauled the leg of the ship's quartermaster. His injury was serious enough that the surgeon had to amputate the tar's leg. The next day the crew sent the bear ashore for good.[30] *Wabash* was not the only vessel to have a bear as a pet. The river gunboat USS *Tyler* also had a bear with an aggressive disposition. Showing its disapproval of the crew's pet dogs, the bear frequently struck the canines with its paws.[31]

Swimming was another popular form of recreation that once proved more dangerous than the bear on *Wabash*. The engineering officer assigned to USS *Kearsarge*, William H. Badlam, described an unfortunate incident that occurred while the crew enjoyed swimming in the Mediterranean Sea one evening: "The crew was piped to bathing, one half of the crew participated in bathing. One man named Tibbetts, was killed by a shark in full view of the crew." Badlam described how the clear water enabled the crew to witness the shark taking the man below the surface of the water. While the shark devoured its victim, the remainder of the men clambered aboard the warship to get out of harm's way.[32]

Sports provided another form of popular physical recreation for the men. The commanding officer of USS *Fort Jackson* sponsored a rowing regatta replete with a two-hundred-dollar purse for the winning boat. The event attracted thirty-one boats, crewed by five hundred men.[33] In 1862, the USS *Flag* crew conducted its own intraship rowing competition as part of a Fourth of July celebration. The winning purse, however, was worth only ten dollars.[34] To break the monotony of life in a Spanish shipyard, the crew of USS *Kearsarge* played "Base Ball," and one sailor used cannonballs for a shot put event.[35]

The sailors' participation in athletic events was sporadic, however. In an effort to provide a constant flow of entertainment and humor, the men often resorted to practical jokes. On one blockading vessel, the ship's surgeon was the recipient of a practical joke one morning. The officer's steward woke the surgeon at 5:00 A.M. and notified him that the ship was in pursuit of a blockade runner. The officer quickly dressed and proceeded to his station only to discover that he was the recipient of a practical joke.[36] As an April Fools' prank on another ship, the officers' black cook baked fresh biscuits for breakfast. The officers, delighted over such a rare delicacy, eagerly broke open the piping hot biscuits to butter them. To their dismay, they discovered that the cook had wrapped potatoes in the biscuits.[37]

One practical joke that affected a civilian's livelihood happened in the waters off Port Royal, South Carolina. The incident involved a navy diver whose duties included removing barnacles from the hulls of ships. This backbreaking work required the diver to spend as many as six hours a day encased in a metal diving suit. He received his air supply through a hose maintained on the surface. One afternoon, the diver surfaced next to a civilian boat selling produce to the fleet. Upon seeing this "river devil" rise out of the water and emit strange noises from the air tube, the petrified civilian panicked, seized his oars, and rowed quickly toward shore. The man, permanently scarred by the encounter, ceased applying his waterborne trade.[38]

Despite the efforts to alleviate the boredom on board ship, the one announcement that immediately brought a smile to the sailor's face was the call for liberty ashore. The granting of liberty for the crew varied from ship to ship, depending on the vessel's operational commitments and maintenance schedule. The commanding officer controlled his vessel's liberty and typically allowed half of the crew to go ashore on liberty after church service. In this manner, each crew member received liberty once every fourteen days when the ship was in port or at anchor.[39]

Unlike the cruisers that patrolled the high seas for weeks on end in pursuit of Confederate commerce raiders, the ships assigned to the blockading squadrons regularly rotated in and out of port for repairs, to receive provisions, and to enjoy some liberty. The periodic reprieve from the rigors of blockading duty improved the morale of the crew. Among the men of the South Atlantic Blockading Squadron, the most popular liberty port was Port Royal. Because it was a logistical base and repair facility for the fleet, this small seacoast town on an island near Charleston, South Carolina, flourished during the war. The sailors' favorite hangout was the Port Royal House, a thriving restaurant, saloon, and hotel offering food, alcoholic beverages, and other amusements to the men. Tars also frequented the Beard and Company sutler store to purchase various toiletry articles, writing material, food, and tobacco products.[40]

Port Royal was not the only liberty port frequented by the South Atlantic Blockading Squadron. The numerous coastal islands also provided some superb liberty opportunities for the men. One Christmas Eve, half of the crew from USS *Fernandina* enjoyed a fine dinner at a mansion then occupied by former slaves. The contrabands served the men a complete dinner replete with ale, cigars, and music from a violin and horn pipe. To the tunes of such songs as "Paddy's Wedding,"

"Columbia, Gem of the Ocean," "Meet Me by the Moonlight Alone," and "Cabin Boy," the men danced away the evening with the local women of the island.[41]

The men of the North Atlantic Blockading Squadron periodically drew liberty in the small town of Beaufort, North Carolina. Although the town did not offer the variety or quality of facilities found in Port Royal, Beaufort sported a small bowling alley and a pool hall saloon that, the sailors complained, served "bad beer." The men stationed aboard ships operating in the Hampton Roads area frequently visited the sutlers and the handful of buildings surrounding Fortress Monroe, Virginia.[42]

For the men assigned to the Gulf Coast Blockading Squadron, liberty ports were rare and restrictive. Even when the men drew liberty in New Orleans, the army general in command of the Crescent City imposed a 9:00 P.M. curfew that seriously curtailed the sailors' liberty. One evening in July 1863, approximately five hundred men ignored the curfew and found themselves thrown in jail for the evening.[43]

The abolishment of grog aboard ship whetted the men's thirst for alcoholic beverages. Excessive drinking by the men on liberty contributed to numerous altercations ashore. On Christmas Day 1862, the crew of *Monitor* enjoyed a fine afternoon ashore, swapping sea stories with sailors from a British man-of-war near Fortress Monroe. As the day wore on into the evening and alcohol began to inebriate the men, a fight broke out. Soldiers from the fort finally suppressed the brawl, and the unruly men sobered up in the confines of the fort's prison cells.[44]

The altercation between the British and American sailors near Fortress Monroe was mild compared to the riot that broke out in the Danish West Indies, where USS *Powhatan* patrolled the Caribbean Sea in search of blockade runners and Confederate commerce raiders. During one extended patrol, the Union ship spent long intervals between liberty ports. The grinding daily routine slowly eroded the men's nerves, and fights frequently broke out between the men. Finally, the commodore authorized liberty in St. Thomas, Danish West Indies, despite the presence of British warships in the harbor. Throughout the war, the United States resented Great Britain's selling of supplies and ships to the Confederacy. Although the two nations remained neutral toward one another, animosity ran high throughout the Union navy.[45]

When *Powhatan* moored in St. Thomas, the commanding officer authorized half of the crew to go ashore on liberty. Approximately 150 men descended upon the small island with zeal and vigor. Within hours fights broke out between the American and British sailors, with the local Danish garrison unsuccessfully attempting to suppress the brawl. At sunset, with the fight out of control, the American commander recalled his crew. By midnight, all hands were on board, and peace returned to the island. Three *Powhatan* sailors were killed and scores injured as a result of the altercation, and British casualties were similar. The American ship departed St. Thomas the next day; her crew did not receive liberty again until the ship reached the United States.[46]

The granting of liberty, at the discretion of the commanding officer, was a privilege and not a right. On numerous occasions a ship's schedule prevented the men from going ashore on liberty. Although USS *Wachusetts* spent Christmas Eve and a portion of Christmas Day 1862 moored in Havana, Cuba, operational commitments prevented the commanding officer from granting liberty. Throughout their entire stay in port, the crew coaled the warship. When the men finally completed the dirty job, the ship got under way in pursuit of the Confederate commerce raider, CSS *Florida*.[47] One week later, *Wachusetts* returned to Havana to enjoy some hard-earned liberty. Unfortunately, the poor condition of the engineering plant required the undivided attention of the engineering division. For three days the engineers labored in the engineering compartments, repairing the condenser and plugging sixty ruptured boiler tubes. The men who did venture ashore did so without cash in their pockets: The ship's paymaster was out of money to pay the crew![48]

As part of its concern about the men's morale, the navy also considered their spiritual well-being. Article 2 of the Navy Regulations directed the commanding officer to conduct religious services on Sunday, weather and operational requirements permitting. Furthermore, the regulation stipulated that any person disturbing the services would face a summary or general court-martial.[49] During the fall of 1862, President Lincoln reemphasized the importance of observing the Sabbath day. In a presidential general order, Lincoln directed the army and navy to reduce physical labor on Sunday to only those activities absolutely necessary.[50]

Sunday routine at sea consisted of a personnel inspection by the commanding officer in the morning, followed by religious services.

The rapid expansion of the navy during the war created a severe shortage of navy chaplains, a shortage so acute in the Western Gulf Blockading Squadron that during the spring of 1863, no ship reported a chaplain aboard.[51] As a result, a commissioned officer, normally reading from the Book of Common Prayer, ministered the more popular Episcopalian service.[52]

Unfortunately, not all the officers were effective orators. One crew member complained, "Well this is Sunday, and I have been to church, as I do every Sunday morning. It is tiresome tho, as the Captain is rather long."[53] A member of USS *Mound City* best described a typical Sunday morning routine found aboard most Union vessels, "A[t] Sabbath morning muster, all hands are assembled, where we await the appearance of the captain. . . . He immediately proceeds to read prayers, after which I call the roll and each man is required to pass before the Captain for inspection. The whole muster requires about an hour."[54]

Sunday was not the only day set aside for formal prayer aboard some vessels. The USS *Macedonian*, for instance, frequently conducted religious services in the evening. The participants of this daily service used religious reading material, tracts, and circulars provided by the U.S. Christian Commission. The unselfish work of these dedicated civilians benefited many sailors. In one incident, a navy lieutenant notified the commission that only one sailor attended church service on Sunday. After receiving and distributing the commission's religious reading material, over one hundred men attended the next church services.[55] Another officer, assigned to USS *North Carolina,* reported that he had enough Bibles and Testaments to give one to each member of the crew if they so desired.[56] An officer aboard USS *Lackawanna* firmly believed that religion had a positive influence on the otherwise "profane, rough and frequently drunken men."[57]

Although participation in religious services was voluntary, the death of a shipmate from combat, accident, or disease always united the crew in the solemn religious service of burying the fallen comrade at sea. For health reasons, the navy seldom had the opportunity to inter its dead ashore. The warm southern climate, which accelerated decomposition, and the fear of disease prevented the storage of the deceased before a ship could reach port. Instead the service followed the time-honored tradition of burying its dead at sea. After the death of a sailor, the ship's surgeon submitted the death certificate to the Navy Department through his chain of command. Meanwhile, the deceased lay in state for a brief period before the crew prepared the body for burial at sea. After the wake, the crew mustered on deck for a brief religious service usually conducted by the commanding officer. At the conclusion of the service, the body was committed to the deep.[58]

The death of a crew member left a lasting impression on the men, reminding them of their own vulnerability and the seriousness of their occupation. One sailor poignantly described the burial of a shipmate: "At sunset we buried him with all the solemnity the occasion required. No eye was dry as we committed our young shipmate to the bosom of the deep."[59] Another sailor aboard USS *Sabina* recounted the details of a comrade's burial: "Connolly was displayed in the cabin until 4:00 P.M. Then at 4:30 all hands received the call to bury the dead. The captain of the "Sabina" held service then [the deceased] was sewn up in his hammock and tossed overboard with 2, 64 lb shots to sink him."[60]

Being near the shore, the Western river squadrons buried their dead on land, with as much solemnity as the at-sea burials. In a letter to his wife, a member of USS *Forest Rose* described in moving detail the burial of a shipmate ashore:

> All hands to bury the dead were piped by the boatswain's mate. All hands assembled on the gun deck amidships, where Capt. Johnston read the Episcopal service. The procession then formed in the following manner: 1st [the] marine escort of twelve men under Ensign Graves; then followed the body borne by six mess mates of the deceased; after which came the boys, sailors, petty officers, and officers according to their rank. . . . At the grave the Capt. read the appropriate portion of the service, after which were fired three rounds by the marines before the body was covered. As the procession left the vessel, a 32-pdr. was fired, and a bell was tolled.[61]

Not all the burials at sea went as smoothly as just described. The USS *Powhatan* was the scene of a macabre burial after the unfortunate death of one of her sailors. When the ship's carpenter received orders to construct a wooden coffin for the deceased, the carpenter was out of screws. He only had nails to hold the coffin lid in place. The next evening, so the story goes, while the crew listened to the reading of the scripture and eulogy, the coffin began to emit a mysterious, high-pitched squeal as the nails, originally holding the lid in place, slowly extracted themselves from the wood. The gases escaping from the

LIFE IN MR. LINCOLN'S NAVY

decomposing body had built to such intensity that they forced the lid partially open. A crew member then secured the lid, however. To make matters worse, the coffin failed to sink when it entered the sea. The crew had to lower a small boat into the water and sent the men to place additional holes in the coffin. Finally, after great trouble and embarrassment, the coffin sank.[62]

Throughout the war, sailors created innovative recreational activities to entertain themselves aboard ship or ashore on liberty. Moreover, the navy's observance of the Sabbath provided an opportunity for the men to satisfy their spiritual needs. Both the recreational and the spiritual opportunities in Mr. Lincoln's navy greatly contributed to the Union sailor's morale.

❖8❖

The Government Gives and the Captain Takes Away

Although the men enjoyed their recreational endeavors and spiritual nourishment, the presence of money and the opportunity to share in the wealth from the adjudication of a prize ship also brought satisfaction to the sailors. When the Civil War began in April 1861, the Union sailor had not received a pay raise since 1854. The lowest rating, that of boy, received $8.00 to $10.00 a month. The navy paid landsmen, ordinary seamen, and seamen $12.00, $14.00, and $18.00 a month, respectively. Engineers fared substantially better. A fireman received $30.00 a month, a second class fireman earned $20.00, and a coal heaver received $15.00.[1]

On the eve of the Civil War, navy wages compared favorably with the civilian labor force. The average laborer made $1.00 a day, or approximately $20.00 to $25.00 a month. A carpenter earned one of the highest salaries during this period. His monthly wages averaged $45.00. A farmhand, with board included, received only $14.73.[2] In the state of New York, leather workers earned $31.00, shipyard workers netted $29.00, while blacksmiths and printers made approximately $30.00. Although a seaman's monthly wage was only $18.00, he received three free meals a day, living accommodations, travel experience, and medical care, which offset his slightly lower pay.[3]

Although the sailor earned a monthly salary, he seldom received the full amount on a monthly basis. His wages accrued monthly as the ship's paymaster made the appropriate entries for each sailor in the pay ledger. When a sailor purchased small items from the ship's store, the paymaster subtracted the amount from the sailor's balance. In addition, the paymaster provided the sailor with a few dollars when he went on liberty. In a letter to his wife, the paymaster aboard USS *Florida* described the hectic pace involving the transaction of money: "Then a hundred times a day I am applied for 'a little money, sir, I've got liberty ashore . . . a pair of shoes, sir, mine are all to pieces . . . a cap, sir, mine has blown overboard' & a thousand wants like these."[4]

The tar received the balance of his monthly pay when he left the service. If the sailor desired, he could establish an allotment and send all or part of his pay to a designated person ashore.[5] The allotment system and the withholding of the sailor's pay until his discharge prevented him from squandering his hard-earned money and eliminated the potential for theft. Alvah Hunter earned $8.00 a month in the boy rating, receiving $98.67 when he mustered out of the naval service after serving one year and ten days.[6] Another more senior sailor remarked, "Today I was paid off $348.00 and discharged. I started for home at half past 5 P.M. by the Fall River route. . . ."[7]

In the event of an emergency, a tar could appeal to the paymaster for a larger sum of money. Paymaster Keeler explained the process to his wife:

> A Sailor is never paid in full till his time of enlistment expires. I usually pay them 3 to 5 dollars a month spending money. Sometimes they come to me with a doleful tale of sickness, death or destitution at home & a request for 15 to 20 dollars to send to their families. "You say your wife wrote you and one of the children was dead?" "Yes sir." "Well, where's the letter?" If their tale was a true one the letter is produced & I give them as I think they need—if on the contrary the letter, as is frequently the case, has been torn up or thrown overboard they meet with a pretty abrupt refusal. If they choose, they can appeal through the 1st Lieutenant to the Capt.; he, however, very seldom changes the decision of the paymaster.[8]

In 1864, sailors received their first pay raise in ten years. The second-class fireman and coal heavers realized a substantial $5.00 a month, or 25 percent, pay raise, while the deck ratings of boy, landsman, ordinary seaman, and seaman all received pay raises ranging from 10 to 12.5 percent (table 8-1).[9] During the Civil War, civilian wages increased by approximately the same amount. Blacksmiths realized a 12.5 percent pay increase, while common laborers and carpenters enjoyed a 20 percent pay raise.[10] Despite these pay increases, wages did not keep pace with inflation. The North experienced an inflation of 80 percent for the entire war.[11]

Unlike their civilian counterparts, however, by 1864, sailors benefited not only from a monthly wage increase, but from several additional monetary allowances unique to the naval service. One of the first allowances paid to the enlisted men stemmed from the abolishment of grog on 1 September 1862. The law prohibiting the issue of spirits aboard ship netted the enlisted man an additional five cents a day in lieu of his grog ration.[12] For the enlisted men assigned to the *Monitor*-class ships in the South Atlantic Blockading Squadron, the secretary of the navy authorized a 25 percent pay increase. The bonus was due to a grateful Navy Department's rewarding the men for successfully operating the ironclads under arduous conditions.[13]

Promotion to the next highest rating was another way for the enlisted man to obtain a pay rise. Unlike today, where Congress and the navy tightly control the number of men advanced each year, during the Civil War the commanding officer normally controlled the individual promotions. He advanced men according to their performance, the needs of the ship, and heroism. For example, the chief engineering officer aboard USS *Wabash* formally requested the promotion of two engineers to the next higher rating because of their outstanding performance and the needs of the division.[14] In another example, Captain Winslow, commanding officer of USS *Kearsarge*, meritoriously promoted Q.M. William Smith to master mate for his heroic actions during the ship's engagement with CSS *Alabama*.[15]

In November 1863, the ironclad USS *Lehigh* ran aground in Charleston harbor. The beleaguered vessel immediately came under a withering fire from the Confederate batteries located at Fort Moultrie. The USS *Nahant* steamed to the assistance of the grounded ship and twice tried unsuccessfully to pull *Lehigh* off the sandbar. Finally, three volunteer sailors from *Nahant* rowed a small boat over to the ironclad, carrying with them a heavier towing line than what the ship had been using. After securing the line while under fire, *Nahant* extracted the ship from her grounded position and towed her out of range from the

TABLE 8-1. Monthly Pay for Enlisted Men, 1864

Engineer ratings

First-class fireman	$30.00
Second-class fireman	25.00
Coal heaver	20.00

Deck ratings

Carpenter's mate	30.00
Master-at-arms	30.00
Chief quartermaster	28.00
Gunners mate	25.00
Quarter gunner	25.00
Quartermaster	25.00
Sailmaker	25.00
Coxswain	25.00
Captain of forecastle	25.00
Captain of afterguard	25.00
Captain of hold	25.00
Cooper	22.00
Painter	22.00
Armorer	22.00
Carpenter	22.00
Seaman	20.00
Ordinary seaman	16.00
Landsman	14.00
Boy	10.00
Cabin steward	35.00
Commanding officer's cabin cook	30.00
Commanding officer's wardroom steward	30.00
Wardroom cook	25.00
Ship's cook	26.00
Baker	22.00
Yeoman	35.00
Ship's writer	20.00
Nurse	14.00

After 1 September 1862, enlisted men twenty-one years old and older received an additional five cents a day as substitution for their abolished grog ration. In addition, the pay scale does not reflect the 25 percent increase in pay for men serving aboard ironclads. From Prize List of USS *Mackinaw,* 5 December 1864, RG 24.

Confederate guns. The three sailors returned to their ship and received a grateful handshake and a promotion from Adm. John Dahlgren. Several days later, each ship read a general order from the admiral, describing the exploits of the three men and their subsequent promotion.[16]

On occasion, the commanding officer's superior overruled the captain's decision regarding a sailor's promotion. Early in the war, a sailor accidentally dropped a sponger, required for the safe operation of the cannon, overboard during the heat of battle. Embarrassed by his action, the sailor jumped overboard and retrieved the sponger, thus enabling the cannon to remain in operation. The commanding officer praised the sailor for his courage in retrieving the instrument but did not believe that a promotion was in order. When Assistant Secretary of the Navy Gustavus Fox learned of the incident, he authorized the commanding officer to promote the man for his heroic actions despite his initial carelessness.[17] In an effort to standardize the promotion system for acts of bravery under enemy fire, the navy established a new award replete with monetary and personal merits.

In the fall of 1861, the navy wanted to recognize its heroes with more than the antiquated Certificate of Merit issued during the Mexican War.[18] The navy drafted, and Congress authorized, a new medal for sailors who accomplished individual acts of bravery. On 21 December 1861, the president signed into law a bill that established the precedent for the navy to award enlisted men the Medal of Honor in recognition for their heroic deeds.[19]

Initially, the Medal of Honor did not stipulate an advancement in rate or a monetary award. The first person in the nation's history to receive the medal was Peter Williams, who received the award for his heroic action during the battle between USS *Monitor* and CSS *Virginia*. During the fiercely contested engagement, Williams, assigned to the ship's pilothouse as wheelsman, remained at his station despite severe damage to the pilothouse. Williams professionally steered the ship during a brief period when the commanding officer, Lieutenant Worden, received a serious injury to both his eyes. Six weeks later, no fewer than twenty sailors received the Medal of Honor as a result of their heroic deeds during the engagement with Forts Jackson and St. Philip, which guarded the entrance to New Orleans.[20] Robert Blake was the first black person to receive the Medal of Honor. An escaped slave, Blake served aboard the gunboat USS *Marblehead* and received the medal on

16 April 1864 for his gallant service on Christmas Day 1863. During a heated engagement with Confederate shore batteries, Blake heroically served as a member of a cannon team that forced the rebels to retire from their position.[21]

On 16 July 1862, the Medal of Honor received additional merit when Congress approved a promotion and a cash award of one hundred dollars for its recipients.[22] During the war, the navy awarded 307 Medals of Honor. Of this number, seven black sailors received the prestigious award.[23]

Although pay raises, unique allowances, and the Medal of Honor all contributed to the monetary fortunes of the enlisted men, sailors could increase their income another way. A great incentive for a man to join the navy instead of the army was the opportunity to share in the profits from the destruction of an enemy warship or sale from a captured blockade runner. The prize money regulation allowed a crew to receive the entire monetary value of an enemy vessel if that vessel was equal to or superior to their ship. The rules governing the distribution of prize money further stipulated that if the enemy vessel was inferior to the capturing force, the navy pension fund received one-half of the adjudicated value of the ship and its cargo. The officers and enlisted divided the remaining one-half in the following manner: The commanding officer of the squadron received one-twentieth; the commanding officers of the capturing vessels received one-tenth or three-twentieths if acting independently; the rest of the officers and crew split the remaining amount, based on their rank or rating. To be eligible to share in the profits, a ship did not actually have to participate in the destruction or capture of the enemy vessel; all a ship had to do was be within signaling distance.[24]

The lure of prize money often drove men to amazing acts of heroism. On the night of 27 October 1864, Lt. William Cushing, accompanied by a crew of fourteen men, proceeded up the Roanoke River near Plymouth, North Carolina, and sank the Confederate ironclad CSS *Albemarle*.[25] Congress initially awarded $80,000 for distribution among the men who participated in the sinking of the rebel ironclad. Eight years later, with the assistance of Admiral Porter, Congress awarded the men an additional cash prize of $202,857. The most junior-rated man, a landsman, whose monthly salary was only $12.00 a month, received $4,019.40 for his participation in the sinking of the Confederate ironclad.[26]

Although the large monetary award for the destruction of the Confederate vessel was the exception and not the rule, several men did profit from the awarding of prize money throughout the conflict.

During the early morning of 17 June 1863, USS *Weehawken* and USS *Nahant* participated in the capture of the Confederate ironclad CSS *Atlanta*. A naval survey board placed the value of the enemy ironclad at $350,829.26.[27] The officers and crew divided the prize money according to the 1862 prize regulations. First-Class Boy Alvah Hunter received a U.S. Treasury warrant for $176.16 for his part in the victory over the Confederate ironclad. Since his monthly pay was then only $10.00, within a short period of several hours he had more than doubled his annual salary.[28] For the men assigned to the USS *Florida*, blockading duty paid handsome dividends. The crew divided $74,369 in prize money for the capture of three enemy vessels.[29] Even small warships accrued some amazing profits from the capture and adjudication of enemy vessels. In the fall of 1864, the union gunboat USS *Acolus* captured two Confederate blockade runners. The commanding officer received $10,000; the officers received between $8,000 and $20,000; and each seaman realized a $3,000 reward.[30]

Not all Union warships sinking or capturing enemy ships received their prize money within a reasonable amount of time. The government did not settle the prize money in USS *Pawnee*'s account for her capture of the Confederate blockade runner *Property* until 16 October 1869, six years after the capture of the ship.[31] For the officers and crew of USS *Kearsarge*, the government failed to reward them for their victory over CSS *Alabama*. The former Acting Master D. H. Summer of *Kearsarge* boldly wrote a letter to the president requesting the payment of prize money to the crew.[32]

Nor did participation in the capture of an enemy ship always guarantee prize money. According to one officer, his ship, USS *Potomac*, assisted USS *Cuyler* and USS *Huntsville* in capturing the blockade runner *Wilder*. An error in the submission of the paperwork through the chain of command failed to mention *Potomac*'s participation. As a result, the officers and enlisted men did not receive one cent for their work.[33]

Although the laws that governed prize money provided the sailors an opportunity to "get rich quick," the sinking of an enemy warship or the capture of a richly laden blockade runner had many inherent dangers. The sailors' quest for prize money frequently exposed them to extreme physical dangers, whether the hazard was an enemy cannon-ball or boarding a blockade runner. If a sailor received a mortal wound or a debilitating injury in the line of duty, Congress and the navy provided the financial means to provide for his surviving family or for himself and his family. On 14 July 1862, Congress created a pension system that laid the foundation for the nation to provide financially for disabled military personnel and their dependents. The Pension Act was retroactive to 4 March 1861. Under the act, disabled military personnel received a graduated amount of money based on rank and degree of disability. For the naval enlisted man, the maximum amount of pension he received for a totally disabling injury was eight dollars a month. If he died in the line of duty as a result of disease or wounds, his widow or children (up to the age of sixteen) also received eight dollars a month.[34]

The Pension Act further stipulated that to be eligible for a pension, the individual had to have medical proof of his disability and an honorable discharge. Along with a number of rules governing the granting of a pension, the unique wording of the act would have a significant impact on both the army and the navy personnel. The act referred to the individuals employed by the army as members of the military service, and the men in the navy as members of the naval service. The act's specific separation of the army and the navy initially benefited the navy. Three days after the Pension Act became law, the navy, with Congress's approval, modified the amount of money that a disabled navy person could receive. Section thirteen in "An Act for the Better Government of the Navy of the United States" increased the amount of pension that a naval member could receive, regardless of rank or rating. The act allowed an invalid person to receive up to his maximum monthly pay based on the severity of the disability. For an enlisted person, this amounted to a substantial increase. Instead of receiving a maximum of only eight dollars a month, a first-class fireman could receive thirty dollars a month (his monthly salary) for a total disability. For two years, the navy enjoyed a financial advantage over the army in the amount of money that could be award for a pension.[35]

In 4 July 1864, Congress authorized an increase in pension money paid to disabled service members. The increase, however, only applied to the army. Section 5 in the Supplementary Pension Act fixed a monetary amount for certain disabilities. A military service member who lost both feet would receive twenty dollars a month, and service members who lost both hands or both eyes would receive twenty-five dollars a month. The revised Pension Act failed to mention the naval service.[36] In December 1864, Secretary Welles mentioned the disparity in his annual report, requesting that the navy be included in the pension increase and stating that the omission of the navy was only an oversight by Congress. One year later, Welles again requested that Congress include the pension increase for sailors who had lost appendages or their eyesight.[37]

Although the navy inexplicably did not benefit from Section 5 of the Supplementary Pension Act, the Navy Department nonetheless superbly administered the pension fund and allocations. Congress authorized the secretary of the navy to invest the pension fund in registered securities of the United States. In addition, a percentage of the proceeds from the sale of captured ships and cargo went into the navy pension fund. By November 1865, the navy had $9 million in the fund, earning $292,783 in interest. The entire pension cost for the navy for 1865 was only $248,529. Thanks to the astute financial management of the pension fund, the navy could pay the pensions of the 2,027 invalids and widows without placing a financial burden on the citizens of the nation.[38] In 1890, Congress expanded the pension criteria to include any honorably discharged veteran who had served a minimum of ninety days and could not earn a living because of a non-service disability.[39] The new pension act greatly increased the number of destitute former soldiers and sailors who received pensions in their later years for nobly serving their country.

For one former tar, admission into the new pension program was impossible. In May 1924, a full fifty-nine years after the Civil War guns fell silent, Congressman Henry E. Barbour of California submitted Bill 811, "For the Relief of Frederick Marshall." Frederick Marshall was a former sailor in the Union navy. At eighty years old, Marshall applied for a pension under the 1890 Pension Act after he was disabled in an automobile accident.[40] Congressman Barbour had submitted the bill when the government had denied Marshall his pension because he did not have an honorable discharge. Navy records listed the former ordinary seaman Marshall as a deserter since 1863. Marshall stated that while on liberty from his ship USS *Cyane* in San Francisco, a man drugged and shanghaied him to the civilian cargo ship *Queen of the East*. After cruising to Germany aboard the civilian ship, Marshall eventually made his way back to the United States by the way of Great Britain and

Australia. Upon his arrival in the States, he offered his services to the navy, which then refused his services because he was deaf.[41] Unknown to Marshall, navy records still listed him as a deserter. Despite the assistance of Congressman Barbour, the House did not overturn his deserter status, thus denying the former sailor his pension.[42]

Throughout the Civil War the navy paid its men a monthly wage that remained competitive with the civilian community. In 1862, with the abolishment of the grog ration, the sailors received an additional $1.50 a month. The navy also recognized and rewarded the men assigned to arduous duty. The 25 percent pay raise for the men assigned to the *Monitor*-class ships laid the foundation for the navy's awarding flight, submarine, and sea pay in the twentieth century. By the end of the war, officer and enlisted wages consumed 39 percent of the navy's budget.[43] The Pension Act of 1862 and the Better Government of the Navy Act of 1862 ensured disabled veterans and their families a modest income for the remainder of their lives. Unfortunately, some committed various violations of the navy's Articles of War, which caused them to forfeit their rate, their wages, and their freedom.

The regulations, or articles, that governed men at sea could be as cruel and unforgiving as the sea itself. The roots of the naval justice system that governed the navy during the Civil War developed from British maritime law and seafaring tradition. As early as December 1775, the Continental Congress authorized the first laws regulating the fledgling navy. The "Rules for the Regulation of the Navy of the United Colonies" contained forty-four articles and provided enormous latitude for interpretation by the individual commanding officers.[44]

Section 8, Article 1, of the U.S. Constitution granted Congress the power to establish rules and regulations for the army and the navy. By the end of the eighteenth century, Congress had established the first rules on how the navy should govern itself. On 23 April 1800, the president signed into law, "An Act for the Better Government of the United States Navy." This act, commonly called the Articles of War, or the "Rocks and Shoals," governed the navy for 150 years with only a few modifications. The abolishment of flogging in 1850 and the abolishment of the grog ration in 1862 were the two major changes to the articles during the century and a half of their existence. In 1950, the Department of Defense replaced the individual judicial systems of the three branches of the military services with the Uniform Code of Military Justice.[45]

On 17 July 1862, the president approved a revision to the original 1800 articles, entitled "An Act for the Better Government of the Navy of the United States."[46] Although the new articles retained a strict measure of discipline, their advantage over the old articles included guidelines that specified the degree of punishment allowed for a particular violation. The 1862 articles also delineated who could impose punishment. Although the new articles were not perfect, they successfully withstood the test of time.

Article 3 of the 1862 regulations combined several old articles that listed offenses carrying the sentence of death if so adjudged by a court-martial. Mutiny, disobeying a lawful order from a superior officer, striking or intending to strike an officer, illegal correspondence with the enemy, desertion, sleeping on watch, hazarding a vessel or crew, and cowardice in the face of the enemy all carried the potential sentence of death.[47] Although the navy during the Civil War did not execute any member of the naval service, several men were tried for violation of Article 3. Instead of imposing the death sentence, court-martial boards opted to punish the convicted men under the guidelines set forth in Article 6, which allowed the board to substitute the death sentence with a maximum sentence of life in prison at hard labor.[48]

Article 7 encompassed the violations of the Articles of War that did not warrant the death penalty but were serious enough to convene a court-martial board. These offenses included cruelty to subordinates, profanity, falsehood, drunkenness, gambling, fraud, theft, fighting, dueling, disrespect to an officer, disobeying orders, and submitting a false muster report. For violating any of these regulations a court-martial board could punish the guilty person with a reduction in rate, confinement at hard labor for a specified period, or expulsion from the naval service.[49]

Article 11 gave the president, the secretary of the navy, and the commanders of the individual squadrons the authority to convene court-martials. The court-martial board required a minimum of five and a maximum of thirteen officers. For a man to receive the death penalty, Article 19 required a vote of two-thirds of the board members and presidential approval. All other convictions required only a majority vote.[50]

Unlike today, when a court-martial can take months to complete, justice at the hands of a Civil War court-martial board was swift. One such board, conveyed at the Philadelphia Navy Yard, consisted of one rear admiral, two commodores, one commander, and one lieutenant.

The presiding judge was Samuel C. Perkins. During one trial session, the board found two sailors guilty of desertion, but it did not award the death sentence. In another case, Landsman John Boyer pleaded not guilty to the charge of desertion. During the sailor's trial, he had no witness in his defense, and after only two days, the board found him guilty as charged. The court likewise tried Ordinary Seaman William Mckay, who also pleaded not guilty to the charge of desertion. After two days, the board also found Seaman Mckay guilty of desertion.[51]

Throughout the Civil War, 4,649 sailors, or 6 percent of all the men who served in the navy, deserted.[52] Many men deserted during the last year of the war. The draft laws, lower quality of recruits, and lucrative bounties all added to the increased numbers of deserters. The navy's difficult transition to a peacetime service in the summer of 1865 also contributed to a number of desertions.

The mustering-out process followed a pattern similar to that of enlisting. A sailor transferred to a receiving ship, where the navy out-processed him. Unfortunately, the navy was ill prepared to handle the large volume of tars seeking to return to their civilian status. In one instance, USS *Florida* transferred a large portion of her crew to the receiving ship USS *North Carolina* for out-processing. Regrettably, eighteen men from the ship deserted because they grew tired of the inactivity aboard the receiving ship and saw no reason to remain in the service with the war over. The USS *Colorado* experienced a similar fate when one hundred men deserted while awaiting their discharges.[53] Unfortunately, this scene repeated itself on numerous occasions after the war and placed a rare black mark on an otherwise impressive service record of the men in Mr. Lincoln's navy.

The Articles of War also contained an article that was all inclusive regarding "other" offenses. Article 8 (similar to today's Article 134) stated that any offenses not covered by Articles 3 or 7, but serious enough to warrant a general court-martial, fell under the guidelines of this article. In this manner, an officer could charge a sailor under the broad context of Article 8 for acts that he perceived to be in violation of the good order and discipline of the navy.[54]

Article 10 was the most important of the several articles concerning discipline aboard ship. It granted the commanding officer the authority to impose limited punishment to members of his crew for minor infractions of the rules in order to maintain good order and discipline. Furthermore, the commanding officer had the authority to reduce a sailor in rate, provided that the officer was the person who had previously advanced him. He could also punish a convicted sailor by confining him with or without leg and wrist irons (manacles). The confinement was not to exceed ten days or solitary confinement on bread and water for five days. Another allowable punishment was to restrict a sailor to the ship without liberty and to assign him extra duties. The article further stipulated that no other punishments were appropriate and that the officer of the deck was responsible for entering into the ship's log all punishments meted out. Although Article 10 was supposed to eliminate the potential for imposing cruel and unusual punishment on a sailor, in reality most Union ships permitted their junior officers to award punishments that violated the article's terms.[55]

The USS *Colorado*, perhaps, violated the rules governing Article 10 more than any other ship did. The warship had a sadistic executive officer commonly called "Erratic Nauticut." It was not unusual for him to place as many as one hundred men in chains on the gun deck for violating a few minor offenses. The psychological climate aboard the ship was so bad that when the executive officer asked a sailor, "How would you like to walk through hell bare foot?" the sailor replied, "A dozen times to get out of this!" Fortunately, the officer was eventually relieved and conditions slowly began to improve on the warship.[56]

The USS *Kearsarge* often violated the rules governing the punishment of men aboard a warship. One of the ship's unique forms of punishment involved drunken tars. Sailors returning from liberty in an inebriated condition often found themselves confined in a canvas strait jacket and secured to a stanchion on the berthing deck as an example to the crew. The man, sweating profusely in the canvas jacket, remained confined until he was sober.[57]

On another ship, a petty thief received a similar punishment. The ship's master-at-arms placed a young sailor in a canvas strait jacket and stenciled the word "Thief" across the jacket. For the remainder of his punishment, the lad had to walk about the deck in full view of the shipmates while wearing his uncomfortable badge of dishonor.[58]

Drunken sailors aboard USS *Nahant* often found themselves used as an example for the rest of the crew. Six of the ship's best enlisted men once illegally purchased some spirits and became intoxicated. As their punishment, the master-at arms placed them in double irons, gagged them, and left them in this pitiful state on the exposed weather deck for the rest of the crew to see.[59]

Although the standard punishment aboard ship for drunkenness was confinement in double irons, for one sailor aboard USS *Monitor*, his indulgence with "John Barley" met with disastrous results. One evening, while being escorted below decks in double irons, the drunken sailor jumped overboard and drowned. The navy found his lifeless body three days later and gave the deceased tar a proper burial ashore.[60]

Paymaster Keeler aboard USS *Florida* frequently violated Article 10. He occasionally punished the boys assigned to the officers' mess by sending them aloft with rifles in the mast at nighttime for several hours. If the boys accidentally broke any wardroom dish, he deducted the cost of the item from their pay.[61]

For the men assigned to a *Monitor*-class ship, confinement in double irons proved to be a hellish experience. Because of the vessel's small confines, the ship had no habitable compartment for use as a brig. Instead, offenders often found themselves placed in double irons and confined to the pitch-black coal bunkers. On board *Nahant*, the punishment for fighting was confinement in double irons in the coal bunker for one to seven days.[62] Not all of the *Monitor*-class ships used the coal bunkers as a brig. The USS *Monitor* chose the damp confines of the chain locker to hold her prisoners. One evening, the steward had too much to drink before serving the officers their supper. To make matters worse, the officers had a distinguished guest aboard for the evening meal. The steward performed badly during the meal and as a result found himself in double irons and locked in the chain locker as his punishment.[63]

Confinement in the ship's brig on one of the larger wooden warships could be as uncomfortable as confinement in the coal bunkers. Several wooden ships used as their brig a very small compartment in the extreme forward part of the ship on the second deck. A prisoner's only source of air and light entered through nine $1/2$-inch small holes.[64] The claustrophobic brig could even be worse if the occupant was prone to seasickness. The bow of a ship is subject to the largest pitching motion on the vessel, which greatly enhances a person's chances of falling victim to seasickness. One can only imagine the discomfort of confinement in irons in a hot, dark space, subject to the constant motion of the ship and the pungent aroma of vomit. Such was the fate of the men who periodically violated the Articles of War.

The officers aboard the receiving ship USS *North Carolina* administered some unusually harsh and, in one case, amusing forms of punishment. For failing to obey an order, a sailor, if lucky, only had to stand at the masthead for three hours. On occasion, the same offense brought a stricter punishment involving hanging a sailor by the arms from the inside of the ratlines for up to two hours. This form of punishment placed a severe strain on the arm and leg muscles, which affected the unfortunate victim for several days. The punishment for spitting on deck was unique and embarrassing. The accused sailor had to wear a barrel cut in half and walk around the ship until he caught someone spitting on deck, in which case he transferred the barrel to the new offender.[65]

The commanding officer of USS *Fernandina* sometimes created unique punishments to fit the crime. For quarreling, he had the two men handcuffed back to back and ordered them to walk the deck for an hour and one-half for their minor offense.[66] The USS *Niagara*'s commanding officer was not as lenient or imaginative with his punishment. A young sailor assigned to his ship received a severe punishment for leaving a candle lighted in an unmanned, locked compartment. For his punishment the captain placed him in double irons with reduced rations until further notice.[67] Captain Winslow of USS *Kearsarge* proved to be a strict disciplinarian, as John Boyle found out one day. The captain placed Boyle in double irons and on bread and water for five days for smuggling liquor aboard.[68]

Not all violations of the Articles of War brought harsh retribution. A favorite form of punishment for minor violations was having the offender's name placed on the blacklist. Men on the blacklist were subject to a variety of extra duties during the day or night, including such dirty work as cleaning the soot from the galley smokestack, washing spittoons, and removing ashes from the galley stove. Worst of all was the suspension of liberty.[69] In addition, the blacklisted had to eat in a separate mess and were not allowed to talk to any other crew member.[70]

Frequently, the rules of evidence did not apply when a sailor was charged with a crime. The accused men sometimes discovered their names on the blacklist even though the commanding officer could not prove their guilt. One such incident occurred aboard a blockading ship operating off the Georgia coast. A washerwoman reported to a Union ship that her pocketbook had been stolen. Even more serious, the pocketbook allegedly contained twelve dollars. The commanding officer charged four men with the crime, although it was never proven that they stole the woman's pocketbook. As their punishment, the captain placed their names on the blacklist and suspended their liberty.[71]

MEN WANTED
FOR THE
NAVY!

All able-bodied men not in the employment of the Army, will be enlisted into the Navy upon application at the Naval Rendezvous, on Craven Street, next door to the Printing Office.

H. K. DAVENPORT,
Com'r. & Senior Naval Officer.

New Berne, N. C.,
Nov. 2d, 1863.

Recruiting poster from coastal North Carolina.

Photo 1. The crew of USS *Miami*. Note the black sailors dispersed throughout the crew, and the sailors in the foreground playing checkers.

Recruiting poster promoting enlistment in the navy as an alternative to conscription.

Photo 2. Young sailor aboard USS *New Hampshire*. The minimum legal age for a boy to join the navy was twelve. Most of these adolescents served in the "boy" rating. During combat they served as "powder monkeys," running black-powder cartridges from the magazines to the cannon. Note the embroidered heart design on the front of his frock.

THE CONSCRIPT BILL!
HOW TO AVOID IT!!
U. S. NAVY.
1,000 MEN WANTED, FOR 12 MONTHS!

Seamen's Pay, - - - - - - - $18.00 per month.
Ordinary Seamen's Pay, ... 14.00 " "
Landsmen's Pay, ... 12.00 " "
$1.50 extra per month to all, Grog Money.

$50,000,000 PRIZES!

Already captured, a large share of which is awarded to Ships Crews. The laws for the distributing of Prize money carefully protects the rights of all the captors.

PETTY OFFICERS,—PROMOTION.—Seamen have a chance for promotion to the offices of Master at Arms, Boatswain's Mates, Quarter Gunners, Captain of Tops, Forecastle, Holds, After-Guard, &c.
Landsmen may be advanced to Armorers, Armorers' Mates, Carpenter's Mates, Sailmakers' Mates, Painters, Coopers, &c.
PAY OF PETTY OFFICERS,—From $20.00 to $45.00 per month.
CHANCES FOR WARRANTS, BOUNTIES AND MEDALS OF HONOR.—All those who distinguish themselves in battle or by extraordinary heroism, may be promoted to forward Warrant Officers or Acting Masters' Mates,—and upon their promotion receive a guaranty of $100, with a medal of honor from their country.
All who wish may leave HALF PAY with their families, to commence from date of enlistment.
Minors must have a written consent, sworn to before a Justice of the Peace.

For further information apply to U. S. NAVAL RENDEZVOUS,

E. Y. BUTLER, U. S. N. Recruiting Officer,
No. 14 FRONT STREET, SALEM, MASS.

FROM WRIGHT & POTTER'S BOSTON PRINTING ESTABLISHMENT, No. 4 SPRING LANE, CORNER OF DEVONSHIRE STREET.

Recruiting poster promising lavish prize money for captured ships.

Photo 3. Black sailors sewing aboard the USS *Miami* and mending their clothes.

Photo 4. USS *Tyler*, a timberclad-class warship assigned to the western rivers. Note laundry hanging out to dry.

Photo 5. Cookstove and crew on the deck of the USS *Monitor*. The oppressive heat inside the *Monitor*-class ships during the summertime frequently forced the men to cook, eat, and sleep on the main deck.

Photo 6. USS *Onondaga*, double-turreted *Monitor*-class ironclad. Note the small, portable outhouse on the stern of the ship.

Photo 7. Conducting religious services on USS *Passaic*. Note the enlisted men sitting on deck while the officers enjoy the comfort of chairs on the opposite side of the ship.

Photo 8. USS *Hartford* at anchor in Mobile Bay, Alabama, in 1864. The ship's hull is coated with gray camouflage paint.

Photo 9. USS *Onondaga,* with rowboat in foreground. Note the three sailors wearing straw hats and seated in the stern of the boat. Note also the low freeboard of the ship. The canvas awnings shielded the metal deck from the sun's rays.

Photo 10. USS *Canonicus* taking on coal from a
schooner. The navy tug SS *Zeta* is in the foreground.

Photo 11. Gun crew for a 9-inch Dahlgren gun. Note the enlisted Marine wearing the white leather cross belts at the rear of the cannon. Marines frequently augmented the gun crews.
Photograph by Matthew Brady. Courtesy of the Brady Collection, National Archives

Photo 12. Officers and crew of the USS *Hunchback*. Almost one-fifth of the enlisted men in this image are African Americans. The sailor standing next to the tar with a paper is holding a dog.

Photo 13. Sailors aboard USS *Monitor.* Note the sailor in the foreground playing checkers, and the tar sitting against the smokestack and reading.

Photo 14. Confederate torpedoes, shot, and shell. *National Archives*

Photo 15. USS *Mendota,* side-wheel gunboat operating close to shore. Ships patrolling along the rivers and estuaries frequently came under deadly sniper fire from Confederate soldiers concealed in the dense foliage.
Photograph by Matthew Brady. Library of Congress

Photo 16. USS *Cairo.*

Photo 17. Naval bombardment of Fort Fisher, North Carolina. Painting by Ens. John W. Grattan, a member of Admiral Porter's staff.
Courtesy of the Naval Historical Foundation, Grattan Collection

⚔ **9** ⚔

Medicine at Sea

Pay, allowances, and the lucrative incentive of prize money helped the enlisted man endure the strict discipline and arduous life at sea. The daily grind and boredom associated with blockading duty contributed to the tar's desire to engage the enemy in battle. To the dismay of the common sailor, however, the enemy did not wear gray or fly the Stars and Bars. Ironically, the major adversary of the men in Mr. Lincoln's navy was small, quick, and deadly—the microbe.

History books are filled with passages dedicated to the valor of men and the clash of arms at sea. Unfortunately, the books fail to mention what percentage of men and ships did not participate in an engagement because of illness and disease. The navy lost 1,800 men in action throughout the war, and approximately 2,550 died from disease. Despite the greater loss of life from a variety of illnesses, the sea service faired considerably better than the Union army in the area of disease-related deaths.[1]

During the Civil War, one out of every twelve soldiers who donned the blue uniform died from disease. The navy, in contrast, lost one out of every fifty from disease.[2] The navy death rate was much lower than that of the army because the sea service entered the conflict prepared for the medical demands that life at sea, and war, placed on the participants.[3]

For decades historians attributed the appalling death rate in the army to the medical community's lack of knowledge. Recent research indicates just the opposite. The army medical profession and officer corps had available to them many medical publications that expressed a need for personal hygiene, vaccination, the consumption of fresh fruits and vegetables, and clean drinking water in order to prevent typhus, smallpox, scurvy, and bowel disorders, respectively.[4] The army's high death rate due to disease was not caused by a lack of medical research or textbooks. In reality, the army doctors were remiss in their professional reading and medical practices.

The antebellum period witnessed the navy actively pursuing a medical program dedicated to the eradication of numerous diseases. Because of the navy's commitment to improving the quality of life for its sailors, the service enjoyed many victories over formerly debilitating diseases. The naval medical community helped pave the way to victory by improving the health of the sailors. With their sailors in good health, ships could remain on station enforcing the blockade and searching for Confederate commerce raiders for prolonged periods.

Another important factor that contributed to the quality of naval medical care was the establishment of the naval hospital system. In 1798, Congress authorized the creation of the U.S. Marine hospital fund to care for sick and disabled merchant seaman. One year later Congress extended the Hospital Service Act to include the navy. To finance the marine hospital service program, each officer and enlisted man had twenty cents deducted from his monthly wages. By 1810, the navy was contributing approximately two-thirds of the money used by the hospital service. The imbalance in the financial support of the program led the navy to pursue its own hospital system.[5]

In February 1811, Congress allowed the navy to establish its own hospital fund. Initially, the fund paid civilian doctors to treat sailors ashore. By 1830, after two decades of limited success using the naval hospital fund, the navy constructed its first hospital in Portsmouth, Virginia. As a result, the navy was no longer dependent on increasingly expensive civilian medical care. The navy continued to deduct twenty cents from the officers' and enlisted men's monthly wages to help finance the hospital system.[6] By the end of the Civil War, the navy was operating eight main hospitals located at Portsmouth, New Hampshire; Chelsea, Massachusetts; Brooklyn, New York; League Island, Pennsylvania; Portsmouth, Virginia; Washington, D.C.; Mound City, Illinois; and Memphis, Tennessee.[7]

In contrast to the army's overcrowded hospitals, the sailors received excellent health care in a congenial atmosphere under the supervision of skilled, professional doctors. After a visit to the naval hospital in Portsmouth, Virginia, an officer described his positive impressions of the medical facility in a letter to his wife:

> Yesterday I made a visit to the Naval Hospital, a very large beautiful building fronting the river, a fine large lawn interspersed with shade trees up front and in the rear an extensive garden and very large grove of pines. . . . The building is some four stories high built of brick and stone and presents a very beautiful and imposing appearance from the river as you approach Norfolk. For comfort, conveyance and good attendance it presents a great contrast to the army hospital.[8]

In 1853, the navy significantly improved its medical care by opening its own laboratory on the grounds of the Brooklyn Naval Hospital. Throughout the Civil War, the laboratory provided a reliable supply of good-quality medicines to the ships and hospitals. The earlier system of purchasing medicines from privately owned pharmacies was unreliable, and the medicines were of dubious quality.[9]

The sailors' health also benefited from the new engineering technology of the day. Steam-operated distilling plants supplied the men with unlimited freshwater. Mechanical ventilation vastly improved the quality of the air on board the ships. With the introduction of iron ships came a sturdier, less drafty dwelling for the sailors. Finally, cold storage compartments were capable of holding large quantities of fresh fruits, vegetables, and meat, thereby ensuring that the men's diet was superior to their army counterparts.[10]

The navy's medical success during the war was the result of proper planning, education, and sound medical procedures based on accepted practices and observations. The naval surgeons owed much of their knowledge to a group of dedicated individuals who laid the medical foundation for these men to draw upon. Of these dedicated men, the most famous pioneer in the field of nautical medicine was the renowned British doctor James Lind, who almost a century before had broken new ground in the eradication of scurvy and several other diseases.

In 1753 Dr. Lind published *A Treatise of the Scurvy,* and subsequent editions brought to the forefront the issues of scurvy, hygiene, ventilation, and drinking water. After years of observation and research Dr. Lind correctly advanced the idea that fresh fruits and vegetables not only cured the disease, but also prevented its onset. In a later edition of his work on scurvy, Dr. Lind wrote about the importance of proper ventilation in preventing the spread of communicable diseases. He also advocated that sailors adopt good hygiene practices in order to prevent typhus. In addition, he strongly promoted the use of distilled water to eliminate intestinal disorders. By 1795, the British navy finally embraced Dr. Lind's theory on the prevention and treatment of scurvy and regularly issued fruit juices to the men. In due time, the American navy also adopted the British technique for dealing with scurvy.[11]

Throughout the eighteenth century the British led the effort to eliminate deadly diseases at sea. Another area in which British doctors significantly improved the health of the seaman was the use of artificial ventilation. Dr. Stephen Hales of the Royal Navy developed artificial ventilation that used a small hand-driven pump capable of delivering fresh air to crewmen below decks. The admiralty soon noticed that the ratio of deaths due to disease dropped more than tenfold on the ships using mechanical ventilation. Unfortunately, not until after the Civil War did researchers discover that airborne microorganisms, and not spontaneous generation, caused the spread of many communicable diseases. As a result of these astute observations, however, the navy learned the benefits of a properly ventilated ship.[12]

Throughout the antebellum and Civil War periods, many men in the medical community refused to embrace the microorganism theory and the work of Louis Pasteur and Joseph Lister. Ironically, the medical profession unknowingly practiced antiseptic procedures when they used various sterilizing agents as deodorants in hospitals and medical compartments aboard ship. Years before the Civil War, the medical profession used chlorine, iodine, turpentine, creosote, and carbolic acid as cleaning agents and deodorants in the hospitals. The continued use of these agents reduced the number of diseases caused by harmful microorganisms.[13]

Unfortunately for the Civil War sailor, the findings of Pasteur and Lister did not receive widespread attention until after the conflict. Although many wartime surgeons encouraged cleanliness, the practice of handling patients with unwashed hands, dirty instruments, and sponges soaked with the blood of several patients was the rule and not the exception. Under such contaminated conditions, diseases and postoperative infection were a common theme that killed almost half a million men.

The naval surgeon went to sea armed with a variety of effective and ineffective drugs to combat the number of illnesses common to a man of war. For pain relief the doctor had at his disposal opium and morphia. The common practice of purging the body of bad fluids remained a popular, although not very effective, way to treat certain fevers and venereal diseases. Doctors used the following chemicals to enhance bowel secretion: blue mass, calomel (a form of mercury), rhubarb, jalop, and sulfate of magnesia. Although a number of these drugs had no positive influence on the recovery of the patient, they did replace the harmful and antiquated practice of bleeding the individual. For sailors experiencing loose bowels, the physician usually prescribed morphia, antimony, or Dover's powder.[14]

The preferred drugs prescribed by the naval surgeon to prevent recurrences of fevers were quinine and arsenic. Astringent drugs used to prevent hemorrhaging were acetate of lead, gallic acid, and nitrate of silver. To induce the sloughing of putrid tissue found in numerous postoperative amputees, the surgeon administered nitric acid or nitrate of mercury. The preferred anesthetic of the period was chloroform because of the chemical's potency and because it was not inflammable. The navy occasionally used ether, but because of its volatility the doctors preferred to stock chloroform aboard their ships.[15]

When medical treatment aboard ship was beyond the capability of the ship's physician, he normally transferred the patient via a northbound ship to one of the six naval hospitals in operation at the start of the hostilities. In December 1862, in an effort to prevent overcrowding of the hospitals and to provide an effective mobile hospital transportation system, the navy commissioned its first hospital ship, USS *Red Rover*. Not only was *Red Rover* the navy's first hospital ship, she also carried the first female nurses to serve aboard a commissioned navy vessel.

On Christmas Eve 1862, several sisters of the Order of the Holy Cross from St. Mary's Convent in South Bend, Indiana, reported on board the ship and offered their services as nurses. Assisting the nuns were two African American female nurses. The navy, grateful for their services, even paid the nurses fifteen dollars a month, three dollars more than the army paid its nurses.[16] Not everyone was initially impressed by the presence of the female nurses. One surgeon skeptically wrote, "These 'sisters' no doubt do much good here as they have charge of the cooking department, but I shall not want them around my wards! They are [a] pale, forlorn looking set, with a downcast look which has anything but cheerfulness about it."[17]

The female nurses, however, proved their value by caring for the sick and wounded. A patient aboard *Red Rover* referred to the sisters as "very kind and attentive to all my wants."[18] Throughout the remainder of the war the female nurses served with courage, kindness, and professionalism. By the end of the war, the nurses serving aboard *Red Rover* had cared for approximately 2,400 patients.[19]

Despite the naval surgeons' concerted efforts to eradicate diseases on board ship and to alleviate the suffering of the sick, the sailors still endured a variety of illnesses throughout the war. Although the doctors normally applied the latest medical techniques and drugs, the crew members frequently suffered cases of dysentery, sexually transmitted diseases, yellow fever, intermittent fevers (malaria), smallpox, scurvy (to a limited extent), heat-related ailments, colds, sore throats, and the one illness that even today has no cure: seasickness.

Even though it is not contagious or the result of a microorganism, seasickness has been nonetheless the curse of seafaring men throughout the ages. The nauseating illness is due to the middle ear's stimulation of the vomiting center located in the brain stem. The middle ear's mistaken signal is a result of the constant movement of the vessel. With no effective cure for the illness during the Civil War, many surgeons did at least prescribe sedatives for the miserable patient. Although lying down helped some crew members affected by the motion of the vessel, this option was not always available while the ship was at sea, since the men had to stand watch and perform other duties while under way.[20]

The constant motion of a ship at sea "laid low" many men during the war, especially the sailors assigned to the ironclads. The low freeboard design of the *Monitors* made them unseaworthy during operations in the open ocean and heavy seas. The continual rolling and pitching of these small ships, plus their poor ventilation, exacerbated the nauseating motion of the claustrophobic ironclads, and even the "saltiest" veteran sailors fell victim to seasickness. In March 1862, during USS *Monitor*'s maiden voyage from New York City to Hampton Roads, Virginia, most of the crew, including the commanding officer, became seasick. To make matters worse, seawater that had leaked through the turret packing soaked the poor sailors' hammocks hanging directly below the turret on the berth deck.[21]

Most sailors eventually acquired their "sea legs" and became accustomed to the constant motion of the ship. Some men, unfortunately, never conquered their vulnerability to motion sickness. The surgeon aboard USS *Florida* fell victim to seasickness every time the ship put to sea. When the doctor suffered from motion sickness, others aboard suffered for a different reason: His condition was so severe that he could not provide proper medical care for the crew. The navy finally transferred the beleaguered physician ashore. Ironically his replacement was no better; he also suffered from the effects of "nausea marina."[22]

Even sailors stationed aboard large ships became seasick from time to time. The majority of the crew of USS *Wachusett,* while operating off the coast of Cape Hatteras, North Carolina, fell victim to motion sickness. The third engineer described in his journal the effects of seasickness on his ship: "At sea, we had a pretty rough time today and things looked quite gloomy for a while, almost everybody was sick. . . ."[23] Although a seasick man felt miserable, the temporary illness was fortunately not life threatening and eventually most men resumed their duties.[24]

Another illness, scurvy, was as familiar to the tars as seasickness itself and was the scourge of all seafaring men. Fortunately for the common sailor, prior efforts by the medical community had all but eradicated this formerly deadly disease. The great nautical disease of the sixteenth through eighteenth century, scurvy had symptoms including included severe fatigue, pain in the joints and limbs, loss of appetite, bleeding gums, loosening of teeth, anemia, and, if the disease were left untreated, a slow and painful death. Scurvy, a noncommunicable disease, is due to a deficiency of vitamin C, a vitamin commonly found in fresh fruits and vegetables.[25] Although the medical profession did not discover the cause of scurvy until 1911, naval surgeons knew from Dr. Lind that consumption of fresh fruits and vegetables not only cured the patient but also prevented the disease.[26] Inexcusably, however, periodic cases of scurvy occurred during the war due to the surgeon's and commanding officer's neglect or the failure of the supply ships to deliver timely shipments of fresh provisions. The USS *Mahaska* experienced an outbreak of scurvy stemming from personal neglect while the vessel was blockading Charleston. The surgeon aboard USS *Fernandina* learned of the presence of scurvy aboard another ship and immediately directed the paymaster to increase the crew's daily ration of fresh vegetables.[27]

Ships enforcing the blockade in the Gulf of Mexico operated at the end of the navy's supply tether. One officer described their tenuous supply situation in his memoirs: "While on blockading duty in the Gulf of Mexico, scurvy was avoided by sporadic arrival of fresh meat and vegetables which lasted several days then back to a diet of salt meat, cheese, hard bread, bad butter, coffee and tea."[28]

Although the navy suffered few cases of scurvy during the war, the same cannot be said for the Union army. The army saw a ratio of thirteen cases of scurvy for every thousand men who were under arms. One-tenth of all disease-related deaths in the army were due to scurvy.[29] The soldiers in Gen. George B. McClellan's Army of the Potomac suffered terribly during his failed Peninsula Campaign of 1862. The Western Army, under the command of Gen. William Rosecrans, suffered a similar fate one year later. Every Rosecrans regiment reported cases of scurvy. During one eight-month period, the soldiers had only received three issues of fresh vegetables.[30] The larger presence of scurvy in the army was partly due to the state-operated militia system that commissioned field and medical officers who lacked the proper training in the prevention and cure of various diseases. The navy's surgeons, on the other hand, received medical training that covered nautical-related diseases, and the nucleus of professional officers and senior enlisted men helped eradicate the once debilitating seafaring disease.

Despite the navy's superb effort in the eradication of scurvy during the war, the constant presence of a variety of different fevers continued to plague the navy and to baffle the medical community as to their cause and treatment. The deadliest disease to strike the navy during the war was yellow fever. This acute, infectious disease, spread by the mosquito, appeared in two stages. During the first stage, the patient experienced a fever as high as 105 degrees, followed by chills. A brief period of remission occurred before the individual entered the second stage, during which the patient suffered terribly from a high fever and vomiting that sometimes produced blood. Death usually followed several days later as a result of exhaustion or uremia. Although even today yellow fever has no cure, during the Civil War, the common practice of treating a yellow fever patient was isolation from the crew, rest, and cooling. A few surgeons followed the antiquated medical practice of prescribing purgatives in an attempt to flush the body of impurities. In reality, these treatments only weakened the patient and reduced his chance of recovery.[31]

LIFE IN MR. LINCOLN'S NAVY

Throughout the war, yellow fever frequently incapacitated a number of ships and periodically threatened the navy's ability to maintain the blockade. In the late summer of 1863, a yellow fever epidemic struck a portion of the Gulf Coast Blockading Squadron at anchor near New Orleans. The epidemic became so severe that the fleet surgeon ordered the ships to sea in an effort to improve the health of the men. Aboard one ship, the fever became so acute that the engineering officer wondered if the ship had enough healthy engineers to get the ship under way.[32] The USS *Powhatan* experienced an outbreak of the dreaded disease while patrolling the Caribbean in search of Confederate blockade runners and commerce raiders. When the ship's surgeon notified the captain that several of the crew had contracted yellow fever, the commanding officer ordered the ship into the open sea. Shortly thereafter, the fever disappeared, and the ship resumed her coastal patrolling.[33]

In the summer of 1864, the East Gulf Coast Squadron suffered terribly from a widespread outbreak of yellow fever. On August 5 of that year the commanding officer of the schooner USS *Chambers,* Acting Master L. Nickerson, reported to his superior, Acting Rear Adm. Theodorus Bailey, that one-third of his crew had contracted yellow fever over the past ten days while blockading the approaches to Indian River, Florida. To make matters worse, the ship's surgeon was also ill with the fever. Four days later, Acting Master Nickerson notified the admiral that four men had died, and thirty-eight men—nearly two-thirds of his crew—were ill with the fever. The remaining healthy crewmen were busy trying to operate the ship, maintain a vigilant lookout for enemy ships, and care for an alarming number of the sick. Fatigue and desperation were slowly overcoming the crew of *Chambers.*[34]

By August 13, yellow fever had claimed the lives of twelve enlisted men and one officer. In addition, the commanding officer and the executive offer had also contracted the disease. Acting Ensign J. Eldredge assumed the duties of commanding officer while the latter was incapacitated with the fever. The schooner was in such a desperate state that after consultation with two visiting surgeons, Ensign Eldredge decided to take the ship north without permission from higher authority. The ship departed the Indian River area on 14 August and arrived at her assigned quarantine anchorage near Philadelphia seven days later. Ensign Eldredge quickly wrote to Secretary Welles explaining his actions as he described the macabre events that transpired aboard *Chambers* during her northbound voyage.[35]

In his correspondence with Welles, Eldredge reported that on 15 August, the commanding officer had died of the fever, and the ship's surgeon had had a mental breakdown from stress and fatigue. Three days later another officer, delirious with fever, jumped overboard and perished. For the officers and men of *Chambers,* the arrival at their anchorage in the Delaware River finally brought an end to their terrible ordeal at the hands of the invisible but deadly virus of yellow fever.[36]

The *Chambers* was not the only ship in the Union navy ravaged by yellow fever while trying to maintain a blockade of the Florida coast. The commanding officer of the bark USS *Roebuck* reported an outbreak of yellow fever on 24 July 1864. Within four days of the initial outbreak, the ship had an additional fifteen cases. During one period of the epidemic, the ship had only six men out of a crew of sixty-nine fit for duty! In September, a medical board ordered the ship north, hoping to restore the men's health. During their voyage, the crew buried the dead at sea and burned all of their clothing. In addition, they liberally disinfected the entire wooden ship, believing that the disease was contagious.[37] As a disinfectant, they used the chemical copperas dissolved in water, and chlorine of lime. They also fumigated the ship by dipping a red-hot piece of iron in tar. Although the use of various disinfectants improved the sanitary conditions of the ship, it did not eradicate the yellow fever. Only rest, plenty of fluids, and cool air could improve the condition of the men stricken by the disease. One can only imagine, however, what the ship smelled like after being fumigated with tar smoke and disinfected with various chemicals.[38]

By the middle of August 1864, Rear Adm. Theodorus Bailey notified Secretary Welles that seven of his ships had to depart their blockading stations and proceed north because of yellow fever. The epidemic had reached such a magnitude that Welles even addressed the issue in his annual report to the president that December.[39] The disease-carrying, pesky little mosquito proved to be a greater adversary to the Union sailors than the Confederate navy.

Another fever that afflicted the navy during the war was malaria, commonly called intermittent fever in the nineteenth century. The medical community of the period also believed that individuals contracted intermittent fever by breathing foul air. As with yellow fever, it was actually the bite from a mosquito that transmitted the disease.

Symptoms included periodic chills, fever, sweating, progressive anemia, and sometimes death. Fortunately, the drug quinine effectively helped both to prevent and to cure the disease.[40] During the sickly summer season of 1862, fleet surgeon for the North Atlantic Blockading Squadron, William Maxwell Wood, ordered the men to take a daily dose of quinine as a preventive measure against intermittent fever. Surgeon Wood encouraged the commanding officers to issue the drug with spirits in order to make the medicine more pleasing to the taste buds.[41]

Another disease to infiltrate the fleet, but less frequently than yellow fever or malaria, was smallpox. Smallpox is a fatal and highly contagious viral disease. Symptoms include headaches, chills, backaches, nausea, vomiting, high fever, and the appearance of red spots after three or four days. As the disease builds in its severity, the red spots enlarge and slowly fill with pus. The disease is spread when an infected person sneezes or coughs, and virus-laden droplets are dispersed into the air. Contact with the red spots also spreads the viral infection. Personal items such as clothing, bedding, and eating utensils can also act as a medium to spread the infection.[42]

Before 1796, the only means of preventing the proliferation of the disease was to quarantine the patient and destroy his or her personal effects. Although smallpox still has no known cure, in 1796, British physician Edward Jenner discovered an effective vaccine against smallpox. On the eve of the Civil War, smallpox vaccination was common in the United States. Hence there were few reported outbreaks of the deadly disease in the Union navy during the war. The potential for an outbreak of the disease, however, required the ship's surgeon to remain on guard and to ensure that the recruits had received smallpox vaccinations prior to their assignment to a ship.[43]

Despite the navy's concerted effort to make sure that each sailor had received the smallpox vaccine, several men slipped past the surgeon during their initial recruiting physical. The flagship of the North Atlantic Blockading Squadron, USS *Dacotah,* reported forty-three cases of smallpox during the fall of 1863, whereupon the fleet surgeon ordered the entire fleet vaccinated.[44] In early December 1863, USS *Commodore Barney* reported four cases of smallpox to the fleet surgeon. When the ship transferred the men to the Norfolk Naval Hospital, however, the physician in charge of the facility refused to admit the men because of the extremely infectious nature of the disease. The army then admitted the men to its so-called pest house, located at Fortress Monroe. In an effort to prevent the possible spread of the disease to the remainder of the North Atlantic Blockading Squadron, the fleet surgeon ordered *Commodore Barney* to a quarantine anchorage and had the entire fleet vaccinated.[45]

In 1864, the North Atlantic Blockading Squadron issued new guidelines in the handling of men stricken with smallpox. The new policy required the transfer of the infected sailor and his personal effects to the army's smallpox hospital. The sailor's ship was then quarantined for three weeks to prevent the spread of the contagious disease to the rest of the fleet.[46] Although the navy experienced isolated cases of smallpox aboard its ships during the war, the use of vaccinations and quarantines prevented wholesale outbreaks of the disease.

The navy was also plagued with typhus, an infectious disease common in crowded living conditions like those on a ship. The disease is spread by the bacterium *Rickettsia prowazeki,* which infects its victims when they are bitten by rat fleas or human body lice. Symptoms include cough, headache, chest pain, followed by sudden high fever and chills. The frequent washing of clothes and the body effectively eliminated the disease-carrying louse and helped prevent typhus. Ridding the ship of rats, however, was a more difficult, nearly impossible task.[47]

Finally, typhoid fever was another disease afflicting the navy during the war. This infectious disease is transmitted by the typhoid bacterium *Salmonella typhi* in shellfish, raw fruit and vegetables, unpasteurized milk, and any other food or drink contaminated by the feces of typhoid victims. Healthy people who harbor typhoid bacteria but who show no symptoms can also spread the disease. Flies also transmit the bacteria as the insects fly from contaminated feces or food to uncontaminated food. The disease's symptoms include chills, high fever, prostration, headache, cough, vomiting, and diarrhea. Although most typhoid victims eventually recover, about one-fifth develop pneumonia or intestinal hemorrhage and may even die.

The only treatment for typhoid fever during the Civil War was isolation, rest, and plenty of fluids. Because of how the disease is spread, good personal hygiene in the handling of foods and in the use of the toilet was critical in preventing typhoid. With the availability of freshwater and saltwater soap aboard ship, the men could practice good hygiene.[48] To prevent outbreaks of typhoid the navy also enlisted the use of the latest technological invention: the freshwater distiller. The navy's ability to distill from seawater large quantities of freshwater for washing greatly aided in its war against typhoid fever.

One of the major reasons that the navy experienced significantly fewer deaths from disease was this capability of the steam-powered ships to distill freshwater. The distilling process required the heating of salt water until it flashed to steam. At this temperature, most harmful bacteria did not survive, although the medical profession did not know this at the time. When the water turned to steam, it left behind a salt brine. When the steam condensed in a heat exchanger, freshwater, free of bacteria, remained for the crew's use. Ships powered only by sail frequently obtained their water from a steamship operating nearby. The surgeon aboard USS *Fernandina* wrote in his diary that the steamship USS *Wamsutta* frequently condensed water for them.[49] For the men assigned to a steamship, water was usually in abundant supply. In a letter to his mother, William Clark wrote, "The ships condensers made so much water that we have twice as much water as the ship requires, this gives us plenty to wash with."[50]

The navy's ability to provide clean freshwater for drinking and washing also had a significant impact on the prevention of dysentery and diarrhea, which were the greatest causes of death from disease in the army. The army reported that three out of every four men at any one time suffered from these diseases, and 44,558 men perished as a result.[51] Although the number of cases of these intestinal disorders was reported by the navy, contemporary documents do not mention dysentery or diarrhea as a problem aboard ship during the war (table 9.1).

The infestation of protozoa or parasitic worms, usually found in dirty water or tainted food, was one cause of these intestinal diseases. Dysentery and diarrhea are intestinal disorders that accelerate the secretion of vital body fluids, and in some cases, even blood is present in the effluent.[52] Although the medical community had no known cure for dysentery and diarrhea during the war, surgeons attempted to treat the symptoms and sometimes succeeded in reducing the effects of the intestinal disorder. The standard medications prescribed by the surgeon were nitrate of silver, Epsom salts, castor oil, calomel, and opium-based medicines.[53]

During the summer of 1862, the ships supporting General McClellan's Peninsula Campaign began to experience an increase in dysentery and diarrhea cases. Although the fleet surgeon did not know the cause

Table 9-1. Quarterly Medical Report for USS *Fernandina*, 1863

1 January to 31 March	vulnus incisum	*1 October to 31 December*
intermittens	vulnus contusum	intermittens (1)
erysipelas	contusio	erysipelas (1)
scrofula	abrasio	urticaria (1)
bronchitis	Daily average number	stomatitis (1)
ulcus	of patients: .9	dyspepsia (1)
anthrax		constipation (2)
tumor	*1 July to 30 September*	dysenteria (1)
psoriasis	intermittens	bronchitis (1)
vulnus contusum	dyspepsia	catarrhus (1)
contusio	cholera	influenza (2)
abrasio	communis	pleuritis (1)
furunculus	constipation	impetigo (1)
catarrhus	dysenteria	herpes (1)
paronychia	acuta	eczema (1)
odontalgia	colica	furunculus (3)
tonsillitis	bronchitis	abscessus (1)
haemorrhois	catarrhus	odontalgia (2)
Daily average number	eczema	synovitis (1)
of patients: 1.4	rheumatis	paronychia (2)
	synovitis	gonorrhoea (1)
1 April to 30 June	paronychia	orchitis (1)
intermittens	enuresis	schofula (1)
cholera	gonorrhoea	otorrhoea (1)
communis	syphilis, primary and	vulnum contusum (1)
constipation	secondary	abrasio (1)
haemorrhois	orchitis	Daily average number
catarrhus	hydrocele	of patients: 2.1
epistaxis	opthalmia	
pleurodynia	conjunctivitis	
cephalalgia	vulnus contusum	
furunculus	fractura	
rheumatism	contusio	
synovitis	abrasio	
paronychia	Daily average number	
otalgia	of patients: 3.5	

The fourth quarter is the only period in which Surgeon Boyer listed the individual number of illnesses. From Samuel Pellam Boyer, *Naval Surgeon: Blockading the South, 1862–1866,* ed. Elinor Barnes and James A. Barnes (Bloomington: Indiana University Press, 1963), 93, 146, 165, 250.

for the disease, his observations led him to believe that the drinking water drawn from the streams in the Tidewater area was the culprit. In an effort to reverse the number of cases, Fleet Surgeon Wood ordered the ships in the area to drink only water condensed on board.[54]

The vessels operating on the western rivers faced similar problems. Since the majority of these ships did not have distilling plants on board, the men were almost entirely dependent on the river for their drinking water. One officer commented on the poor quality of water in the shallower Black and Red Rivers and how the crew made a concerted effort to obtain drinking water from the deeper Mississippi River.[55] By the end of the summer, however, even the Mississippi river was low. A surgeon stationed aboard a hospital ship described the predicament: ". . . we have no water but that which we obtained from the river [Mississippi] and has been for some time, very low and filthy."[56]

The shallow rivers decreased the quality of drinking water, which inherently led to an increase in the number of intestinal disorders. In his third-quarter report, surgeon Edward Kershner aboard USS *Choctaw* reported that 25 percent of the men admitted to the ship's infirmary suffered from diarrhea. As the summer gave way to the fall and the approach of the rainy season, the quality of drinking water increased and with it the health of the men. By the end of the fourth quarter, all the sailors suffering from diarrhea were returned to duty.[57]

The combination of technology and sound medical procedures enabled the navy to remain relatively free of the debilitating intestinal disease. Unfortunately, technology and medical procedures could not prevent the sailor from contracting potentially dangerous venereal diseases such as syphilis and gonorrhea, frequently associated with liberty and promiscuity. Although the discovery of penicillin as an effective cure for venereal disease was almost a century away, surgeons attempted to treat the disease with various other drugs. One common practice was the injection of lead, sulfate of zinc, or nitrate of silver every twelve hours for five days. Several other forms of treatment included the use of purgatives, rest, low diet, and bathing the genitals in salt water three times a day.[58]

In the summer of 1863, the crew of the brig USS *Fernandina* fell victim to venereal disease. After eight months of operating with the South Atlantic Blockading Squadron, the ship finally received orders to proceed to her home port at Portsmouth, New Hampshire, for liberty and ship repairs. Upon arrival in port, the commanding officer granted the crew one week's liberty. When the men reported back for duty the ship's surgeon, who commonly called the diseases "relics of old decency," treated for venereal disease 28 men out of a crew of 110. In the opinion of the ship's surgeon, 2 men were suffering severely enough from the disease to warrant hospitalization.[59]

Colds and sore throats were illnesses less severe than the fevers, intestinal disorders, and venereal diseases but unpleasant enough for the sailor to require treatment. The common treatment for sore throats in the mid-nineteenth century required the patient to gargle several times a day with a mixture of vinegar, water, salt, and cayenne pepper. Other physicians treated the illnesses with opium-based drugs.[60]

Despite the attempts of the ship's surgeon to treat and alleviate the effects of the common cold and sore throat, the cooperation of the patient played a major factor in the sailor's discomfort and recovery. One sailor, suffering from a cold while assigned to the supply ship USS *Circassion,* eloquently described his treatment and subsequent reaction to the prescribed medication:

> The doctor felt my pulse, looked at my tongue and into my throat, gave me a few powders to take, and told me to come to the dispensary three times during the day to gargle my throat with a mixture the dispensary steward would give me, and to keep quiet and get rested. I tossed the powders overboard as soon as I was out of sight of the dispensary, but reported a couple of times for the gargle, and fully obeyed the instruction to keep quiet and rest.[61]

The one "disease" that occasionally afflicted sailors, but had no known cause or cure other than an unsympathetic surgeon, was malingering. A few surgeons during the war developed some creative treatments to prevent the spread of the perceived illness. One doctor called malingerers "old sagers" and treated the sailors feigning illness with a strong dose of purgatives. After a week of "loose bowels" the sailor usually decided that work was better than the medicine the doctor was giving him. In addition, the surgeon noticed a significant decline in the number of men reporting for the daily sick call on Sunday, when the crew anticipated liberty.[62]

Not all the illnesses experienced by the Union tar were due to motion sickness or the microbe. Although the Navy Department never

LIFE IN MR. LINCOLN'S NAVY

diagnosed a number of illnesses by its veterans, years after the war, many men, especially engineers, reported job-related illnesses in their advanced years. A study published in 1917 showed that engineers were susceptible to a higher rate of respiratory diseases from breathing coal dust in confined and poorly ventilated engineering spaces. This study also concluded that steam engineers suffered from a higher rate of digestive illnesses because of fatigue, the constant exposure to extreme high temperatures, and a lack of sunshine.[63] One can only wonder at the number of Civil War sailors who suffered from similar service-related disabilities, but never received compensation.

The daily grind associated with life at sea and the harsh working conditions not only stressed the immune system, it also strained the mental health of the men. A coal heaver assigned to the steam warship USS *Mattabesett* reached his mental breaking point and attempted suicide not once but on three separate occasions. One afternoon the distraught man jumped overboard; fortunately his shipmates rescued him. The ship's surgeon, after questioning the individual, ordered him to his hammock for rest. Several days later the coal heaver tried again to commit suicide by suffocating himself with an overcoat in that part of the fire room where the temperature reached 160 degrees. For a second time his comrades rescued the tar. This time the surgeon administered a sedative and placed the man in his hammock.[64] The next day, the disturbed engineer, still determined to escape from the harsh conditions of working in the fire room, hurled himself through the entrance to the engine room. For a third time he failed to accomplish his death wish when he landed on the shoulders of a watchstander who broke his fall. This time, the surgeon directed the ship's master-at-arms to shackle the poor fellow to an iron ring in the crew's berthing compartment until he could transfer the mentally disturbed man to a hospital ashore.[65]

To ensure that only physically fit men served aboard its ships, the navy created a medical board to screen men who had potentially debilitating diseases or injuries. The review board consisted of three medical officers who determined the future status of a sailor, based on his degree of infirmity and his prognosis for further useful service. After reviewing the man's medical record, they either returned him to full duty, discharged him without a pension recommendation, or discharged him with a recommendation for pension, provided his infirmity was service connected.[66] The navy's ability to screen handicapped men from serving aboard ship as a result of debilitating disease or injury contributed to the effectiveness of the ship and enabled many men to receive their justly earned pensions.

The sailors' physical health was not the only concern of the navy, which also provided corrective dental work for the men, utilizing the surgeon's questionable dental expertise.[67] The tar's ability to chew his food and work without the constant throbbing of a toothache contributed to his health and morale. During the 1860s, very few sailors understood the importance of preventive dental care. If a tar did possess good oral hygiene habits, he probably brushed his teeth with a wooden- or ivory-handled toothbrush sporting pig bristles. Toothpaste or tooth powder formula consisted of powdered chalk, red chalk, powdered myrrh, and orris root.[68]

To relieve the pain of a toothache, the surgeon frequently treated the tooth with oil of cloves. Periodically, a doctor tried to save a decaying tooth by treating the root with creosote. As a general practice, however, once a toothache developed, the surgeon had little recourse other than to extract the tooth. Men who progressively lost their teeth because of work-related incidents or poor oral hygiene could obtain an ill-fitted denture made from silver and ivory.[69] Sailors primarily sought the services of the ship's surgeon only when the pain of a decayed tooth exceeded the fear of dentistry. This fear contributed to the long-term pain and suffering of many men. Surgeon Boyer commented on the "joy" of removing a tooth from a sailor because the tar could bear the pain no longer. Several days later two more sailors in pain and "cursing their teeth" rejoiced when the surgeon extracted the offending teeth and relieved them of their suffering.[70]

Throughout the war the navy had amazingly few sick men, according to the ship's surgeon from the brig USS *Fernandina* and later the steam warship USS *Mattabesett*. According to Surgeon Boyer in his quarterly report to the Bureau of Medicine and Surgery, both vessels averaged only 3 percent of the crew reporting daily for sick call. Of this number, only a few actually missed any working days. In 1863, while operating off the coast of northern Florida and Georgia, *Fernandina* averaged only 2 men a day at sick call. The USS *Choctaw* had an almost equally impressive record, averaging 3.6 men reporting to daily sick call for the third quarter of 1863. This number dropped slightly in the fourth quarter to 3.4, a remarkably small number of sick even by today's standards (table 9.1).[71]

LIFE IN MR. LINCOLN'S NAVY

Surgeon Boyer attributed the excellent health of the crew to their steady diet of fresh meat and vegetables. *Fernandina* continued to enjoy a healthy environment during her 1863 blockading duties. On 25 March 1863, Surgeon Boyer placed Ordinary Seaman John Murphy on the sick list. He was the first one to go on the list in almost a month.[72] *Fernandina* was not the only ship to experience good health while blockading the Confederate coast. Paymaster Keeler, in a letter to his wife in June 1863, mentioned that although the captain was suffering from dysentery, the rest of the crew were in good health.[73]

Surprisingly, the *Monitor*-class vessels had the fewest sick men. Contrary to the perceived medical belief of the period, the *Monitors* provided healthier environments than did the wooden vessels. A thirty-month study conducted by the Bureau of Medicine and Surgery revealed that the *Monitor*-class ships reported fewer illnesses than did the wooden ships. As an example, the ironclad USS *Saugus* had only four sick men during a four-month period. The USS *Montauk* did even better. She had only one illness in a six-month period! No wooden vessel could match these impressive statistics. The metal construction of the *Monitors* was one reason for their better health record. The all-metal ships lacked wooden timbers for bacteria to inhabit. In addition, the *Monitors* had the distilling equipment that provided clean drinking water.[74]

The navy's low morbidity rate was attributable to several factors. First was the dedicated effort to supply the ships with fresh provisions and the men's ability to forage, both of which strengthened the men's immune system and prevented scurvy. The capability of steamships to distill freshwater greatly reduced the number of intestinal disorders. Because the ships were mobile, they could escape the disease-carrying mosquito. Further aiding the battle against infectious disease was the cadre of professional officers and senior enlisted men who grasped the essentials of good hygiene and passed this knowledge on to the new recruits. The strict qualifications for a doctor to receive his commission screened out incompetent physicians, and the low patient-to-doctor ratio ensured that the sailor received timely medical care. Finally, the operation of hospitals and laboratories also contributed to the overall health of the men.

❖ 10 ❖

"To Meet the Elephant"

Despite the efforts of the naval community to eradicate diseases and provide quality medical care, the best medicine for sailors aboard ship was the news that their ship was homeward bound. Although disease, not Confederate shells or bullets, claimed far more Union sailors' lives, the men enforcing the blockade or pursuing Confederate commerce raiders faced weapons capable of enormous carnage.[1] Throughout the war, enemy ordnance exposed the sailors to destructive power unparalleled in the annals of warfare. Large-caliber solid shot and exploding shells weighing 100 pounds or more were capable of sending walls of lead and wooden splinters hurtling through the air. For the men assigned to the ironclads, red-hot shrapnel replaced the lethal wooden splinters as a hazard from enemy ordnance. The presence of silent but deadly mines lurking near the surface of the water; bursting cannon; exploding black powder; and the threat of fire, drowning, and scalding from bursting boilers all contributed to the hazards that the tars faced aboard ship.[2]

During the war, the navy had 1,804 men killed in action. Of this number, one-third died from drowning or scalding during combat.[3] The tars had a one in sixty-five chance of being killed in combat. This risk of death in combat was the same as that of their army counterparts.[4] Although naval engagements did not have the enormous number of casualties normally associated with land combat, the ratio of killed to wounded sometimes exceeded the army's casualty figures. At the battle of Mobile Bay on 5 August 1864, for example, 30 percent of the navy's casualties were fatal, compared to approximately 14 percent for the Union army at Gettysburg.[5]

The high percentage of sailors killed in action at the battle of Mobile Bay was partially attributed to the waterborne mine (commonly called a torpedo during the Civil War), which the Confederate military used quite effectively throughout the war. The relatively new weapon provided a fledgling country with an inexpensive way of protecting its harbors while sometimes passively sinking enemy warships (photo 14).

The typical Confederate torpedo consisted of a wooden beer keg, which the manufacturer waterproofed by applying tar along the wooden seams. Filled with black powder as the primary explosive, the torpedo exploded when the hull of a ship struck a cap (filled with fulminated mercury) protruding from the keg. Upon impact with the hull, the chemical in the cap created a small spark that ignited the black powder in the keg. The force of the explosion was usually great enough to inflict a mortal wound to the vessel. With a hole in her hull, the unfortunate ship would uncontrollably flood and sink.[6] A second type of contact exploding system used by the Confederate Torpedo Bureau consisted of a glass vial filled with sulfuric acid. When the hull of a ship struck the glass ampule, it broke, releasing the sulfuric acid into a small amount of sugar just below the glass vial. The chemical reaction between the sulfuric acid and sugar created a spark that ignited the black powder in the keg.

A third type of ignition system used an electric current produced by a galvanic battery. A person stationed ashore determined when to send the electric current generated by the battery along a wire attached to the waterborne torpedo.[7] Naturally, the use of these torpedoes was limited, since they could only be placed in waters near enough to shore and calm enough to prevent the wire's breaking.

On the Western rivers, the Union navy frequently removed all three types of these "infernal machines" by having sailors, rowing ahead of the warships in small boats, drag the river with grappling hooks. This arduous assignment often proved fatal to the men exposed to Confederate rifle fire from the shoreline (photo 15). Although this primitive method of mine clearance was successful throughout the war, USS *Cairo* (photo 16) became the first Union warship to fall victim to a Confederate torpedo. On 12 December 1862, while operating along the Yazoo River, she struck an electrically operated torpedo and sank in 12 minutes.[8]

Although all three ignition systems worked well, the Achilles' heel of the torpedo was its vulnerability to seawater leakage, which rendered the black powder ineffective. Despite this design deficiency, the torpedoes succeeded in sinking or damaging forty Union ships during the war. The Confederate torpedoes' success led Secretary Welles at the end of the war to comment about their effectiveness: "[They were] always formidable in harbors and internal waters, and . . . have been more destructive to our naval vessels than all other means combined."[9]

For the officers and enlisted men assigned to Admiral Farragut's fleet that forced its way into Mobile Bay, the knowledge that numerous Confederate mines were blocking the approaches to the bay was unnerving. As the ships passed through the mouth of the bay, the men aboard USS *Hartford* and USS *Brooklyn* reported that they heard the snapping of the torpedo primers against the hulls of their ships, but because of the leakage and corrosion, the lethal weapons failed to explode.[10] Although several Confederate torpedoes failed during the epic battle, one torpedo worked well enough to cause the navy, and not the army, to suffer the largest loss of life in a single action during the war.

When the *Monitor*-class USS *Tecumseh* struck a Confederate torpedo early in the morning of 5 August 1864, just offshore from Fort Morgan, she sank in 30 seconds, taking 93 out of a crew of 114 (81.5 percent) to their watery graves.[11] Over the years, authors have written scores of books and articles about the great loss of life suffered by several army regiments, both Northern and Southern. For example, at the Battle of Gettysburg, the 24th Michigan Volunteer Regiment suffered 80 percent casualties. However, only 18 percent died in the battle or several days later as a result of their wounds. For the South, the 26th North Carolina Infantry Regiment sustained a staggering 86 percent casualties, but only 17 percent were battle-related deaths.[12] *Tecumseh*'s 81.5 percent fatality remained the largest loss of life from one command in a single action for the entire war.

Torpedoes continued to take their toll on Union ships and their crews throughout the conflict. On the evening of 15 January 1865, USS *Patapsco* lost 59 percent of her crew when she struck a torpedo and sank near the entrance of Charleston, South Carolina.[13] During the final weeks of the war, the Union navy lost several more ships in Mobile

Bay to the infernal machines of war.[14] The torpedoes were such a deadly weapon primarily because of the absence of watertight compartments below the ship's main deck. If a vessel received a substantial hull penetration below the waterline, the volume of water entering the ship progressively flooded the vessel, and she usually sank in less than a minute. In the United States, naval architects did not begin designing ships with watertight compartments as a defensive measure against torpedoes until the 1880s.[15]

Unlike the army, which fought most of its battles during the daylight hours, the sailors at sea had no time limit on their combat. Most Confederate blockade runners preferred to slip in and out of port under the cover of darkness. In addition, many naval engagements occurred at night. Throughout the war, the men regularly awoke from a deep sleep to the piercing sound of the boatswain's whistle or rattle calling them to their battle stations in anticipation of pursuing a blockade runner or engaging an enemy warship. On the evening of 4 May 1862, while at anchor in the Hampton Roads area, the men aboard *Monitor* received the call to general quarters (battle stations). In a letter to his wife, the paymaster described the furious action of the men:

> down came the awnings—off came the smoke stacks following the bo'-sun's whistle and horse and prolonged call of "a-l-l h a n d s prepare ship for action"—odds and ends were gathered up and stowed away—the iron hatches placed in readiness to cover the openings— magazines opened—additional hand grenades filled—everybody seemed to step with a livelier gait. . . .[16]

The call to general quarters required an enormous amount of effort to ready the ship for battle. The men assigned to the *Monitor*s experienced the unpleasant task of covering the entire main deck with approximately $1/8$ inch of grease. The officers believed that an enemy shot would readily glance off the greased deck, thus reducing the chance of damage from the projectiles. After battle, the men then had to clean the grease from the deck.[17] To protect their vital engineering spaces, the crew on the wooden ships frequently hung anchor chain along the side of the ship. When standing watches in the exposed areas of the ship, the men periodically stacked hammocks as a barrier against Confederate snipers patrolling the riverbanks.[18]

For the men assigned the task of engaging the forts that protected New Orleans, the sound of the rattle rousted the men from their sleep

in the middle of the night as they prepared their warships for the anticipated battle. One sailor assigned to USS *Hartford* described the action:

> A little before 1 A.M. the men were served with hot-coffee and hard tack,
> many thought that grog ought to be served but the flag officer was
> opposed to it. After that those that had any remaining preparations for
> the battle commenced to make them. The carpenters gang commenced
> preparing plugs and patches to stop [plug] shot holes. The carpenters
> mate had canvas overhauls with leaden shoes suspended from long lines,
> that he might be suspended at any place over the ships side where a hole
> would occur. The gunners mate was busy looking after the lock strings of
> the guns, filling the division tubs with water for use in case of fire, or to
> drink, and buckets of sand which were placed near the rear of the guns
> to be scattered on the bloody deck to keep the men from slipping.[19]

Despite the efforts taken by the crew in preparing their ships for
battle, nothing proved to be as effective in protecting the ship and
crew than the actual thickness of the iron plate that encased the *Monitor*s. Lieutenant Greene, executive officer of USS *Monitor,* described
the effectiveness of the iron plate after his ship's struggle with CSS *Virginia*: "The turret and other parts of the ship were heavily struck, but
shots did not penetrate. . . . A look of confidence passed over the men's
faces and we believed the *Merrimac* [CSS *Virginia*] would not repeat the
work she had accomplished the day before. . . ."[20] In his after-action
report to John Ericsson, the designer of *Monitor,* the chief engineering
officer described the effectiveness of the iron plating in repelling the
enemy's shot and shell: "We were struck 22 times—pilot house twice,
turret nine times, side armor 8 times, deck 3 times. The only vulnerable point was the pilot house."[21]

The impressive performance of *Monitor* in neutralizing the Confederate ironclad *Virginia* inspired the navy to invest large amounts of capital in building a series of *Monitor*-class ships. In the spring of 1863, the
Confederate gunners severely tested the remarkable protection
afforded by the new class of ironclad *Monitor*s. On 7 April, the South
Atlantic Blockading Squadron, under the command of Adm. Samuel
Du Pont, ordered nine ironclads to enter Charleston Harbor to engage
and, he hoped, to neutralize the Confederate forts and batteries protecting the city. The duel lasted two hours, and during this time the
slow-firing Union ironclads fired only 139 rounds. On the other hand,
the combined Confederate cannon returned in kind approximately

2,000 rounds at Admiral Du Pont's fleet. The USS *Weehawken* managed to fire only 26 rounds, while Confederate shot and shell struck the Union vessel 53 times. Although the Union attack failed to achieve its goal, the engagement illustrated the inordinate amount of hits that a *Monitor*-class vessel could receive and still remain operational.[22]

The enormous size of the ammunition, the complex mechanics involved in operating the great guns, the close quarters inside the turret, and the fatiguing nature of the work explained why the *Monitor*s could not fire any faster. Although the iron-encased turret provided excellent protection for the men, the noise and heat proved challenging to the sailors operating the cannon. Harris Webster, a member of USS *Manhattan,* described the action inside a *Monitor*-class vessel during the battle of Mobile Bay:

> With the recoil of the gun a sudden tremor ran through the ship as though in collision followed an instant later by the roar of the explosion mingled with [the] deep voiced rushing note of the shot as it leaves the muzzle of the gun. The turret chamber, or space directly below the gun was instantly filled with blinding smoke mingled with particles of burning powder, and in a few minutes the smell was found in every part of the ship by the blowers which take their air for ventilation through the turret. The effect in the engine room was perhaps more marked than in other parts of the ship, being near the extreme after part of the vessel. . . .
>
> The sounds produced by the shot striking our turret were far different from what I anticipated. The scream of the shot would arrive at about the same time with the projectile, with far from a severe thud and then the air would be filled with that peculiar shrill singing sound of violently broken glass, or perhaps more like the noise made by flinging a nail violently through the air. The shock of discharge of our own guns was particularly especially hard on the ears of those in the turret. . . . But it was really a place of perfect safety, and no one was injured at his station throughout the battle.[23]

Operating the great guns in battle, either in the confines of a *Monitor* or on the gun deck of a wooden ship, was dangerous, hot, and demanding work. One Union officer, during USS *Monitor*'s epic engagement with CSS *Virginia,* described the appearance of the men working the cannon in the turret as "stripped to their waist and . . . covered with powder and smoke, the perspiration falling from them like rain."[24] In addition to the heat's sapping the men's strength, the large-caliber cannon used aboard the warships could also injure the men's eardrums. A crew member from USS *Hartford* tried to describe the deafening noise of battle after his ship's heated action against the Confederate forts protecting New Orleans: "The noise and roar at the time was terrible, and cannot be described, but to help the imagination there was two hundred guns and mortars of the largest caliber in full blast, double this by the explosion of shells, then add to this the hissing and crashing through the air, and shipping, confine this in a half mile square, it may give some idea of the noise and uproar that has taken place."[25] Another sailor aboard a man-of-war described the preventive actions taken by the gun crew moments before firing one large cannon: "After they load, they all go as far aft as they can get, they stand on their tiptoes, hold their hands or arms above their heads, open their mouths so that when it is fired, the noise will not affect them. . . ."[26]

Although the men on the *Monitor*s experienced fear, noise, smoke, and exhaustion during battle, nothing equaled the nightmare endured by the men assigned to wooden man-of-war ships. For those on the beleaguered steam frigate USS *Cumberland*, trading shots with CSS *Virginia* was a devastating experience unparalleled in the history of naval warfare. On 8 March 1862, as the Confederate ironclad *Virginia* methodically pounded the wooden *Cumberland* at close range, the Union tars refused to give quarter. After-action reports described the carnage and heroism as the defenseless ship tried in vain to destroy the revolutionary new enemy warship. One report mentioned two enlisted gunners who refused to leave their cannon and rode the ship beneath the waves. Another episode described a sailor who had both legs carried away by a Confederate round. The mortally injured man painfully made his way to a cannon on his bloody stumps and fired a cannon before he fell back dead from his wounds. A third sailor, also suffering from the loss of his appendages, refused medical assistance, all the while urging his comrades on, shouting, "Back to your guns, boys! Give 'em —! Hurrah for the flag!"[27] The brave tar perished when the ship sank.

The surgeon assigned to *Cumberland* described the terrible ordeal: "The sanded deck is red and slippery with the blood and wounded and the dying; they are dragged amidships. There is no time to take them below. Delirium seizes the crew; they strip to their trousers; tie handkerchiefs around their heads, kick off their shoes; fight and yell like demons; load and fire at will."[28]

During the war, many soldiers wrote about the whining of the minie balls as they whizzed past their heads in battle. Although lethal, the soft lead minie ball weighed only half an ounce. For the sailors serving aboard a warship during combat, however, the sound and pressure wave of a 100-pound shell racing past their heads certainly proved to be an unnerving experience. In April 1862, as Admiral Farragut ran the forts protecting New Orleans, a sailor commented on the effects of the large-caliber shells flying through the air: "And now the shot and shell were flying and bursting around us in all directions, crashing through our ship, scattering splinters and bolts on all sides, killing and wounding our men in a terrible manner. . . . I must confess for my part, though, I cordially disliked the business, as these big 100-pound shells, moving with a fiendish velocity within a few feet of a man, make the most hellish and disagreeable noise imaginable. I thought every shot was within a few inches of my head, or aimed directly at me, and, as a matter of course, I felt, as it were, compelled to dodge frequently to avoid them."[29]

Perhaps no Union ship received as much from the Confederate gunners and still remained afloat as did USS *Galena*. In conjunction with General McClellan's 1862 Peninsula Campaign, the navy tried unsuccessfully to open a water route to the Confederate capital of Richmond, Virginia. The only obstacle preventing the Union ships from reaching Richmond was Fort Darling, situated high on a bluff overlooking the James River. Unfortunately for the Union ships, the fort's cannon had a commanding field of fire over the river.

On 15 May 1862, when the navy tried to neutralize the fort, an engagement ensued. One ship participating in the battle was the experimental ironclad sloop *Galena*. The ship was unique in that her sides were covered with iron bars. Unfortunately this left the ship vulnerable to plunging fire, because the iron sides were not strong enough to withstand impacts from projectiles at right angles.[30]

Despite her shortcomings, *Galena* covered herself in glory during the battle. One of her crew members, Cpl. John F. Mackie, U.S. Marine Corps, who would receive the Medal of Honor for his actions on this day, described the carnage:

> They [Confederates] sprang to their guns and reopened fire on the fleet, particularly on the *Galena*, smashing every one of our six small boats, cutting so many holes in the smokestack that it reminded one of a nutmeg grater, tearing great gaps in our spar deck and smashing all

the spars. One shot struck the quarter deck wheel and binnacle, knocking them overboard. The ship began to fly all to pieces, and in a short time we were all a complete wreck. But no officer or man flinched from his duty, and our work went bravely on. . . .

As the gunner turned to go below an 8-inch solid shot pierced the port side, killing him and four other men instantly and wounding several others. This was followed almost within a moment by another 8-inch solid shot hitting a little further forward, killing and wounding another six men. After this shell came one which exploded on our deck, killing and wounding several men. Among these was a powder monkey in the act of passing a cartridge, which exploded.

While this dreadful work was going on forward the after division fared still worse. A 10-inch solid shot struck this part of the ship, killing and wounding the entire after division of twenty five men and disabling all the guns. . . .

As soon as the smoke cleared away a terrible sight was revealed to my eyes: the entire after division down and the deck covered with dead and dying. . . .

A captain of the gun was thumbing the vent of a 9-inch Dahlgren as the men rammed home a 10 pound cartridge of powder, when he was knocked down by a splinter uncovering the vent. George Smith, a seaman, placed his bare thumb on the hot gun and kept the vent closed until the men finished loading; he was burned severely, but never left his station. . . .

A part of a shell entered the boiler room, cutting the steam escape pipe and unseating the safety valve, filling the fire-room with steam and driving everybody out. The boilers were losing steam at a terrible rate, when a young fireman, Charles Kenyon, rushed in at great risk of his life and seated the valve, a most heroic act.[31]

During the battle, *Galena* received 132 hits; the damage was so great that the men had to brace up a portion of the main deck to prevent a cannon from falling through. Two months after the navy's failed attempt to pass Fort Darling, President Lincoln visited the battle-scarred *Galena*. Upon seeing the extent of damage from the Confederate cannon, Mr. Lincoln remarked, "I cannot understand how any of you escaped alive." While on board, the president met with the crew, authorized several men to receive the Medal of Honor, and promoted them to the next highest rate for their valor.[32]

The *Galena* was only one of several ships that received an inordinate amount of damage during the war. The men serving on board Admiral Farragut's flagship, USS *Hartford,* constantly found themselves in some of the heaviest fighting of the war. In March 1863, in an attempt to pass the Confederate gun emplacements around Port Hudson, Mississippi, Admiral Farragut's fleet became heavily engaged with the well-fortified Confederate batteries. During the engagement, one of the many enemy shells that struck *Hartford* sent a wall of debris hurtling indiscriminately through the air. After surviving the ordeal, a sailor noted in his diary the potential effect that a splinter of oak measuring 5 feet long by 4 inches wide could have on his fellow shipmates.[33]

This wooden splinter was not the largest missile to grace the decks of *Hartford.* After the Union's victory at Mobile Bay, a Confederate surgeon, upon boarding Farragut's flagship, noticed among other things, a splinter of wood 10 feet long and 4 inches wide. Indeed, life aboard a wooden warship during combat proved to be a harrowing and dangerous job.[34]

While some Union warships frequently found themselves the target of Southern gunners, other ships seemed to live a charmed life. The USS *Kearsarge* was one such ship. During her monumental battle with the celebrated Confederate commerce raider, CSS *Alabama,* only 31 out of approximately 350 enemy shells struck *Kearsarge,* causing minimal damage.[35] For the crew of *Kearsarge,* luck was more useful than military skill on that summer day. Early in the engagement, a Confederate shell struck the Union warship in the critical rudder post, but fortunately for the crew, the shell failed to explode. Without this stroke of luck for the Union side, the battle might have had a different ending![36]

During the engagement, *Kearsarge* suffered only three casualties, and only one proved mortal. William Gouin, ordinary seaman, received a grievous wound in the leg when a Confederate shell found its mark and exploded. Gouin painfully dragged himself to the hatch leading below deck to sick bay, where he passed out from exhaustion and loss of blood. When he regained consciousness in sick bay, the wounded sailor cheered his shipmates on as the cannon roared above. As the surgeon prepared to treat the severely wounded Gouin, the tar bravely said, "Doctor I can fight no more, and so come to you, but it is all right; I am satisfied for we are whipping the *Alabama.*"[37]

After *Kearsarge*'s victory over the Confederate raider, the ship's surgeon transferred Gouin to a French hospital for additional medical care. Although it appeared that the sailor would survive his wound, he died several days later under the care of the French physicians. The sailor's commanding officer, Capt. John Winslow, was attending a dinner in the lad's honor when he received word of Gouin's death. Upon receiving the tragic message, Captain Winslow gave a brief eulogy and drank a toast in honor of his fallen comrade.[38]

The *Kearsarge* was fortunate to sustain only modest damage during her battle with *Alabama*. USS *Hartford* was not as fortunate in her assault on Mobile Bay and her engagement with the Confederate gunners of Fort Morgan and crew of the ironclad CSS *Tennessee*. First Lt. John Kinney, acting as signal officer aboard *Hartford* on that fateful morning, described the carnage aboard the flagship:

> Shot after shot came through the side, mowing down the men, deluging the decks with blood, and scattering fragments of humanity so thickly that it was difficult to stand on the deck, so slippery was it. The old expression of the "scuppers running blood," the slippery deck, etc., gives but the faintest idea of the spectacle on the *Hartford*. The bodies of the dead were placed in a long row on the port side, while the wounded were sent below until the surgeons quarters would hold no more. A solid shot coming through the bow struck a gunner on deck, completely severing his head from body. One poor fellow lost both legs by a cannon ball; as he fell he threw up both arms, just in time to have them carried away by another shot which came crashing through the bulwark. A shell burst between the two forward guns in charge of Lieutenant Tyson, killing and wounding fifteen men.[39]

While the Union ships endured the cacophony of cannon fire from Fort Morgan, an officer described the conditions of *Hartford*: "mangled fragments of humanity . . . scattered across the decks." One enemy round killed ten men, and the explosion was so great that mangled limbs and wooden splinters rained down on USS *Metacomet,* which was steaming alongside the admiral's flagship.[40]

Admiral Farragut ordered his fleet to anchorage after their successful passage of Fort Morgan. The brief respite from battle enabled the crew to eat breakfast while the surgeons continued their grim task of amputating the arms and legs of the wounded. In addition, the men removed the wreckage of battle inflicted by enemy shot and shells. The sailors cast overboard wooden splinters 10 feet long, rope, block and tackle, shell fragments, parts of gun carriages, and various collections of anatomical appendages. The tars then washed the decks of the slippery blood and prepared for action again. This time the formidable enemy was the Confederate ironclad CSS *Tennessee*.[41]

During the Union fleet's engagement with *Tennessee*, the participants fought with courage, perseverance, and audacity. At one point in the battle, the Confederate ironclad and USS *Lackawanna* were so close together that the Union ship could not depress her guns low enough to fire upon *Tennessee*. John Smith, in charge of the forecastle, became so frustrated that he threw a holystone through one of the enemy's gun ports because he heard a Confederate sailor cursing the crew of his ship.[42] Despite the tenacious defense put forth by the men of the *Tennessee*, the ironclad finally surrendered to the overwhelming Union superiority in ships and firepower.

After the ship surrendered to Farragut's flagship, the medical officer from *Tennessee* went aboard *Hartford* and was overwhelmed at the carnage that lay before his eyes: "The spar deck was covered and littered with gun carriages, shattered boats, disabled guns, and a long line of grim corpses dressed in blue lying side by side. The officer accompanying me told me that these men—two whole gun crews— were all killed by splinters, and pointed to a piece of weather-boarding ten feet long and four inches wide. . . ."[43]

A number of other Union warships suffered terribly during their costly victory at Mobile Bay. George Maulsby, surgeon aboard USS *Brooklyn*, submitted an after-action report that summarized the devastating injuries wrought by the large-caliber shells and debris:

> Killed—William Cook, acting master mate, splinter wood of both legs and thigh, the left carried away; Charles B. Seymour, seaman, upper half of head carried away; Thomas Williams, seaman, spine and ribs carried away; Lewis Richards, seaman, back part of chest and head carried away; William Smith, private Marine, struck by a shot and knocked overboard; Richard Burke, coal-heaver, back part of chest carried away, and compound fracture of left leg; Anthony Dunn, first-class fireman, abdomen and chest opened by shell; James Modermott, landsman, left side of abdomen carried away.[44]

Without a doubt, the wooden splinters created by the force of a solid shot or explosion of a shell created the greatest hazard to the men assigned to the wooden warships. Edmund H. Stevens, an enlisted man assigned to USS *Philippi*, described in his memoir his inopportune meeting with several wooden missiles during the battle of Mobile Bay:

During the firing many shot and shell went through the boat which was a side wheeler steamer. One man's leg was shot off and while I attempted to control the hemorrhage a heavy timber struck my leg fracturing the fibula. Having on only a flannel shirt my back was filled with large and small splinters about as thick as they could be put in. Upon reaching the hospital ship Surgeon Atkins found great difficulty in removing my shirt as it was pinned to my back by splinters. My back was terribly cut and blood flowed freely from the punctures made by the splinters. The surgeon bathed my back thoroughly with alcohol. These wounds were many weeks in healing and caused more suffering than the fractured leg.[45]

The engineers, toiling below decks as the battle raged above, were not immune to the carnage of battle. During the battle of Mobile Bay, three-quarters of the severely wounded aboard USS *Oneida* received their wounds from scalding.[46] During the battle between the Confederate ram CSS *Albemarle* and USS *Sassacus*, a well-placed shot pierced the side of the Union ship and ruptured her boiler. The escaping steam quickly filled the fire room, scalding and seriously injuring a number of the engineers as they tried to escape the inferno. To make matters worse, when the engineers evacuated the steam-filled space, the Confederates greeted them with small-arms fire.[47]

During this same engagement, USS *Mattabessett* received several rounds from the pesky *Albemarle*'s cannon. One round struck the side of the ship, sending a rain of splinters over the main deck. Two men died from loss of blood due to the wounds received from the splinters. Several other men had injuries of varying severity from these lethal projectiles. The ship's surgeon treated these men by applying cold water dressings to their wounds and a shot of whiskey to numb the pain.[48]

The last large-scale battle fought by the navy occurred in January 1865, when the combined forces of the navy and army attempted to seize Fort Fisher and close the Confederates' last major port, Wilmington, North Carolina. Adm. David Dixon Porter, fleet commander for the Fort Fisher operation, directed each large warship to provide 200 sailors, and the smaller vessels a lesser number of men, for the amphibious assault on the seaward side of the fort while the army attacked from the landward side. Porter's landing force consisted of 1,600 sailors and 400 marines. On the morning of 15 January 1865, the navy began an unprecedented naval bombardment of the fort (photo 17). Just before noon, the amphibious landing force received orders to proceed ashore. Approximately 2,000 men from thirty-five ships rowed toward the enemy fortification under the protective fire of their ships.[49]

Amazingly, the heterogeneous group of men reached shore without the benefit of a rehearsal invasion. Unfortunately for the landing force, the majority of the men had only pistols and cutlasses to attack the fort. These extremely short-range weapons were ill suited for attacking fixed fortifications. As the men debarked from their small boats, Capt. Thomas O. Sefridge described the heated action:

> At a preconcerted signal the sailors sprang forward to the assault. . . . We were opened upon in front by the great mound battery and in the flank by artillery of the half-moon battery, and by fire of a thousand rifles. Though many dropped rapidly under this fire, the column never faltered, and when the angle where the two faces of the fort unite was reached the head halted to allow the rear to come up. This halt was fatal, for as the other came up they followed suit and lay down till the space between the parapet and the edge of the water was filled. . . . The situation was a grave one. The rush of the sailors was over; they were stacked like sheep in a pen, while the enemy were crowding the ramparts not forty yards away, and shooting into them as fast as they could fire. There was nothing to reply with but pistols. . . . Flesh and blood could no longer endure being killed in the slaughter-pen, and the rear of the sailors broke, followed by the whole body, in spite of all efforts to rally them. It was certainly mortifying, after charging for a mile, under a most galling fire, to the very foot of the fort, to have the whole force retreat down the beach.[50]

Heroism knew no rank on the bloody beaches before Fort Fisher. Following the failed naval assault, the sailors and marines lay prostrate before the guns of the Confederate stronghold. Some of the physically fit desperately tried to extract the wounded from the beaches while under deadly sniper fire from the fort. Once, a fireman tried to move a severely wounded officer to the water's edge, where a small boat would ferry the wounded back to the safety of the ships. The fireman, armed only with a coal shovel, used the tool as a stretcher, placed the wounded officer on the tool, and pulled him toward the surf. After a few steps, an enemy bullet cut the sailor down, piercing both arms.[51]

One officer described the scene in front of Fort Fisher as "dead and wounded officers and men as far as one could see." The same officer graphically described the terrible suffering endured by the wounded: "As a rule they lay quiet on the sand and took their punishment like brave lads they were, but occasionally the thirst brought on by loss of blood was more than one could bear, and a sound-wave would drift along, 'water, water, water!' and then all would be quiet again."[52]

Although the naval assault failed to penetrate the fort, the attack was not in vain. The naval bombardment coupled with the naval amphibious assault tied down many enemy soldiers who otherwise could have aided in repulsing the army's simultaneous land assault. The army eventually pierced the fort's wall, and Fort Fisher capitulated that evening. The heroic seaborne attack cost the navy 20 percent of its assaulting force.[53] All that remained was the surgeons' grizzly task of treating the wounded and the burying of the dead.

To treat the wounded before their evacuation, the navy erected a makeshift hospital at the water's edge. Several ships stood nearby to transfer the wounded to northern hospitals. It took the navy two days to treat and remove the wounded from the shore. USS *Florida* helped transfer fifty wounded sailors from the Fort Fisher battle to the northern hospitals. One of her injured passengers had survived five gunshot wounds; other patients were victims of the surgeon's knife and were minus legs and arms. The carnage was a grim and foreboding sight for some of the new recruits aboard *Florida.*[54]

Naval combat was not the only danger sailors experienced. A Union warship in pursuit of a blockade runner at nighttime and in shallow water always had the potential for running aground. The result could be damage to the ship and possible injury or capture at the hands of the enemy. The actual capture of a blockade runner proved to be equally dangerous. In June 1863, when *Florida* captured the Confederate blockade runner *Calypso,* the Union tars discovered upon boarding the vessel that the crew had intended to destroy their ship. The *Calypso* crew gagged[55] the safety valves on the boiler and increased the fire, which consequently increased the pressure in the boiler. The *Florida*'s sailors quickly removed the gags and manually lifted the safeties, thus eliminating the potential for a catastrophic boiler explosion.[56]

Throughout the war, many Union tars served their country heroically as a result of their training, quick thinking, and aggressive actions during periods of crises. The first naval hero of the conflict actually emerged on the eve of the war. When the navy surrendered the Pensacola naval yard on 12 January 1861, Q.M. William Conway, a thirty-eight-year navy veteran, refused to lower the U.S. flag. The yard's executive officer, Ebenezer Farrand, arrested Conway and had him placed in irons for failing to obey his order. Shortly after the surrender, Farrand resigned his commission and offered his services to the fledgling Confederate naval service. When Secretary Welles heard the story of Conway's refusal to lower the flag, he immediately issued a general order praising Conway's patriotism and dedication to duty. Conway faithfully served his country throughout the war; he died on active duty, on 30 November 1865, at the age of sixty.[57]

One of the greatest acts of heroism during the Civil War occurred on the evening of 12 May 1862, when Robert Smalls commandeered a Confederate ship. Smalls was a black slave who piloted the Confederate-armed dispatch and transport steamer *Planter*. The South used the vessel to transport officers and supplies to the various forts located in the Charleston area. On the evening of 12 May, Smalls and several other slaves, including women and children, seized *Planter* while the captain and crew were ashore. Smalls successfully navigated the vessel past various Confederate strong points and into the open sea, where he turned the vessel over to the South Atlantic Blockading Squadron. As a reward for his courage and skill in piloting the vessel, Admiral Du Pont appointed Smalls as a navy pilot and captain of *Planter*. Throughout the remainder of the war, Smalls provided valuable service as a pilot in the various estuaries around Charleston. Following the war, Smalls served in the South Carolina legislature and later as a U.S. congressman.[58]

Most sailors who received the nation's highest award for valor earned their medals because of their courageous actions during periods of danger to their ship and crew. John Davis, quarter gunner aboard USS *Valley City*, received the Medal of Honor for sitting down during a critical moment involving the safety of his ship! While *Valley City* engaged the Confederate shore batteries in Pamlico Sound, North Carolina, a well-placed enemy shell started a fire near the ship's powder magazine. Gunner Davis observed the sparks from the fire spreading toward the magazine and, in particular, an open barrel of highly explosive black powder. Davis, without concern for his life, sat on top of the open barrel, thus sealing it off from the sparks and preventing a cataclysmic explosion. While Davis's shipmates attempted to extinguish the fire, numerous sparks singed Davis and caught his clothes on fire. Although severely burned, Davis did not leave his perch until his shipmates had extinguished the fire. For his action, Davis received the Medal of Honor.[59]

One group of navy heroes who received no recognition were the poor sailors who languished in Confederate prisons during the war. Although postwar authors have written numerous excellent books about the soldiers, both Northern and Southern, who suffered in prisoner-of-war camps, the writers failed to mention the sailors who also shared the same morbid conditions as did their army contemporaries. In October 1864, fifteen enlisted men described to navy officials their terrible ordeal as prisoners of war:

> After our capture we were put in the Charleston city prison, where we remained four days, our food while there was one table-spoonful of mush each day, and at night we had nothing to lie on. From Charleston we were sent to Columbus, S.C.; during our journey we received nothing to eat, and here we were placed in the city barracks, wooden shed.
>
> We were then sent to Andersonville, Georgia, seventy-five or eighty being placed in each cattle car, some of us were in open cars; and the weather was very cold during the time; when we arrived there we were placed in the stockade or cattle pen, with a fence eighteen feet high; we were here without any covering. The stockade comprised about sixteen acres, nearly one-half of which was swamp; we had to use the swamp water for drink. Our ration was one pint corn meal and one third of a pound of meat each day. We had no means of cooking our food, most of the time; when we had no other means we would make a kind of gruel with the meal and eat our meat raw. . . . In the month of August there were from one hundred to one hundred and fifty that died daily . . . we forgot to mention about the dead, when in the stockade at Andersonville, during the later part of our stay; when a man would die we would bury him just where he fell. Stripped of all clothing without coffins, boxes or anything, sometimes hundreds were placed in the same ditch. We were chained and made to drag heavy balls, sometimes for two or three weeks at a time, for the slightest offenses, and if we attempted to desert were hunted with blood-hounds; some of our men were brought back, torn in pieces by these hounds.[60]

One of the more inhumane actions taken against a captured Union tar occurred in May 1864. A beleaguered sailor taken prisoner from the gunboat USS *Little Rebel* was first sent to Mobile, Alabama. From Mobile, his captors made him walk barefoot to Andersonville prison, a distance of approximately 300 miles. On one day, the sailor had to walk 35 miles![61]

As living conditions deteriorated at Andersonville prison during the summer of 1864, a number of men formed into roving bands that preyed on their fellow prisoners in order to improve their own plight. The prisoners called this collective band of desperadoes "the raiders." The raiders became so successful at stealing and the manipulation of the other prisoners that the men feared the raiders more than they feared the prison guards. Lawlessness prevailed throughout the summer until the prison commandant, Capt. Henry Wertz, demanded the identity of the raiders and ordered them brought to trial by a jury of their peers.[62] During the first week of July, a jury of Union prisoners found six of the raiders guilty of crimes against their fellow prisoners. The jury sentenced the six criminals to death by hanging. One of the six, Andrew Muir, was a sailor. On 10 July 1864, the Confederate prison guards hanged the convicted raiders.[63]

It is hard to imagine a group of men who suffered a worse fate at the hands of their captors or rogue countrymen than did the soldiers and sailors incarcerated at Andersonville prison. Black sailors and their white naval officers, however, suffered even greater deprivation than did their white shipmates. Throughout the war, the Confederate policy toward black soldiers and sailors and their white officers was extremely harsh and inhumane. In one instance, the Confederates denied a naval lieutenant a parole because he had commanded black sailors.[64] In another incident, Southern officials refused to transfer a naval officer interned at Andersonville to an officers' prison because he had led black men. The naval officer's captors even refused the man medical treatment and continually belittled him during his internment.[65]

Black sailors also suffered terribly at the hands of the Confederate prison guards. In January 1863, Admiral Dahlgren received word that the Confederacy had hanged George Brinsmaid, a black sailor from USS *Perry*. Another event illustrated the poor treatment of black Union sailors. The acting assistant surgeon from USS *Morning Light* wrote to Secretary Welles about the events surrounding the capture and incarceration of the crew from the Union ship in January 1863. The surgeon reported that upon their capture, the Confederates respected the personal effects of the white officers and crew, but robbed and abused the black sailors. The surgeon stated that they "were robbed of everything and treated with much indignity."[66]

Finally, on 30 July 1863, the Northern administration issued an "Order of Retaliation" because of the Southern atrocities against Union prisoners of war, especially their extreme abuse of the black soldiers and sailors. Unfortunately, the "Order of Retaliation" failed to curtail the continued poor treatment of the black military members.[67]

During the summer of 1863, the North secured a prison exchange with the South for the entire crew of USS *Isaac Smith*. Unfortunately, Confederate officials refused to exchange three black sailors and kept them under close confinement in a prison cell in Charleston. As a retaliatory measure, Northern officials notified the Confederates that they were placing three Southerners under similar conditions until they exchanged the three black sailors from *Isaac Smith*.[68] Despite the Union's threats of retaliation and the sporadic exchange policy, Union sailors continued to suffer at the hands of their captors throughout the remainder of the war.

During the four years of conflict, the Union tars fought with unparalleled courage, determination, and bravery. The following excerpt from the journal of the commanding officer of USS *Augusta* best summarizes the overall performance of the enlisted man in combat: "Before leaving station I think it my duty to testify to the gallantry and good conduct displayed on that occasion by the officers and men of the *'Augusta,'* they were as cool as they are at any time and I was well satisfied with their precision and their rifle fire."[69]

For a grateful nation, the hours of training, drilling, and discipline had paid off. When called to action, the Union tars proved their mettle and served their country with extraordinary courage and professionalism.

❖11❖

Legacy

When peace finally settled over the nation in 1865, the navy was quite different in its composition and level of professionalism than it was four years earlier. The officers and enlisted men had met the challenge of war, had expanded and applied new technology, and had defeated a courageous, innovative foe. By the spring of 1865, the navy had 51,500 enlisted men in uniform and approximately six hundred ships in commission. During the conflict, the navy conducted the largest blockade that any country had attempted to date as its ships vigilantly patrolled over 3,500 miles of enemy coastline. In addition, the naval service actively pursued several Confederate commerce raiders on the high seas and conducted combined operations with the army along the coast and on the Western rivers.[1]

The combined army-navy operations greatly enhanced the Northern war effort. The Union navy's ability to conduct a successful blockade also played a significant role in the defeat of the South. Furthermore, the blockade was recognized internationally: Great Britain and France, for example, remained neutral throughout the war. In addition, the sailors' endurance of the daily grind of blockading duty denied the Confederate war machine its much-needed material and medical supplies. As the Union navy progressively tightened the blockade by closing Southern ports and increasing the number of ships on station, the blockade began to cause a spiraling rise in the South's inflation, which eventually helped lower Southern morale. By the end of the war, the Union navy had captured or destroyed approximately 1,500 blockade runners, worth almost thirty-one million dollars.[2] Although the blockade in itself did not win the war, its political, military, and economic impact on the South greatly augmented the Northern wartime strategy and contributed to its final victory.

The navy also conducted combined operations with the army. The navy thwarted the Confederates' first serious threat to the blockade by neutralizing their ironclad CSS *Virginia*. Through this naval success, the Union maintained its control of the sea lanes, and Gen. George B. McClellan could launch his Peninsula Campaign in the spring of 1862. Not only did the navy transport McClellan's army by sea, it also maintained the army's supply line, covered its flanks along the James River, and evacuated the army after the campaign had failed in July.

As early as the summer of 1861 and throughout the remainder of the war, the navy maintained a presence along the coastal islands of the Eastern Seaboard, requiring the Confederacy to siphon off thousands of badly needed troops to protect its ocean frontiers. By 1864, Gen. Ulysses S. Grant's spring offensive against Gen. Robert E. Lee's army and Grant's eventual siege of Petersburg, Virginia, depended on the navy's ability to support Grant's numerous flanking movements, both tactically and logistically.

In the west, the navy actively participated in General Grant's successful 1862 spring campaign in Tennessee, and Union ships and sailors played a major role in the capture of New Orleans in 1862 and Vicksburg, Mississippi, in 1863. By the fall of 1864, the navy continued to support the army's major land campaigns when Secretary Welles ordered the commander of the South Atlantic Blockading Squadron, Admiral Dahlgren, to "render any assistance he could," in support of Gen. William T. Sherman's famous "March to the Sea."[3] Following Sherman's capture of Savannah, Georgia, in December 1864 and Charleston, South Carolina, in February 1865, the navy continued its support of Sherman's army as the troops methodically moved north through the Carolinas.

Although the defeat of the Confederate nation remained the primary contribution of the sailors manning Mr. Lincoln's ships, they also successfully demonstrated the military application of steam and iron ships that changed naval warfare forever. In 1862, a journalist for the

Times of London astutely realized the impact that iron ships would have in shaping future navies. He called the engagement between USS *Monitor* and CSS *Virginia* the "most significant and important event in the Naval annals for many a year."[4] Even the naval officers aboard the French frigate *Gassendi,* at anchor in Hampton Roads during the battle of 9 March, referred to the *Monitor* as "invulnerable."[5] For over a century, historians and authors marked the battle between *Monitor* and *Virginia* as the birth of the age of iron ships and the end of the wooden sailing era for warships. In reality, it was the enlisted sailors' ability to successfully operate the *Monitor*-class warships on a daily basis throughout the war, not in battle alone, that marked the true beginning of the age of iron warships.

The *Monitors* operated by the officers and men of the Union navy marked the greatest naval innovation to emerge from the war. The North built sixty-two *Monitor*-type warships during the war. Of this number, the Union navy lost only six to enemy action or adverse weather. After the war, the United States sold fifteen *Monitors* and scrapped eleven. Thirty such ships remained in commission as late as 1899.[6] A number of the warships, including Alvah Hunter's USS *Nahant,* again saw service in defense of her nation as harbor defense ships during the Spanish-American War.[7]

The enlisted sailors' role in defeating the South and proving the feasible application of the *Monitor*-class ships was not their only contribution during the war. In the area of naval engineering, the proliferation of navy ships provided an invaluable opportunity for the Bureau of Engineering to experiment with new designs. As the sailors successfully operated numerous new inventions, they were molding the navy of the future, a navy that would help shape America's foreign policies.

The enlisted engineers' experimentation with various boiler tube configurations and the search for the most efficient types of coal provide a good example of how technical innovation in the navy could ultimately influence other aspects of naval policy. Because of the engineers' experimentation, boiler pressures on the ships increased. This subsequent increase in boiler pressures, coupled with improved condensing methods, increased the horsepower of the vessels. The increase in horsepower and the successful application of the *Monitors'* revolving turrets greatly influenced the navy's development of the larger and more powerful pre-Dreadnought warship of the 1880s. The new ships of the 1880s were a tribute to the hard work and determination of the enlisted men serving in the Union navy during the Civil War. Their successful application of the all-steam-powered warships not only influenced future ship designs, but also encouraged some navy and civilian officials to pursue an ambitious foreign policy during the last decade of the nineteenth century.

Successful application of new technology was only a part of the legacy of the enlisted men. The Union tar proved that large-scale racial integration was not only feasible, but practical in the military. The black sailor gained many social benefits from serving in the Union navy during the war. Not only did the navy actively seek his services, but the free black sailor and, eventually, the runaway slave received pay, clothing, food, medical attention, and job opportunities equal to their white shipmates (photo 12). Unfortunately, in the decades following the Civil War, the black sailor slowly lost his equal status. As Reconstruction gave way to increased levels of discrimination and the rise of Jim Crow laws near the end of the nineteenth century, the number of black sailors serving in the navy steadily declined. During the Civil War, African Americans constituted approximately 20 percent of the Union navy's enlisted force. By the 1890s only 9 ¹/₂ percent of the enlisted force were black.[8]

Prejudices against black sailors and potential recruits continued to increase under the Democratic leadership of President Woodrow Wilson. Under his tutelage, the government reduced the job opportunities for African Americans to work for the government. President Wilson's secretary of the navy, Josephus Daniels, a Southern Democrat from North Carolina, followed suit and reduced the number of black enlistments in the navy. To make matters worse, Secretary Daniels continued the practice of restricting black recruits from serving in any billet except the lower engine room and messmen ratings. On 4 August 1919, Daniels stopped recruiting African Americans altogether. By 1932, only 0.55 percent of the enlisted naval force was black.[9]

Despite all the hardships endured by the common sailor in Mr. Lincoln's navy, he never forgot that he joined the navy to fight, and fight he did. When the boatswain piped the crew to general quarters in anticipation of battle with the enemy, all hands answered the call to duty, all wondering if they would see the next sunrise. For some tars, victory brought personal glory and prize money, for others, battles introduced the unfortunate sailor to the grim reaper or the surgeon's knife. John M. Browne, surgeon on USS *Kearsarge* during her engagement with CSS *Alabama,* described the dedication of the enlisted sailor: "when the *Kearsarge* was cleared for action every man on the sick list went to his station."[10]

When the Civil War finally ended after four terrible years, most sailors turned in their hammocks and returned to the civilian community. As the years passed and youth gave way to age, the common sailor took solace knowing that he had helped save the Union, secured the freedom of all, and, perhaps more important, laid the solid foundation for the future world-class navy, upon which the nation would build.

Notes

Chapter 1. The Antebellum Navy

1. E. B. Long and Barbara Long, *The Civil War Day by Day: An Almanac, 1861–1865* (New York: Doubleday, 1971), 711.

2. U.S. Department of Navy, *Report of the Secretary of the Navy with an Appendix Containing Reports from Officers, December 1865* (Washington, D.C.: Government Printing Office, 1865), xxxiii.

3. "An Act for the Regulation of Seaman on Board the Public and Private Vessels of the United States" (chap. 42, 3 March 1813), in *Public Statutes at Large of the United States of America,* ed. Richard Peters (Boston: Charles C. Little and James Brown, 1848) 2:809.

4. Harold D. Langley, *Social Reform in the United States Navy, 1798–1862* (Chicago: University of Illinois Press, 1967), viii.

5. Ibid., 273–79.

6. Ibid., 60.

7. Ibid., 50–66.

8. Ibid., 61–64.

9. Ronald G. Walters, *American Reformers, 1815–1860* (New York: Hill and Wang, 1978), 37.

10. Only a court-martial could award more than twelve lashes to a sailor for violation of rules and regulations. James E. Valle, *Rocks and Shoals: Naval Discipline in the Age of Fighting Sail* (Annapolis, Md.: Naval Institute Press, 1996), 81. Although a commanding officer in the American navy could award a maximum of twelve lashes per flogging, the Royal Navy averaged thirty-three lashes per flogging in 1860. Eugene L. Baker, *Reform in the Royal Navy: A Social History of the Lower Deck, 1850–1880* (Hamden, Conn.: Archer Books, 1976), 128–29.

11. Langley, *Social Reform,* 172.

12. David J. Rothman, *The Discovery of the Asylum: Social Order and Disorder in the New Republic* (Boston: Little, Brown, 1990), 101–2.

13. Langley, *Social Reform,* 144.

14. Ibid., 169.

15. Ibid.

16. Ibid., 172–204.

17. *Congressional Globe,* 31 Cong., 1st sess. (Washington, D.C.: John C. Rives Printing Office, 1850) 21 (part 2): 2057.

18. Ibid.: 2060; "An Act Making Appropriations for the Naval Services for the Year Ending the 30th of June, 1851" (chap. 80, 28 September 1850), in *Statutes at Large and Treaties of the United States of America,* ed. George Monot (Boston: Charles C. Little and James Brown, 1851) 9:515–23; Langley, *Social Reform,* 190–93, 205–6. Ironically, the navy abolished flogging over a century before the civilian society outlawed the whip as a form of punishment. Public flogging was still legal in the state of Delaware as late as 1964! *World Book Encyclopedia,* s.v. "flogging."

19. Constance Lathrop, "Grog: Its Origin and Uses in the United States," U.S. Naval Institute *Proceedings* 61 (March 1935): 377–78; *Almanac of Naval Facts* (Annapolis, Md.: Naval Institute Press, 1964), 282; Gershom Bradford, *A Glossary of Sea Terms* (New York: Dudd, Mead, 1946), 81; William P. Mack and Royal W. Connell, *Naval Ceremonies, Customs, and Traditions,* 5th ed. (Annapolis, Md.: Naval Institute Press, 1980), 254–55.

20. *Almanac of Naval Facts,* 282; Bradford, *A Glossary of Sea Terms,* 81; Mack and Connell, *Naval Ceremonies,* 254–55; C. Keith Wilbur, *Pirates and Patriots of the Revolution: An Illustrated Encyclopedia of Colonial Seamanship* (Old Saybrook, Conn.: Globe Pequot Press, 1973), 29, 51.

21. Walters, *American Reformers, 1815–1860,* 125.

22. Langley, *Social Reform,* 217.

23. Ibid., 240.

24. "An Act to establish and regulate the navy ration," (chap. 267, 29 August 1842), in *Public Statutes at Large of the United States of America,* ed. Richard Peters (Boston: Little, Brown and Company, 1860) 5:546–47.

25. Reuben Elmore Stivers, *Privateers and Volunteers: The Men and Women of Our Naval Forces, 1776–1866* (Annapolis, Md.: Naval Institute Press, 1975), 169.

26. Langley, *Social Reform,* 78–80.

27. Frederick S. Harrod, *Manning the New Navy: The Development of a Modern Naval Enlisted Force, 1899–1940* (Westport, Conn.: Greenwood Press, 1978), 13.

28. "An Act to regulate the pay of pursers and other officers of the navy," (chap. 206, 26 August 1842), in *Public Statutes at Large of the United States of America,* ed. Richard Peters (Boston: Little, Brown and Company, 1860) 5:535–36.

29. Langley, *Social Reform,* 82–83. The disparity in salary was due to the navy's paying pursers a higher annual salary for serving on a large vessel.

30. When a ship is placed in ordinary, it is removed from active service and decommissioned. Today, the navy refers to a ship in ordinary as mothballed.

31. U.S. Department of Navy, *Dictionary of American Naval Fighting Ships,* vols. 1–8 (Washington, D.C.: Government Printing Office, 1969–81); Paul H. Silverstone, *Warships of the Civil War Navies* (Annapolis, Md.: Naval Institute Press, 1989), 20–27.

32. Stivers, *Privateers and Volunteers*, 312; Peter Karsten, *The Naval Aristocracy: The Golden Age of Annapolis and the Emergence of Modern American Navalism* (New York: Free Press, 1972), 65–69. This superb work provides an interesting review of the continual friction between the line and engineering officers during the fledgling development of marine engineering throughout the nineteenth century.

33. U.S. Department of Navy, *American Naval Fighting Ships*, vols. 1–6; Silverstone, *Warships*, 20–27.

34. Summer B. Besse, *C.S. Ironclad "Virginia" and U.S. Ironclad "Monitor"* (Newport News, Va.: Mariners Museum, 1978), 9–10.

35. Langley, *Social Reform*, 78–80.

36. *Official Records of the Union and Confederate Navies in the War of the Rebellion*, series 1 (Washington, D.C.: Government Printing Office, 1894–1927) (hereafter cited as ORN) 1:xv; *Report of the Secretary of the Navy with an Appendix Containing Reports from Officers, December 1861* (Washington, D.C.: Government Printing Office, 1861) (hereafter cited as SECNAV Report), 613–17.

37. *Statutes at Large*, 37th Congress, 1st session, 1861, ed. George P. Sanger (Boston: Little, Brown and Company, 1861), appendix 4, p. ii.

38. SECNAV Report, 4 July 1861, 1–2; SECNAV Report, December 1864, p. iii; Ella Lonn, *Foreigners in the Union Army and Navy* (Baton Rouge, La.: Louisiana State University Press, 1951), 620. Men on USS *Niagara* on deployment during the spring of 1861 did not realize that the nation was at war until they arrived in Boston in early May. Word of hostilities precipitated a Southern exodus of nine officers and several enlisted men. Winfield Scott Schley, *Forty-Five Years under the Flag* (New York: Appleton and Company, 1904), 21–23.

39. *Statutes at Large*, 37 Cong., 1st sess., appendix 6, p. iii.

40. "An Act Authorizing Additional Enlistments in the Navy of the United States" (chap. 50, 5 August 1861), in *Statutes at Large*, 37 Cong., 1st sess., p. 315.

Chapter 2. Manning the Fleet

1. Lonn, *Foreigners in the Union Army and Navy*, 618.

2. SECNAV Report, 4 July 1861, 8–9.

3. ORN 1:22, 385–86. Ironically, with the exception of manning and weapons, the War Department was responsible for construction, supplies, maintenance and operation of the vessels on the western rivers. On 2 October 1862, the army officially transferred the Western Gunboat Fleet, including the "vessels, stores, supplies and property" to the navy (thereafter called the "Mississippi Squadron"). ORN 1:23, 388–89.

4. ORN 1:22, 433–35, 451–52, 464–65, 468, 498, 579; Henry R. Browne and Symmes E. Browne, *From the Fresh Water Navy, 1861–1864: The Letters of Acting Master's Mate Henry R. Browne and Acting Ensign Symmes E. Browne*, ed. John D. Milligan (Annapolis, Md.: Naval Institute Press, 1970), 23, 27, 29; Edwin C. Bearss, *Hardluck Ironclad*, rev. ed. (Baton Rouge, La.: Louisiana State Press, 1980), 27–35; John D. Milligan, *Gunboats Down the Mississippi* (Annapolis, Md.: U.S. Navy, 1863), 25–28.

5. William N. Still Jr., "The Common Sailor," *Civil War Times Illustrated* 23 (February 1985): 26; Lonn, *Foreigners in the Union Army and Navy*, 618.

6. Engineering Officer McCleary to Admiral DuPont, 12 November 1862, Schoff Civil War Collection, box 35, item 29, William L. Clements Library, University of Michigan.

7. W. Jeffrey Bolster, *Black Jacks: African American Seamen in the Age of Sail* (Cambridge: Harvard University Press, 1997), 7–43. This brilliant new book is a must for anyone interested in the social and maritime history of the African American sailor during the sailing era. See also Benjamin Quarles, *The Negro in the American Revolution* (New York: W. W. Norton, 1961), 83–89.

8. Quarles, *The Negro in the American Revolution*, 89.

9. Langley, *Social Reform*, 93.

10. David L. Valuska, "The Negro in the Union Navy, 1861–1865" (Ph.D. diss., Lehigh University, 1971), 25–28.

11. "Contraband" was a name that the Lincoln administration used for runaway slaves. Ibid.

12. ORN 1:12, 210. One ration during the Civil War consisted of three meals a day: breakfast, dinner, and supper. Additionally, all sailors twenty-one years old and older received one ration of grog until its abolishment from the navy on 1 September 1862.

13. L. M. Goldsborough to subordinate commanders, 6 May 1862, Record Group (hereafter cited as RG) 45, box 356, National Archives (hereafter cited as NA).

14. ORN 1:18, 269.

15. "Act to surpress insurection, to punish Treason and Rebellion, to seize and confiscate the property of Rebels, and for other Purposes" (chap. 195, 17 July 1862), *Statutes at Large*, 37 Cong., 2nd sess., p. 592.

16. ORN 1:5, 210.

17. Valuska, "The Negro in the Union Navy," 76.

18. The number of black sailors serving in the Union navy remains a subject of debate today. In 1947, Herbert Aptheker placed the number of blacks in the navy at 25 percent, based on a review of three ships' muster reports. In 1972, Valuska, in "The Negro in the Union Navy," placed the figure at only 8 percent. Joe Reidy, professor at Howard University, is currently reviewing every ship's muster report available at the National Archives. Reidy places the number of blacks serving in the navy during the war at 20 percent. The major problem in conducting this demographic research is the inconsistencies in the muster reports themselves. A close review of the USS *Kearsarge* muster report for 20 November 1864 clearly illustrates this problem. The muster shows only two "Negro" and one "black" on board. However, seven crew members are listed as "mallato," and fourteen as "dark." Several of the "dark" men hailed from foreign countries. Were the foreigners blacks or just dark-skinned? The number of blacks serving also varied greatly from ship to ship. Muster reports for USS *Louisiana*, *Kearsarge*, and *Morning Light* show the percentage of black enrollment at 42, 13, and 20, respectively.

19. Valuska, "The Negro in the Union Navy," 131–33; Still, "The Common Sailor," 33.

20. ORN 1:25, 327–28; Bolster, *Black Jacks*, 218.

21. Valuska, "The Negro in the Union Navy," 131–35.
22. Bolster, *Black Jacks*, 215.
23. SECNAV Report, December 1864, iv.
24. Schley, *Forty-Five Years under the Flag*, 27.
25. "An Act Repealing Certain Provisions of Law Covering Seamen on Board Public and Private Vessels of the United States" (chap. 170, 28 June 1864) *Statutes at Large*, 38 Cong., 1st sess., 201–2.
26. James R. MacDonald & Co. to W. H. Webb, 18 February 1862, RG 45, box 356, NA; Gideon Welles to James R. MacDonald & Co., 9 July 1862, RG 45, box 356, NA.
27. James R. MacDonald & Co. to Gideon Welles, 31 July 1862, RG 45, box 356, NA; Welles to James R. MacDonald & Co., 14 August 1862, RG 45, box 356, NA.
28. Austin, Baldwin & Co. to Welles, 18 August 1862, RG 45, box 356, NA; Welles to Austin, Baldwin & Co., 21 August 1862, RG 45, box 356, NA.
29. Welles to Austin, Baldwin & Co., 21 October 1862, RG 45, box 356, NA; Welles to Secretary of State, 25 September 1863, RG 45, box 356, NA; James R. MacDonald & Co. to Welles, 18 January 1864, RG 45, box 356, NA.
30. SECNAV Report, December 1864, 672–73.
31. Muster Report, USS *Kearsarge*, 20 November 1864, RG 24, NA.
32. Muster Report, USS *Hartford*, 30 September 1864, RG 24, NA; David F. Riggs, "Sailors of the U.S.S. *Cairo*: Anatomy of a Gunboat Crew," *Civil War History: A Journal of the Middle Period* 28 (Sept. 1982): 269; Muster Report, USS *Louisiana*, 1 January 1863 and 30 December 1863, RG 24, NA.
33. Muster Report, USS *Hartford*, 30 September 1864, RG 28, NA.
34. William Frederick Keeler, *Aboard the USS "Florida," 1863–1864: The Letters of Acting Paymaster William Frederick Keeler, U.S. Navy, to His Wife, Anna*, ed. Robert W. Daily (Annapolis, Md.: Naval Institute Press, 1964), 70.
35. *Boston Daily Journal*, January 1862; General Order Advertisement Prescribed by the Navy Department, 22 December 1861; Check from Navy Department to *Boston Daily Journal*, 31 December 1861; Check from Navy Department to *New York Times*, 26 December 1861, RG 45, box 356, NA.
36. Navy Recruiting Poster, 1863, RG 45, box 356, NA.
37. Bureau of Equipment and Recruiting to Commanding Officer, USS *Rhode Island*, 13 March 1864, RG 45, box 356, NA.
38. ORN 1:22, 434.
39. Robert M. Browning, *From Cape Charles to Cape Fear: The North Atlantic Blockading Squadron during the Civil War* (Tuscaloosa: University of Alabama Press, 1993), 202.
40. Adam Mayers, "Stolen Soldiers," *Civil War Times Illustrated* 34 (June 1995): 56.
41. L. Baker, Adjutant for the War Department, to Provost Marshall General, 26 May 1865, RG 45, box 356, NA.
42. Browning, *Cape Charles to Cape Fear*, 205.
43. "An Act for enrolling and calling the national Forces, and for other purposes" (chap. 75, 3 March 1863), *Statutes at Large*, 37 Cong., 2nd sess., 731.
44. *Statutes at Large*, presidential proclamation no. 9, 17 October 1863, appendix, vi–vii.
45. Citizens of Gloucester, Massachusetts, to Secretary of the Navy, 22 October 1863, RG 45, box 356, NA.

46. "An Act to Amend an Act Entitled 'An Act for Enrolling and Calling the National Forces, and for Other Purposes,' Approved March 3rd, 1863" (chap. 13, 24 February 1864), *Statutes at Large*, 38 Cong., 1st sess., 6.

47. Gideon Welles to Hannibal Hamlin, 30 March 1864, RG 45, box 356, NA.

48. Headquarters, Department of the Gulf, Field Orders 35, 37, 38, 39; and Headquarters, 159 Regiment, N.Y.S. Volunteers, to Rear Admiral Porter, 8 May 1864, RG 45, box 356, NA.

49. Browning, *Cape Charles to Cape Fear*, 206–7.

50. Valuska, "The Negro in the Union Navy," 492–522.

51. Keller, *USS "Florida,"* 158,169.

52. Flag Officer Louis Goldsborough to Commander, 2nd Division, U.S. Expedition, Pamlico Sound, 31 January 1862, RG 45, box 356, NA.

53. ORN 1:7, 606.

54. Thomas O. Selfridge Jr., *What Finer Tradition: The Memoirs of Thomas O. Selfridge, Jr., Rear Admiral, U.S.N.* (Columbia: University of South Carolina Press, 1987), 57.

55. Schley, *Forty-Five Years under the Flag*, 54.

56. Gideon Welles, *Diary of Gideon Welles*, ed. Howard K. Beale (New York: W. W. Norton, 1960) 2:120. Secretary Welles's only concern regarding the amended act was the potential for corruption and bounty jumpers. A bounty jumper was a man who enlisted for bonus money only to desert and reenlist in a different town in order to collect another bonus payment. Unfortunately, the navy did have its fair share of bounty jumpers. For example, a bounty jumper from USS *Powhatan* jumped ship one day. The next day several of his former crew members discovered his body under the docks with his throat sliced open. Robert D. Evans, *A Sailor's Log: Recollections of Forty Years of Naval Life* (London: Smith, Elder, and Company, 1901), 72–73.

57. SECNAV Report, December 1864, xxxiv–xxxv.

58. Browning, *Cape Charles to Cape Fear*, 205.

59. Bureau of Equipment and Recruiting to Commander, North Atlantic Blockading Squadron, 15 May 1865, RG 45, box 356, NA.

60. Stivers, *Privateers and Volunteers*, 211.

61. Frederick H. Dyer, *A Compendium of the War of the Rebellion* (New York: Thomas Yoseloff, 1959), 11, published in Stivers, *Privateers and Volunteers*, 211.

62. J. N. O. Robertson, *Michigan in the Civil War* (Lansing: W. S. George and Company, State Printers and Binders, 1882), 988. Secretary of the Interior, *Population of the United States, 1860* (Washington, D.C.: Government Printing Office, 1864), 598–99.

63. Muster roles for USS *Hartford*, USS *Kearsarge*, and USS *Louisiana*; Riggs, "Sailors of the U.S.S. *Cairo*," 272–73; Long and Long, *Civil War Day by Day*, 707.

64. Long and Long, *Civil War Day by Day*, 707.

Chapter 3. Metamorphosis

1. "'Shipping Articles,' for the Naval Service for Persons Shipping on Sea-going Vessels, Bureau of Equipment and Recruiting," 1 July 1864, RG 45, box 356, NA; *Almanac of Naval Facts*, 298.

2. Stephan F. Blanding, *Recollections of a Sailor Boy on the Cruise of the Gunboat "Louisiana"* (Providence, R.I.: E. A. Johnson, 1886), 49; Silverstone, *Warships of the Civil War Navies,* 24, 125, 181.

3. Alvah F. Hunter, *A Year on a "Monitor" and the Destruction of Fort Sumter,* ed. Craig Symonds (Columbia: University of South Carolina Press, 1987), 7–9.

4. Blanding, *Recollections of a Sailor Boy,* 8–36.

5. Ibid., 58.

6. Ibid., 36–95.

7. Still, "The Common Sailor," 30.

8. *Boston Daily Journal,* January 1862. Today, a new male recruit receives seventy-eight items at a cost to the government of $862.82. U.S. Department of Navy, "BUPERSNOTE [Bureau of Personnel] 1020 of 3 October 1995, FY-96 Seabag Requirements for Navy Enlisted Personnel (E1–E6) and Initial Clothing Allowance for Chief Petty Officers (CPOS)," (Washington D.C: Defense Printing Office, 13 October 1995).

9. U.S. Department of Navy, *Regulations for the Uniform and Dress of the Navy and Marine Corps of the United States* (Philadelphia: Lippincott, Grambo, 1852);U.S. Department of Navy, *Regulations for the Uniform of the Navy of the United States, 28 January, 1864,* reprinted in *Illustrated Catalog of Arms and Military Goods; Containing Regulations for the Uniform of the Army, Navy, Marine and Revenue Corps of the United States* (1864; reprint, New York: Dover, 1985).

10. The navy did remarkably well in securing contracts to meet the needs of the service. It originally had contracts for the outfitting of 8,500 men with clothing. The increase in manpower required by the blockade had placed a strain on the system, and several contractors failed to meet their quotas. In his annual report to Congress, however, Secretary Welles stated that no squadron was short of clothing or provisions.

11. Blanding, *Recollections of a Sailor Boy,* 36.

12. Frederick P. Todd, *American Military Equipage, 1851–1872* (New York: Scribner's, 1980), 531.

13. Nina Hyde, "Fabric of History: Wool," *Journal of the National Geographic Society,* 173 (May 1988): 557–61.

14. Todd, *American Military Equipage,* 531.

15. Kurt Allen, "Navy Uniforms," *Dolphin,* 2 February 1995, 16.

16. Ibid.

17. Todd, *American Military Equipage,* 531; the author viewed an original white frock uniform at the U.S. Naval Museum, Washington, D.C.

18. Ibid., 534.

19. Keeler, *USS "Florida,"* 18.

20. Mack and Connell, *Naval Ceremonies,* 214.

21. Henry Woodhead, *Echoes of Glory: Arms and Equipment of the Union* (Alexandria, Va.: Time-Life Books, 1991), 88–91; the author viewed an original pair of enlisted shoes at the U.S. Naval Museum, Washington, D.C.

22. Keeler, *USS "Florida,"* 19. "Lucky bag" was a term given to a locker that contained articles of clothing left out or not identifiable. The lucky bag locker was under the control of the ship's master-at-arms. Bradford, *A Glossary of Sea Terms,* 111.

23. William Frederick Keeler, *Aboard the USS "Monitor," 1862: The Letters of Acting Paymaster William Frederick Keeler, U.S. Navy, to his Wife, Anna,* ed. Robert W. Daly

(Annapolis, Md.: Naval Institute Press, 1964), 92–93. There is no exchange of currency during this process. The items drawn by the sailor were charged to his account in the receipt book. When the sailor left the navy his account was settled. When USS *Monitor* sank off Cape Hatteras on 31 December 1862, the paymaster could not carry the cumbersome receipt books with him. He spent many agonizing hours trying to reconstruct the pay accounts from memory. Keeler, *USS "Florida,"* 3.

24. Log, USS *Hartford,* 14 July 1864, RG 45, NA.

25. Keeler, *USS "Monitor,"* 7.

26. Keeler, *USS "Florida,"* 18–19; Samuel Pellum Boyer, *Naval Surgeon: Blockading the South, 1862–1866,* ed. Eleanor Barnes and James A. Barnes (Bloomington: Indiana University Press, 1963), 27; Hunter, *A Year on a "Monitor,"* 30–31. A "housewife" was the name given to a small sewing kit that contained an assortment of needles, thread, buttons, and scissors. The men could purchase a housewife from the ship's store or sutler, or they may have received one from home. Hunter, *A Year on a "Monitor,"* 19.

27. Sailing vessels usually required the men to wash with salt water because of the limited amount of freshwater carried on board for drinking. The increased inventory of steam-powered ships enabled the vessel to distill freshwater for drinking, cooking, and bathing. Despite the increase in steam-powered vessels, the navy still sold saltwater soap to the crew. Saltwater soap possessed a high alkali content, which allowed the soap to lather when mixed with salt water. Unfortunately, the soap left a residual soap film on the skin. As a result, many sailors purchased freshwater soap from merchants or received soap from home. Hunter, *A Year on a "Monitor,"* 90; Bradford, *A Glossary of Sea Terms,* 158.

28. Henry A. Simmons Journal, USS *Sophrinia,* 2 February 1862, Schoff Civil War Collection, Clements Library, University of Michigan.

29. Issac Degraff Diary, Copy of General Orders Relating to Duties of Engineers, RG 45, NA.

30. Keeler, *USS "Monitor,"* 158–59.

31. Valuska, "The Negro in the Union Navy," 128–29.

32. Prior to Christopher Columbus's voyage to the New World, sailors used to sleep wherever they could find room to lie down on the wooden deck. Columbus noticed that the natives of the various Caribbean Islands used woven cotton nets suspended above the ground for their beds. The islanders called the beds *hammacs.* Columbus introduced the "hammock" (over the years Europeans modified the spelling) on his return voyage. During the reign of Elizabeth I, the English navy began using the new beds in increasing numbers. Over the years the netting gave way to canvas as the primary material because of the abundance of canvas on board a sailing vessel. By the eighteenth century, the canvas hammock was the common form of bedding used by mariners. The American navy still used hammocks throughout the first half of the twentieth century. Although the hammock was practical, it was also dangerous. Statistics are not available for the Civil War period, but the annual report of the surgeon general in 1926 reported ninety-four sailors injured from falling out of their hammocks. Mack and Connell, *Naval Ceremonies,* 258; "Annual Report of the Surgeon General, 1926," in Frederick S.

Harrod, *Manning the New Navy: The Development of a Modern Naval Enlisted Force, 1899–1940* (Westport, Conn.: Greenwood Press, 1978), 149.

33. Hunter, *A Year on a "Monitor,"* 11–12.
34. Ibid., 12–13.
35. Ibid., 13–14; William C. White and Ruth White, *Tin Can on a Shingle* (New York: Dutton, 1957), 57–58.
36. Hunter, *A Year on a "Monitor,"* 11–16.
37. Keeler, *USS "Monitor,"* 137
38. Ibid., 139.
39. Ibid., 19–20.
40. Ibid., 233, 236.
41. Hunter, *A Year on a "Monitor,"* 13–17; U.S.S. Iron Clad Steamer, *Monitor,* General Plans, Provided by the *Monitor* National Marine Sanctuary, National Oceanic and Atmospheric Administration.
42. Hunter, *A Year on a "Monitor,"* 16–17.
43. Ibid., 16; A. A. Hoehling, *Thunder at Hampton Roads* (Englewood Cliffs, N.J.: 1976; reprint, New York: Da Capo Press, 1993), 53.
44. White and White, *Tin Can on a Shingle,* 57; Bradford, *A Glossary of Sea Terms,* 87.
45. U.S.S. Iron Clad Steamer, *Monitor,* General Plans.
46. White and White, *Tin Can on a Shingle,* 57–58; Dana Wagner, David Taylor Research Engineering Center, Bethesda, Maryland, telephone interview with author, 10 July 1996.
47. Photograph, USS *Onondaga,* NH 43067 and NH 60210; Dana Wagner, telephone interview with author, 10 July 1996; Colon Ratcliffe, U.S. Department of Navy, Naval Historical Center, Washington, D.C., telephone interview with author, 10 July 1996.
48. USS *Monitor* Drawing Catalog Data Sheet, Catalog No. 97, Deck Light Locations, 260–1, Thomas F. Rowland Jr., Collection, Newport News, Va.
49. Hunter, *A Year on a "Monitor,"* 18; White and White, *Tin Can on a Shingle,* 57–58.
50. William N. Still Jr., "Technology Afloat," *Civil War Times Illustrated* 14 (November 1975): 5–8.
51. L. Franco, Acting Assistant Surgeon, USS *Delaware,* to Commander and Senior Officer in Sounds of North Carolina, 8 January 1863, RG 45, box 298, NA.
52. H. H. Savage, Acting Master Commanding USS *General Putman,* to Captain Smith, Commanding 2nd Division, North Atlantic Blockading Squadron, 26 September 1864, RG 45, box 298, NA.
53. Boyer, *Naval Surgeon,* 153.
54. Keeler, *USS "Monitor,"* 203.
55. George Dewey, *Autobiography of George Dewey, Admiral of the Navy* (New York: Charles Scribner's Sons, 1913), 84.
56. John E. Patterson to His Mother, 9 September 1863, John E. Patterson Papers, Duke University, William Perkins Library, Special Collections Library.
57. Boyer, *Naval Surgeon,* 113–14, 128.
58. Browne and Browne, *From the Fresh Water Navy,* 82.
59. Ibid., 111.
60. Thomas H. Dickson to His Mother, 17 September 1864, Dickson Papers, published in Stivers, *Privateers and Volunteers,* 377.

Chapter 4. Shipboard Routine

1. Hunter, *A Year on a "Monitor,"* 22.
2. F. A. Roe, *Naval Duties and Discipline with the Policy and Principles of Naval Organization* (New York: D. Van Nostrand, 1865), 26–27.
3. Ibid., 26.
4. Boyer, *Naval Surgeon,* 274–75.
5. Uriah Phillips Levy, *Manual of Rules for Men-of-War,* (New York: D. Van Nostrand, 1862), 6–9.
6. Ibid., 26–29.
7. Keeler, *USS "Florida,"* 185–96.
8. George M. Ransom Journal, Schoff Civil War Collection, Clements Library, University of Michigan.
9. Asa Beethman to His Sister Emma, 5 July 1861, Beethman Papers, Library of Congress, Manuscript Division, published in Valuska, "Negro in the Union Navy," 130.
10. Mack and Connell, *Naval Ceremonies,* 259–60.
11. Blanding, *Recollections of a Sailor Boy,* 58.
12. Selfridge Jr., *What Finer Tradition,* 82–83.
13. Edward L. Beach, *The United States Navy: Two Hundred Years* (New York: Holt, 1986), 150.
14. Robert J. Plumb, "Yankee Paymaster," U.S. Naval Institute *Proceedings* 103 (October 1977): 54–55.
15. Boyer, *Naval Surgeon,* 59.
16. Evans, *A Sailor's Log,* 67.
17. Keeler, *USS "Florida,"* 128–29.
18. Browne and Browne, *From the Fresh Water Navy,* 126–27.
19. Levy, *Men-of-War,* 10–12.
20. Roe, *Naval Duties,* 33; Muster Report, USS *Kearsarge,* June and 20 November 1864; Muster Report, USS *Hartford,* 30 September 1864, RG 28, NA; Prize List, USS *Mackinaw,* 3 December 1864; Prize List, USS *Huron,* 25 January 1865, RG 45, NA; ORN 1:19, 557–58, 21, 491–93. Bearss, *Hardluck Ironclad,* 190–91.
21. William J. Clark to His Mother, 8 June 1862, William J. Clark Papers (hereafter cited as Clark Papers), Manuscript Department, Historical Society of Pennsylvania, Philadelphia, Pa. (hereafter cited as HSP); Besse, *C.S. Ironclad "Virginia,"* 36–37. Fuel consumption varied with several internal and external conditions. The external conditions included wind, the sail set for vessels carrying both types of motive force, current, humidity, sea state (height of waves), water depth, the course steered, and the amount of fouling of the hull. Internal factors included the weight of the ship, the heating factor of the coal, the temperature of the feed water, the scaling of the boiler tubes, the vacuum of the main engines, and the amount of steam-driven auxiliary equipment in operation.
22. B. F. Isherwood, *Experimental Researches of Steam Engineering,* (Philadelphia: William Hamilton, Hall of the Franklin Institute, 1863) 1:335.
23. Bearss, *Hardluck Ironclad,* 190.
24. Joseph H. Keenan and Frederick G. Keys, *Thermodynamic Properties of Steam: Data for Liquid and Solid Phases* (New York: John Wiley and Sons, 1936), 42.

25. Joseph P. Upham to George C. Kimbell, 2 July 1864, published in Stivers, *Privateers and Volunteers*, 315.

26. The impurities found in the water used in a boiler operated under high temperatures and pressures eventually caused the minerals in the water to come out of solution and deposit themselves on the inside of the boiler tubes. These deposits, called scale, reduced the thermal efficiency of the boiler and eventually led to tube failure. The engineers understood this problem and routinely scrubbed the inside of the tubes with specially designed brushes. In one recorded instance, a second engineering officer requested another, larger ship to fabricate six spring tools for use in scaling boiler tubes. Robert Talbot Letters, Schoff Civil War Collection, Clements Library, University of Michigan.

27. Isaac Degraff Journal, 25 February 1862, RG 45, NA.

28. Thomas H. Stevens, "Cruise of the *Sonoma*," *Cosmopolitian*, December 1890, published in Stivers, *Privateers and Volunteers*, 317–19.

29. Myron H. Knapp Journal, 12 December 1862, Myron H. Knapp Papers, Burton Historical Library, Detroit, Mich. (hereafter cited as BHL).

30. Isaac Degraff Journal, 5 March 1862, RG 45, NA.

31. Keeler, USS *"Monitor,"* 29–30.

32. Edward W. Sloan, *Benjamin Franklin Isherwood, Naval Engineer* (Annapolis, Md.: Naval Institute Press, 1965), 10–11,

33. Myron H. Knapp Journal, 7 August 1862, Myron H. Knapp Papers, BHL.

34. John C. Huntly Diary, vol. 3, 4–5 September 1863, pp. 20–21, HSP.

35. Hunter, *A Year on a "Monitor,"* 97–110.

36. Charles Ellery Stedman, *The Civil War Sketchbook of Charles Ellery Stedman, Surgeon, United States Navy,* ed. Jim Dan Hill (San Rafael, Calif.: Presidio Press, 1976), 172.

37. ORN 1:14, 322.

38. Harris Webster, "An August Morning with Farragut at Mobile Bay," in U.S. Department of Navy, Naval History Division, *Civil War Naval Chronology, 1861–1865* (Washington, D.C.: Government Printing Office, 1971) 6:93. Today, the navy has established a maximum exposure time limit to excessive heat. The navy "safe stay time" chart only goes as high as 125 degrees. At this temperature, an engineering watch stander can remain in the space exposed to this temperature for only twenty-five minutes. The Civil War engineer was constantly exposed to temperatures over 125 degrees and for much longer than twenty-five minutes. U.S. Department of Navy, "Physiological Heat Exposure Limits (PHEL)," *OPNAVINST 5100.20C* (Washington, D.C.: Government Printing Office, 5 March 1985), enclosure 5, p. 2.

39. Steam Log, USS *Wachusetts*, BHL.

40. John C. Huntly Journal, vol. 3, 26 September 1863, p. 25, HSP; Log, USS *Lexington*, 2–3 May 1862, RG 24, NA. George M. Ransom Journal, 5 May 1862, Schoff Civil War Collection, Clements Library, University of Michigan; Beach, *The United States Navy*, 150.

41. Isaac DeGraff Journal, Copy of General Orders relating to duties of engineers, RG 45, NA.

42. Ibid.; John C. Huntly Journal, vol. 3, 3–5 September 1863, pp. 20–21, HSP.

43. John B. Marchand, *Charleston Blockade: The Journals of John B. Marchand, U.S.*

Navy, 1861–1862, ed. Craig L. Symonds (Newport, R.I.: Naval War College Press, 1976), 157.

44. ORN 1: 9, 224.

45. Captain Percival Drayton to A. Hamilton, 22 April 1864, Captain Percival Drayton Letters, New York Public Library, Manuscript and Archives Division.

46. Schley, *Forty-Five Years under the Flag,* 20; Defense Mapping Agency Hydrographic and Topographic Center, *Distance between Ports, Publication 151,* 5th ed. (1995), 31, 63, 151.

47. SECNAV Report, December 1864, 673.

48. William J. Clark to His Mother, vol. 1., 14 July 1863, Clark Papers, HSP.

49. Myron H. Knapp Journal, 8 March 1862–7 September 1862, Myron H. Knapp Papers, BHL.

50. Engineering Logbook for CSS *Florida,* 7 October 1864–18 November 1864, Myron K. Knapp Papers, BHL.

51. ORN 1:3, 637.

52. William H. Badlam, *"Kearsarge" and "Alabama"* (Providence, R.I.: Providence Press, Snow and Farnkam Printers, 1884), 35.

53. Lester L. Swift, ed., "Letters from a Sailor on a Tinclad," *Civil War History,* March 1961, 52.

54. Charles Wilkes, *Autobiography of Rear Admiral Charles Wilkes, U.S. Navy, 1798–1877,* ed. William James Morgan et al. (Washington, D.C.: U.S. Department of Navy, Naval History Division, 1978), 832.

55. Hunter, *A Year on a "Monitor,"* 68, 88.

Chapter 5. Shipboard Training

1. Riggs, "Sailors of the U.S.S. *Cairo,"* 271.

2. Frank W. Hackett Papers, Civil War to Spanish-American Wars, Historical Reference, (ZO), box 8, Naval Historical Center, Washington, D.C.

3. Levy, *Men-of-War,* 31.

4. Evans, *A Sailor's Log,* 60.

5. W. M. C. Philbrick Journal, vol. 3, 14 January 1863, RG 45, NA.

6. Browne and Browne, *From the Fresh Water Navy,* 219.

7. Boyer, *Naval Surgeon,* 218.

8. Log, USS *Kearsarge,* 16 June 1864, RG 45, NA.

9. Keeler, *USS "Monitor,"* 40.

10. U.S. Department of Navy, *Report of the Chief Bureau of Ordnance* (Washington, D.C.: Government Printing Office, October 1863), 18.

11. Robert H. Rankin, *Small Arms of the Sea Service* (New Milford, Conn.: N. Flaygerman, 1972), 2–5; Todd, *American Military Equipage,* 560.

12. Rankin, *Small Arms of the Sea Service,* 5–9; Todd, *American Military Equipage,* 559–60.

13. Rankin, *Small Arms of the Sea Service,* 14–17; Todd, *American Military Equipage,* 167–68; Marchand, *Charleston Blockade,* 70.

14. U.S. Department of Navy, *Report of the Chief Bureau of Ordnance,* 18; Rankin, *Small Arms of the Sea Service,* 73; Todd, *American Military Equipage,* 167–68.

15. Rankin, *Small Arms of the Sea Service,* 76–80; Todd, *American Military Equipage,* 169–73; Racine and Laramie, *A Short History of Civil War Revolvers.*

16. Rankin, *Small Arms of the Sea Service*, 114–21; Todd, *American Military Equipage*, 554–55; U.S. Department of Navy, *Report of the Chief Bureau of Ordnance*, 18: Keeler, *USS "Monitor*," 46.

17. Keeler, *USS "Florida,"* 128.

18. Hunter, *A Year on a "Monitor,"* 44.

19. Still, "Technology Afloat," 45.

20. Spencer Tucker, *Arming the Fleet: U.S. Navy Ordnance in the Muzzle-Loading Era* (Annapolis, Md.: Naval Institute Press, 1989), 217–23; U.S. Department of Navy, *Report of the Chief of the Bureau of Ordnance*, 20 October 1863. The great guns found aboard Union warships were enormous weapons capable of delivering massive destructive power. The cannon were also quite rugged. One 11-inch Dahlgren barrel, weighing 15,778 pounds and located aboard USS *Oneida*, was struck by three confederate cannonballs and still operated. The cannon is currently on display at the U.S. Naval Base, Great Lakes, Illinois. Gunpowder, or black powder, consisted of 75 percent salt peter, 15 percent charcoal, and 10 percent sulfur. Extremely volatile, the powder required great caution in handling, as the slightest spark could set off an explosion. John C. Reilly Jr., *The Iron Guns of Willard Park, Washington, Navy Yard* (Washington, D.C.: National Historic Center, 1991), 30.

21. Still, "Technology Afloat," 8.

22. Francis T. Miller, *Photographic History of the Civil War: The Navies*, reprint ed., (New York: Castle Books, 1957), 294.

23. Hunter, *A Year on a "Monitor,"* 34–36.

24. Boyer, *Naval Surgeon*, 99.

25. Evans, *A Sailor's Log*, 74.

26. U.S. Department of Navy, Naval History Division, *Civil War Naval Chronology, 1861–1865* (Washington, D.C., 1971) 5:11; *Harper's* 14 January 1865, 23.

27. Anonymous, "Life on a Blockader," *Continental Monthly* 6 (August 1864): 50.

Chapter 6. Pork and Beans

1. Anonymous, "Life on a Blockader," *Continental Monthly* 6 (August 1864): 50.

2. During the Civil War a ration consisted of three meals a day: breakfast, dinner (noon meal), and supper.

3. "An Act to Alter and Regulate the Navy Ration," *Statutes at Large*, 37th Cong., 1st sess., 1861, 264–65.

4. U.S. War Department, *Revised Regulations for the Army of the United States, 1861* ([date]; reprint, Harrisburg, Pa.: National Historical Society, 1980), 243, 279. The Union navy's meat ration was also larger than the British navy's. The Union sailor received four ounces more per day than did the British tar. Eugene L. Rasor, *Reforms in the Royal Navy: A Social History of the Lower Deck, 1850–1880* (Hamden, Conn.: Archer Books, 1976), 128–29.

5. SECNAV Report, 4 July 1861, 10–11.

6. ORN 1:27, 357. The navy's ability to resupply its ships on a biweekly basis is a remarkable accomplishment, even by today's standards!

7. Keeler, *USS "Florida,"* 21, 41. Keeler also wrote in a letter to his wife that he regularly purchased fresh provisions for the crew of USS *Monitor* semi-weekly. Keeler, *USS "Monitor,"* 70.

8. Anonymous, "Life on a Blockader," 51.

9. Browne and Browne, *From the Fresh Water Navy*, 215, 219.

10. Ibid., 219.

11. Ibid., 235.

12. USS *Mississippi* Pay Voucher to Mr. Jose Vallejo Jr., William Perkins Library, Special Collections, Duke University.

13. Keeler, USS *"Florida,"* 77.

14. Log, USS *Hartford*, 12, 13 May 1864, RG 24, NA.

15. Keeler, USS *"Florida,"* 205. In 1892, USS *Olympia* was the first U.S. Navy ship to have mechanical refrigeration. USS *Olympia* Historical Center, Philadelphia, Pa.

16. ORN 1:27, 367–68; Browning, *Cape Charles to Cape Fear*, 177.

17. ORN 1:27, 367–68.

18. Hunter, *A Year on a "Monitor,"* 42–43. One of the great disparities between the living conditions of officers and enlisted men was in their food. On board the larger wooden sailing ships, there was usually room set aside in the forward part of the vessel for livestock, namely, sheep, cows, pigs, and chickens. When slaughtered, these animals normally ended up on the plates of the officers. Only rarely did the enlisted receive freshly slaughtered meat. Boyer, *Naval Surgeon*, 31.

19. Frank J. Allston, *Ready for Sea: The Bicentennial History of the U.S. Navy Supply Corps* (Annapolis, Md.: Naval Institute Press, 1995), 80.

20. ORN 1:13, 655–56.

21. Boyer, *Naval Surgeon*, 154–55.

22. Owen Connelly, *The French Revolution and Napoleonic Era*, 2nd ed. (Fort Worth, Tex.: Holt, Rinehart and Winston, 1991), 217; Valerie-Anne Giscard d'Estaing, *The World Almanac Book of Inventions* (New York: World Almanac Publications, 1985), 77–78.

23. Reay Tannahill, *Food in History* (New York: Crown Publishing, 1986), 310.

24. Virginia Mescher, *Dates of Selected Inventions and Occurrences during the Latter Part of the Eighteenth Century and Nineteenth Century* (Burke, Va.: Virginia Mescher and Nature's Finest, 1993), 4, 8.

25. The canning process of the day required the canner to seal fresh meat in a container. The manufacturer then submerged the product in a water bath heated to 270 degrees Fahrenheit. The can's lid contained a small hole that allowed for the release of vapors during the heating process. After the water bath, the can cooled, thus creating a vacuum. During this cooling process the manufacturer sealed the hole with lead solder. John J. Keevil, *Medicine and the Navy, 1200–1900* (Edinburgh: E. and S. Livingstone, 1957–63), 4:99–100.

26. Frank Hastings Hamilton, *A Practical Treatise on Military Surgery* (New York: Bailliere Brothers, 1861), 67, 603.

27. James M. Sanderson, *Camp Fires and Camp Cooking or Culinary Hints for the Soldier* (Washington, D.C.: Government Printing Office, 1862), iv; Palmer H. Boeger, "Hardtack and Burnt Beans," *Civil War History* 4 (1958): 73–92.

28. Blanding, *Recollections of a Sailor Boy*, 66.

29. U.S. Department of Navy, Naval History Division, *Civil War Naval Chronology, 1861–1865*, 6:53–64.

30. Hunter, *A Year on a "Monitor,"* 36, 48.

31. Blanding, *Recollections of a Sailor Boy*, 66.
32. Ibid., 60.
33. Keeler, *USS "Monitor,"* 64.
34. "An Act for the Better Government of the Navy of the United States" (chap. 204, 17 July 1862), *Statutes at Large* 13:564. The new law did not prohibit officers from maintaining and consuming alcoholic beverages on board ship. In 1914, the secretary of the navy, Josephus Daniels, permanently outlawed all spirits, except for medicinal purpose, aboard navy ships. Harrod, *Manning the New Navy*, 156.
35. Blanding, *Recollections of a Sailor Boy*, 61.
36. Lathrop, "Grog," U.S. Naval Institute *Proceedings* 61:3, n. 19; U.S. Naval Institute, *The Book of Naval Songs* (Annapolis, Md.: Naval Institute Press, 1955), 86–87. The term "splicing the main brace" originally referred to the arduous and dangerous evolution that required the sailors to repair the main cable that helped secure the largest mast, the main mast, in place aboard a sailing vessel. Over the years this term has become synonymous with any difficult task successfully completed by the crew. Before the abolishment of alcohol in the navy, the crew usually received a reward in the form of an extra ration of grog. Mack and Connell, *Naval Ceremonies*, 283.
37. E. G. Parrott Journal, 31 August 1862, RG 45, NA.
38. James M. Merrill, "Men, Monotony, and Mouldy Beans: Life on Board Civil War Blockaders," in *Thirty Years of the "American Neptune"* (Cambridge: Harvard University Press, 1972), 203.
39. Boyer, *Naval Surgeon*, 123.
40. ORN 1:12, 741–42.
41. Ibid. 1:3–4, 12, 13, 741–42; Boyer, *Naval Surgeon*, 15.
42. Boyer, *Naval Surgeon*, 123.
43. ORN 1: 14, 418–19. The engineers' practice of drinking a mixture of water and oatmeal appeared to be standard. For example, the chief engineering officer of USS *Wabash* requested fifty barrels of oatmeal for his engineers (Chief Engineer McCleery to Admiral Dupont, 22 March 1863, Schoff Civil War Collection, box 35, item 39), and the second assistant engineer on board USS *Pensacola* wrote that the engineering division received 100 pounds of oatmeal in cans (John T. Hawkins Memorandum Book, p. 24, New York Public Library, Manuscripts and Archives Division).
44. Frazer Kirkland, *Anecdotes and Incidents of the War of the Rebellion* (Hartford, Conn.: Hartford Publishing, 1866), 383–84.
45. Hunter, *A Year on a "Monitor,"* 43.
46. Roe, *Naval Duties*, 30; Hunter, *A Year on a "Monitor,"* 43; W. M. C. Philbrick Journal, vol. 3, 7 October 1862, RG 45, NA; James A. Chesley to the People of Wakefield, 6 February 1862, Library of Congress, Manuscript Division, published in Valuska, "The Negro in the Union Navy," 129; Dewitt Papers, published in Stivers, *Privateers and Volunteers*, 371.
47. Charles Poole Papers, 17 October 1863, published in Stivers, *Privateers and Volunteers*, 371.
48. Hunter, *A Year on a "Monitor,"* 42–43.
49. Blanding, *Recollections of a Sailor Boy*, 88.
50. W. M. C. Philbrick Journal, vol. 3, 21, 25 December 1862, RG 45, NA.

51. Browne and Browne, *From the Fresh Water Navy*, 130.
52. Blanding, *Recollections of a Sailor Boy*, 66–67.
53. Private Charles Brother Journal, published in U.S. Navy, Naval History Division, *Civil War Naval Chronology* 6:48–81.
54. Hunter, *A Year on a "Monitor,"* 82.
55. ORN 1:13, 139.
56. Keeler, *USS "Florida,"* 91.
57. Boyer, *Naval Surgeon*, 69.
58. Ibid., 139, 190.
59. Willaim J. Clark to His Mother, 25 April 1862, vol. 1, Clark Papers, HSP.
60. James L. B. Blauvelt to His Mother, 12 October 1863, Duke University, William Perkins Library, Special Collections.
61. Schley, *Forty-Five Years under the Flag*, 55–56.
62. S. P. Lee, Commander, North Atlantic Blockading Squadron, to Captain Smith, Commanding 2nd Division, 18 July 1864, RG 45, box 298, NA.
63. Invoice of Poultry from the Office, U.S. Navy Yard, New York, to Admiral Porter, Commanding North Atlantic Blockading Squadron, 8 November 1864, RG 45, box 298, NA.
64. Robert J. Plumb, "Yankee Paymaster," U.S. Naval Institute *Proceedings* 103 (October 1977): 55. The Thanksgiving tradition continues to be a bountiful annual event. For Thanksgiving Day dinner of 1996, the ship's cooks of the aircraft carrier USS *John F. Kennedy* prepared 180 whole turkeys weighing 25 pounds each. The men and women assigned to the guided missile cruiser USS *Vicksburg* ate even better, feasting on a quarter-ton of 24-pound turkeys, several hundred pounds of prime rib and Virginia ham, 800 pounds of fresh shrimp, plus corn on the cob, corn bread stuffing, cranberry sauce, and pumpkin pie. The U.S. Navy still remains the best-fed service in the world. Hugh A. Mulligan, "Military Turkeys Do Tasty Duty Overseas," *Detroit Free Press* 24 November 1996, sec. F, p. 7.
65. Boyer, *Naval Surgeon*, 34, 36.
66. Ibid., 242–45.
67. Merrill, "Mouldy Beans," 196–97.
68. Bartholomew Diggins Recollections, p. 244, New York Public Library, Manuscript and Archives Division.
69. William Marvel, *The "Alabama" and "Kearsarge,"* (Chapel Hill: University of North Carolina Press, 1996), 98, 147.

Chapter 7. Entertainment, Liberty, and the Lord's Day

1. Marchand, *Charleston Blockade*, 157.
2. Keeler, *USS "Monitor,"* 54–57, 65, 107; Lt. Samuel Dana Greene to His Father, 4 May 1862, Mariners Museum Research Library and Archives, Newport News, Va.
3. Marvel, *The "Alabama" and "Kearsarge,"* 155–56.
4. Hunter, *A Year on a "Monitor,"* 42; Boyer, *Naval Surgeon*, 170–71.
5. Browne and Browne, *From the Fresh Water Navy*, 229.
6. Henry A. Simmons Journal, 9 April 1862, Schoff Civil War Collection, Clements Library, University of Michigan.

7. Keeler, USS *"Monitor,"* 252.

8. Lonn, *Foreigners in the Union Army and Navy* (Baton Rouge: Louisiana State University Press, 1951), 639.

9. Boyer, *Naval Surgeon,* 316.

10. Ibid., 317.

11. Ibid., 84.

12. Blanding, *Recollections of a Sailor Boy,* 68.

13. U.S. Navy, Naval History Division, *Civil War Naval Chronology* 6:112–80; Victory Music, *Victory Sings at Sea: The Curse of the Somers,* (Bonney Lake, Wa.: Victory Music, 1995).

14. Merrill, "Mouldy Beans," 199.

15. Ibid., 200.

16. *Sailor's Magazine* 37 (December 1862): 108.

17. Keeler, USS *"Monitor,"* 59; Boyer, *Naval Surgeon,* 172.

18. Stephan Lee, Commander, North Atlantic Blockading Squadron, to Captain Smith, Commanding 2nd Division, North Atlantic Blockading Squadron, 24 September 1864, RG 45, box 298, NA.

19. Browning, *Cape Charles to Cape Fear,* 211.

20. Hunter, *A Year on a "Monitor,"* 30; Boyer, *Naval Surgeon,* 27, 31.

21. John C. Huntly Diary, 9 June 1863, HSP.

22. U.S. Postal Service, *We Deliver: The Story of the U.S. Postal Service* (Washington, D.C.: U.S. Postal Service, 1986), 10–11; Boyer, *Naval Surgeon,* 27, 31; Browning, *Cape Charles to Cape Fear,* 178.

23. Anonymous, "Life on a Blockader," 51–52.

24. "An Act to Authorize the Employment of Volunteers to Aid in Enforcing the Laws and Protecting Public Property" (chap. 9, 22 July 1861), *Statutes at Large,* 269–71.

25. "An Act in Relation to the Letters of Sailors and Marines in the Service of the United States" (chap. 9, 21 January 1862), *Statutes at Large,* 332.

26. Hunter, *A Year on a "Monitor,"* 168; Richard W. Kaeuper, "The Forgotten Triumph of the Paw Paw," *American Heritage* 46 (October 1995): 89.

27. "An Act for the Better Government of the Navy of the United States" (chap. 204, 17 July 1862), *Statutes at Large,* 602; Francis A. Lord, *Civil War Collector's Encyclopedia: Arms, Uniforms and Equipment of the Union and Confederacy* (Secaucus, N.J.: Castle Books, 1982), 203–6.

28. William N. Bock to His Family, 5 March 1864, published in Stivers, *Privateers and Volunteers,* 454.

29. Boyer, *Naval Surgeon,* 65, 90, 201, 204.

30. Evans, *A Sailor's Log,* 48–49.

31. Browne and Browne, *From the Fresh Water Navy,* 123.

32. Badlam, *"Kearsarge" and "Alabama,"* 7–9. Edward H. Tibetts, a nineteen-year-old ordinary seaman from Brunswick, Maine, died on 13 July 1862 at 6:45 P.M. His death certificate stated that "A shark seized and carried Tibetts down, while he was swimming."

33. Keeler, USS *"Florida,"* 180.

34. Anonymous, "Diary of the Cruise of USS *Flag,* June 2, 1862–November 25, 1863," Mariners Museum Research Library and Archives, Newport News, Va.

35. Marvel, *The "Alabama" and "Kearsarge,"* 147.

36. Boyer, *Naval Surgeon*, 92.

37. Ibid., 93.

38. Kirkland, *Anecdotes and Incidents*, 383.

39. Boyer, *Naval Surgeon*, 65.

40. Hunter, *A Year on a "Monitor,"* 122; Merrill, "Mouldy Beans," 203–4.

41. Boyer, *Naval Surgeon*, 50.

42. Merrill, "Mouldy Beans," 204.

43. John C. Huntly Diary, 5 July 1863, vol. 3, p. 9, H SP.

44. Keeler, USS *"Monitor,"* 250.

45. Evans, *A Sailor's Log*, 65.

46. Ibid., 65–66.

47. Knapp Journal, 25 December 1862, in Myron K. Knapp Papers, BHL.

48. Ibid., 1–3 January 1863.

49. "An Act for the Better Government of the Navy of the United States" (chap. 204, 17 July 1862), *Statutes at Large*, 602.

50. Abraham Lincoln, General Order Respecting the Observance of the Sabbath Day in the Army and Navy, Executive Mansion, Washington, 15 November 1862, RG 45, box 298, NA.

51. *Sailor's Magazine* 35 (March 1863): 208.

52. Henry A. Simmons Journal, 18 February 1862, Schoff Civil War Collection, Clements Library, University of Michigan; Hunter, *A Year on a "Monitor,"* 28; Boyer, *Naval Surgeon*, 58; Karsten, *The Naval Aristocracy*, 73.

53. Phyllis H. Haughton, ed., *Dearest Carrie: Civil War Letters Home* (Lawrenceville, Va.: Brunswick Publishing, 1995), 40.

54. Browne and Browne, *From the Fresh Water Navy*, 69.

55. Logbook, USS *Macedonian*, Mariners Museum Research Library and Archives, Newport News, Va.; Stivers, *Privateers and Volunteers*, 353–54.

56. *Sailor's Magazine* 35 (September 1862): 16.

57. Still, "Common Sailor," 32.

58. Boyer, *Naval Surgeon*, 292; Keeler, USS *"Florida,"* 74.

59. Henry A. Simmons Journal, 17 July 1862, Schoff Civil War Collection, Clements Library, University of Michigan.

60. Author Unknown, diary of a sailor enlisted in the navy on 21 August 1862, age, 14 years, 5 months. Assigned to USS *Sabina*. Diary entry describing burial at sea, 30 June 1863. This diary is in the custody of the U.S. Department of Navy, Naval Historical Center, Washington, D.C.

61. Browne and Browne, *From the Fresh Water Navy*, 259.

62. Evans, *A Sailor's Log*, 67–68.

Chapter 8. The Government Gives and the Captain Takes Away

1. "An Act Making Appropriations for the Naval Service for the Year Ending the 30th of June, 1855" (chap. 268, 5 August 1854), *Statutes at Large* 10:583, 587; Langley, *Social Reform*, 78–81.

2. Secretary of the Interior, *Statistics of the United States (Including Mortality, Property & c.) in 1860 of the Eighth Census* (Washington, D.C.: Government Printing Office, 1866), 512; U.S. Department of Commerce, *Historical Statistics of the United States, Colonial Times to 1970,* (Washington, D.C.: Government Print-

ing Office, 1976), part 1, series D, pp. 728–34. Monthly wages based on twenty-four days of work per month. Even the low wages of a farmer exceeded that of a female. A women, with board included, received $1.85 a week, or $7.40 a month, as a common laborer.

3. Secretary of the Interior, *Manufacturing of the United States in 1860, Eighth Census* (Washington, D.C.: Government Printing Office, 1865), 352. Monthly wages based on twenty-four workdays per month.

4. Keeler, *USS "Florida,"* 98. Prior to a ship's deployment, the paymaster drew money from the Navy Department to purchase supplies and provide small stipends to the sailors. Keeler signed for two million dollars in greenbacks before USS *Florida* got under way in 1865. Ibid., 207. Rarely did a sailor go ashore after the spring of 1862 with gold or silver in his pockets. To prevent the hoarding of gold during the war, the government authorized the issue of non-interest-bearing notes, commonly called greenbacks, with the passage of the Legal Tender Act: "An Act to Authorize the Issue of United States Notes, and for the Redemption or Funding Thereof, and for Funding the Floating Debt of the United States" (chap. 33, 25 February 1862), *Statutes at Large,* 37 Cong., 2nd sess., 345–47; Patricia L. Faust, *Historical Times Illustrated Encyclopedia of the Civil War* (New York: Harper and Row, 1986), 323, 432–33. The greenbacks did not reach the fleet immediately after the passage of the Legal Tender Act. William Clark, in a letter to his mother on 26 March 1862, wrote that he was paid in gold. William J. Clark Letter to His Mother, 26 March 1862, Clark Papers, HSP.

5. Keeler, *USS "Florida,"* 98; "An Act to Authorize the Equipment of Volunteers to Aid in Enforcing the Laws and Protecting Private Property" (chap. 9, 22 July 1861), *Statutes at Large,* 37 Cong., 2nd sess., 271.

6. Anonymous, USS *Flag* Diary, 23 November 1863.

7. Hunter, *A Year on a "Monitor,"* 180.

8. Keeler, *USS "Florida,"* 98.

9. Prize List, USS *Mackinaw,* 3 December 1864, RG 45, NA, and Prize List, USS *Huron,* 25 January 1865, RG 45, NA; Navy Officers Pay Table, reproduced in Schuyler, Hartley & Graham, *Illustrated Catalog of Civil War Military Goods: Union Weapons, Insignia, Uniform Accessories and Other Equipment* (1864; reprint with slight alterations, New York: Dover, 1985), 89–90. The ship's prize list reported coal heavers receiving $20.00 a month, while Schuyler, Hartley & Graham showed that coal heavers received only $18.00 a month. Naval pay was better than the army's. The top enlisted infantry rating, sergeant major, received $21.00 a month. The navy's pay for the rates of boatswain, gunner, carpenter, cook, quartermaster, and fireman all exceeded the army's highest monthly wage and did not even take into account the grog substitution pay, *Monitor* duty, or the opportunity for prize money.

10. U.S. Department of Commerce, *Historical Statistics of the United States,* series D, pp. 728–34; J. G. Randall and David Donald, *The Civil War and Reconstruction* (Lexington, Mass.: D. C. Heath, 1969), 484; Donald D. Jackson, *Twenty Million Yankees: The Northern Home Front* (Alexandria, Va.: Time-Life Books, 1985), 77.

11. Patrick O'Brien, *The Economic Effects of the American Civil War* (Atlantic Heights, N.J.: Humanities Press International, 1988), 54–55; Randall and Donald, *Civil War,* 480–83.

12. "An Act Making Appropriations for the Naval Service for the Year Ending 30th of June, 1863, and for Other Purposes" (chap. 164, 14 July 1862), *Statutes at Large*, 37 Cong., 2nd sess., 561–63.

13. ORN 1:14, 414–15, 444.

14. Robert W. McCleery to Thomas Corbin, Commanding Officer, USS *Wabash*, 20 January 1863, William L. Clements Library, University of Michigan.

15. Log, USS *Kearsarge*, 8 July 1864, RG 24, NA.

16. ORN 1:15, 120.

17. Ibid. 1:6, 133.

18. Melanie Billings-Yun et al., eds., *Above and Beyond: A History of the Medal of Honor from the Civil War to Vietnam* (Boston: Boston Publishing, 1985), 4.

19. "An Act to Further Promote the Efficiency of the Navy" (chap. 1, 21 December 1861), *Statutes at Large*, 37 Cong., 2nd sess., 329–30. The army did not receive authorization to issue its own version of the navy's Medal of Honor until Congress approved a bill containing a section on the medal in July 1862.

20. Billings-Yun et al., *Above and Beyond*, 5, 316.

21. Joseph B. Mitchell, *The Badge of Gallantry* (New York: Macmillian, 1968), 134.

22. "An Act to Establish and Equalize the Grade of Line Officers of the United States Navy" (chap. 183, 16 July 1862), *Statutes at Large*, 37 Cong., 2nd sess., 583–85.

23. Joseph Reidy, professor at Howard University, 19 May 1997, letter to Paul Wilderson, Naval Institute Press, Annapolis, Md. The seaman rating earned 18 percent of the 307 medals awarded to navy sailors during the war, coxswains 12 percent, quartermasters 11 percent, boatswain's mates 10 percent, ordinary seaman 9 percent, firemen 3.5 percent, coal heavers 3 percent. U.S. Bureau of Naval Personnel, *Medal of Honor, 1861–1949* (Washington, D.C.: U.S. Navy, 1950), 13–57; Billings-Yun et al., *Above and Beyond*, 5, 316. In 1863, the army authorized its officers to receive the award, but the navy did not allow officers to receive the award until 1915.

24. "An Act for the Better Government of the Navy of the United States" (chap. 204, 17 July 1862), *Statutes at Large*, 37 Cong., 2nd sess., 606. Congress abolished the awarding of prize money in 1900, citing that the system was unjust because some navy billets required men to remain ashore in support of the fleet. These men were thus unable to share in the quest for prize money.

25. ORN 1:10, 611–23.

26. Robert W. Daly, "Pay and Prize Money in the Old Navy," U.S. Naval Institute *Proceedings* 74 (August 1948): 970.

27. ORN 1:14, 265–302.

28. Hunter, *A Year on a "Monitor,"* 84.

29. Keeler, USS *"Florida,"* 53–54.

30. James McPherson, *Battle Cry of Freedom: The Civil War Era* (New York: Oxford University Press, 1988), 378.

31. William J. Clark, vol. 2, Clark Papers, HSP.

32. ORN 1:3, 82.

33. Schley, *Forty-Five Years under the Flag*, 31.

34. "An Act to Grant Pensions" (chap. 166, 14 July 1862), *Statutes at Large*, 37 Cong., 2nd sess., 566–69.

35. "An Act for the Better Government of the Navy of the United States" (chap. 204, 17 July 1862), *Statutes at Large*, 37 Cong., 2nd sess., 608.

36. "An Act Supplementary to an Act Entitled, 'An Act to grant Pensions,'" (chap. 247, 4 July 1864), *Statutes at Large*, 38 Cong., 1st sess., 387.

37. SECNAV Report, December 1864, xxxviii, and December 1865, xxx.

38. SECNAV Report, December 1865, xxx.

39. "An Act Granting Pensions to Soldiers and Sailors Who Are Incapacitated for the Performance of Manual Labor, and Providing Pensions to Widows, Minor Children, and Dependent Parents" (chap. 634, 27 June 1890), *Statutes at Large*, 51 Cong., 1st sess., 182; Maris A. Vinovskis, ed., *Toward a Social History of the American Civil War: Exploratory Essays* (reprint, Cambridge, England: Cambridge University Press, 1990), 22–25.

40. Frederick Marshall Navy Discharge Authorization, and Witness Notations, *House of Representative Bill 811*, 68 Cong., 1923–24, 2241.

41. Ibid., 2242.

42. Library of Congress, *General Index to Pension Files, 1861–1934* (Washington, D.C.: National Archives and Records Service, 1993).

43. SECNAV Report, December 1856, xxxii.

44. Edward M. Byrne, *Military Law*, 3rd ed. (Annapolis, Md.: Naval Institute Press, 1981), 2–4.

45. Ibid., 4–5. U.S. Naval Academy, Department of Law and Leadership, *Naval Law* (Dubuque, Iowa: Kendall/Hunt Publishing, 1995), 1–28.

46. "An Act for the Better Government of the Navy of the United States" (chap. 204, 17 July 1862), *Statutes at Large*, 37 Cong., 2nd sess., 601–10.

47. Ibid., 601–2.

48. Ibid., 602. The navy has not executed a single member of the naval service since 1849. U.S. Naval Academy, Department of Law and Leadership, *Naval Law*, 1–13.

49. "An Act for the Better Government of the Navy" (chap. 204, 17 July 1862), *Statutes at Large*, 37 Cong., 2nd sess., 602.

50. Ibid., 603–5.

51. Samuel C. Perkins, Private Docket, Historical Society of Pennsylvania, Naval General Court Martial at Philadelphia, Pa.

52. Still, "Common Sailor," 39.

53. Keeler, USS *"Florida,"* 228; Dewey, *Autobiography*, 137.

54. "An Act for the Better Government of the Navy" (chap. 204, 17 July 1862), *Statutes at Large*, 37 Cong., 2nd sess., 603.

55. Ibid.

56. Dewey, *Autobiography*, 123–24.

57. Quinby Papers, 23 December 1863, published in Stivers, *Privateers and Volunteers*, 358.

58. Boyer, *Naval Surgeon*, 316.

59. Hunter, *A Year on a "Monitor,"* 20.

60. Keeler, USS *"Monitor,"* 216.

61. Keeler, USS *"Florida,"* 98.

62. Hunter, *A Year on a "Monitor,"* 40, 114.

63. Keeler, USS *"Monitor,"* 22.

64. Quinby Papers, 17 June 1862, published in Stivers, *Privateers and Volunteers*, 358.

65. Blanding, *Recollections of a Sailor Boy*, 61.
66. Boyer, *Naval Surgeon*, 138.
67. Log, USS *Niagara*, 13 March 1863, RG 24, NA. The log mentioned the sailor's start of confinement, but there is no deck entry for his release.
68. Log, USS *Kearsarge*, 4 July 1864, RG 24, NA.
69. Dewitt Papers, 8 April 1862, published in Stivers, *Privateers and Volunteers*, 358.
70. Roe, *Naval Duties and Discipline*, 67.
71. Boyer, *Naval Surgeon*, 119.

Chapter 9. Medicine at Sea

1. William F. Fox, *Regimental Losses in the American Civil War* (Albany, N.Y.: Albany Publishing, 1889), 537.
2. Ibid.; Richard Gabriel and Karen S. Metz, *A History of Military Medicine* (New York: Greenwood Press, 1992), 182–83; Long and Long, *Civil War Day by Day*, 705–13.
3. In 1842, the navy established the Bureau of Medicine and Surgery to enhance the medical care of its sailors. By 1861, the bureau was capable of handling the proliferation of enlistments needed to enforce a 3,000-mile blockade.
4. James Lind, M.D., "A Treatise of the Scurvy," reprinted in *The Health of Seamen: Selections from the Works of Dr. James Lind, Sir Gilbert Blane, Dr. Thomas Trotter*, ed. Christopher Lloyd (London: Navy Records Society, 1965), 7–62; Thomas Gurnsey, *Homeopathic Domestic Practices* (London: Turnee, 1861); Frank Hastings Hamilton, *A Practical Treatise on Military Surgery* (New York: Bailliere Brothers, 1861); Samuel D. Gross, *A Manual of Military Surgery*, 2nd ed. (Philadelphia: J. B. Lippincott, 1862), 139–50.
5. "An Act in Addition to 'An Act for the Relief of Sick and Disabled Seamen'" (chap. 36, 2 March 1799), *Statutes at Large*, ed. Richard Petters (Boston: Little, Brown, 1854) 1:729; Roddis, *Nautical Medicine*, 258–60.
6. "An Act Establishing Navy Hospitals" (chap. 26, 26 February 1811), *Statutes at Large* 2:650–51; SECNAV Report, December 1865, xxxiii.
7. The only army hospital in operation at the start of the Civil War was at Fort Leavenworth, Kansas. The hospital had only forty beds. Without a doubt, the army medical service was ill prepared for war in 1861. Roddis, *Nautical Medicine*, 260–63; Gabriel and Metz, *History of Military Medicine*, 187; Browne and Browne, *From the Fresh Water Navy*, 185.
8. Keeler, USS *"Florida,"* 92.
9. Roddis, *Nautical Medicine*, 208–9.
10. Ibid., 156–57.
11. Lind, "A Treatise of the Scurvy," 2, 20, 47–48, 63; Langley, *Medicine in the Early U.S. Navy*, 53, 368.
12. Gabriel and Metz, *History of Military Medicine*, 117.
13. Ibid., 152–53. From 1857 through 1863, Louis Pasteur conducted research that led to the discovery of microorganisms as the cause of infections and many diseases. Following on the heels of Pasteur's research was Dr. Joseph Lister, who experimented with amputation patients by applying carbolic acid as an antiseptic to the injury. In 1867, he published his results in the *Lancet*.

Physicians remained skeptical about Pasteur's and Lister's work until 1879, when Robert Koch published *Etiology of the Traumatic Infectious Diseases*. Koch's landmark work confirmed the former research that microorganisms, and not spontaneous generation, caused infections. Koch asserted that by following aseptic procedures, doctors could eradicate these harmful microbes and improve the patients' opportunity for recovery.

14. Gross, *Manual of Military Surgery*, 35–37.

15. Ibid., John L. Margreiter, "Anesthesia in the Civil War," *Civil War Times Illustrated* 6 (May 1967): 22–23.

16. Barbara Mann Wall, "Grace Under Pressure: The Nursing Sisters of the Holy Cross, 1861–1865" *Nursing History Review* 1 (1993): 79–80.

17. John Vance Lauderdale, *The Wounded River: The Civil War Letters of John Vance Lauderdale, M.D.*, ed. Peter Joseph (East Lansing: Michigan State University Press, 1993), 128.

18. Browne and Browne, *From the Fresh Water Navy*, 185.

19. U.S. Department of Navy, *American Naval Fighting Ships*, 51–52; Roddis, *Nautical Medicine*, 227.

20. Clayton L. Thomas, ed., *Taber's Cyclopedic Medical Dictionary*, 15th ed. (Philadelphia: F. A. Davis, 1985), 1537; Roddis, *Nautical Medicine*, 59–61.

21. Keeler, USS *"Monitor,"* 27; Hunter, *A Year on a "Monitor,"* 20.

22. Keeler, USS *"Florida,"* 119, 170.

23. Knapp Journal, 23 September 1862, in Myron K. Knapp Papers, BHL.

24. Francis B. Butts, a survivor of the sinking, wrote an article years later describing in great detail the sinking of USS *Monitor.* In the article, Butts mentioned that an officer, S. A. Lewis, was suffering so badly from the effects of seasickness that he chose to go down with the *Monitor.* Recent findings by the *Monitor* National Marine Sanctuary, however, show that Lewis in fact did survive the sinking. Perhaps it was another officer whom Butts was referring to. Francis B. Butts, "The Loss of the *Monitor,*" *Century Illustrated Monthly Magazine* 31 (November 1885–86): 300; William C. Davis, *Duel between the First Ironclads* (Baton Rouge: Louisiana State University Press, 1975), 162.

25. Thomas, *Taber's Cyclopedic Medical Dictionary*, 1536.

26. Lind, "A Treatise of the Scurvy," 3.

27. Boyer, *Naval Surgeon*, 196.

28. Schley, *Forty-Five Years under the Flag*, 31.

29. U.S. War Department, *The Medical and Surgical History of the War of the Rebellion* (Washington, D.C.: Government Printing Office, 1870–83) 2:18–23.

30. Frank Hastings Hamilton, *A Treatise on Military Surgery and Hygiene* (New York: Bailliere Brothers, 1865), 80.

31. Thomas, *Taber's Cyclopedic Medical Dictionary*, 1889; Keevil, *Navy Medicine, 1200–1900*, 4:186–87.

32. John C. Huntly Diary, 25, 28–30, September and 1–8 October 1863, vol. 3, HSP. The medical community during the Civil War believed that fevers, including yellow fever, were caused by foul air common to swampy areas, and not by the virus-carrying mosquito. When the fleet surgeon ordered the ships to sea, he correctly but unknowingly placed the ships beyond the range of the disease-carrying insect. It would be almost another forty years before the mosquito was identified as the carrier of the dreaded yellow fever virus. The

United States has not had a death from yellow fever since 1905, when 1,000 people died of the disease in Louisiana. Unfortunately, yellow fever is making a comeback in Africa, with an estimated 200,000 new cases each year. Frederick F. Cartwright, *Disease and History* (New York: Dorset Press, 1972), 147–50; "Yellow Fever Is on the Rise Again in Africa," *Detroit Free Press*, 9 October 1996, sec. A1, p. 5A.

33. Evans, *A Sailor's Log*, 63.
34. ORN 1:17, 744.
35. Ibid., 17, 745.
36. Ibid., 17, 744–49.
37. Ibid., 17, 761–2.
38. Ibid., 17, 762.
39. Ibid., 17, 746; SECNAV REPORT, December 1864, ix.
40. Thomas, *Taber's Cyclopedic Medical Dictionary*, 998–99.
41. Keeler, *USS "Monitor,"* 204.
42. Thomas, *Taber's Cyclopedic Medical Dictionary*, 1576–77.
43. Ibid., 1576–7, 1828; John A. Hutson, *The Sinews of War: Logistics, 1775–1956*, (Washington, D.C: Office of the Chief of Military History, 1966), 41–42.
44. Keeler, *USS "Florida,"* 104; ORN 1:9, 346.
45. ORN 1:9, 345–46.
46. Ibid., 9, 418.
47. Thomas, *Taber's Cyclopedic Medical Dictionary*, 1794–95.
48. Ibid., 1795. Roddis, *Nautical Medicine*, 34–35.
49. The surgeon aboard USS *Fernandina* wrote in his diary that one day they received 800 hundred gallons of freshwater from the steam-powered ship USS *Wamsutta*. Boyer, *Naval Surgeon*, 91.
50. William J. Clark to His Mother, 3 March 1863, vol. 1, Clark Papers, HSP.
51. George Worthington Adams, *Doctors in Blue: The Medical History of the Union Army in the Civil War* (1952; reprint, Dayton, Ohio: Morningside Press, 1985), 226–27, 241–42; Gabriel and Metz, *History of Military Medicine*, 182–83.
52. Thomas, *Taber's Cyclopedic Medical Dictionary*, 458–59, 503.
53. Edward Kershner, Case Book, Duke University, William Perkins Library, Special Collections; Boyer, *Naval Surgeon*, 294: Adams, *Doctors in Blue*, 226–27.
54. Keeler, *USS "Monitor,"* 204.
55. Browne and Browne, *From the Fresh Water Navy*, 267.
56. John E. Patterson to His Mother, 9 September 1863, John E. Patterson Papers, Duke University, William Perkins Library, Special Collections Library.
57. Edward Kershner Papers, Report of Sick, 3rd and 4th Quarter, 1864, for the USS *Choctaw*, Duke University, William Perkins Library, Special Collections.
58. Gross, *Military Surgery*, 129–31.
59. Boyer, *Naval Surgeon*, 162.
60. Ibid., 256. Gross, *Military Surgery*, 130.
61. Hunter, *A Year on a "Monitor,"* 178.
62. Boyer, *Naval Surgeon*, 13–14, 31.
63. James C. Pryor, *Naval Hygiene* (Philadelphia: P. Blakiston's Sons, 1918), 198.
64. Boyer, *Naval Surgeon*, 319–20.
65. Ibid., 320–21.
66. Ibid., 336–48.

67. The navy commissioned and assigned its first dentist to a ship in 1873. The ship's surgeon performed the collateral duty of dentist during the Civil War. The Naval Dental Corps was established in August 1912. U.S. Department of Navy, Bureau of Medicine and Surgery, *The Dental Corps of the United States Navy* (Washington, D.C.: U.S. Navy, 1962), 5–6.

68. Gordon Dammann, *Pictorial Encyclopedia of Civil War Medical Instruments and Equipment* (Missoula, Mont.: Pictorial Histories Publishing, 1988), 77–83.

69. Ibid., 77–83. Boyer, *Naval Surgeon,* 82–83, wrote in his diary that he removed a sailor's tooth that had broken off during a fire drill.

70. Boyer, *Naval Surgeon,* 82, 113, 115.

71. Ibid., 312; Edward Kershner Papers, Report of Sick, 3rd and 4th Quarter, 1863, for the USS *Choctaw,* Duke University, William Perkins Library, Special Collections. Unfortunately, the Navy Department never tabulated all the quarterly medical reports submitted by the ship's surgeons, as the army did in its six-volume *Medical and Surgical History of the War of the Rebellion.* Perhaps someday a graduate program will undertake this massive but important project.

72. Boyer, *Naval Surgeon,* 65–68.

73. Keeler, *USS "Florida,"* 64.

74. SECNAV Report, December 1865, xxiii.

Chapter 10. "To Meet the Elephant"

1. "To meet the elephant" was a nineteenth-century term that referred to a recruit about to experience combat for the first time. A veteran of combat was said to have seen the elephant. Farmers originally coined the phrase after seeing pachyderms at a traveling circus for the first time. The size and power of the elephants so impressed the farmers that they were "bowled over" by their presence. Paul Dickson, *War Slang, Fighting Words and Phrases of Americans, from the Civil War to the Gulf War* (New York: Pocket Books, 1994), 9.

2. Fox, *Regimental Losses,* 537; Gabriel and Metz, *History of Military Medicine,* 118–21.

3. Fox, *Regimental Losses,* 537.

4. Ibid.; Long and Long, *Civil War Day by Day,* 713.

5. SECNAV Report, December 1864, 463; U.S. War Department, *War of the Rebellion: A Compilation of the Official Records of the War of the Union and Confederate Armies* (Washington, D.C.: Government Printing Office, 1880–1901), series 1, part 1, vol. 27, p. 187.

6. U.S. Navy, Naval History Division, *Civil War Naval Chronology* 1:19, 2:105; Ian Drury and Tony Gibbons, *The Civil War Military Machine: Weapons and Tactics of the Union and Confederate Forces* (New York: Smithmark, 1993), 186–89.

7. U.S. Navy, Naval History Division, *Civil War Naval Chronology* 2:71, 106; Francis X. Walter, *The Naval Battle of Mobile Bay, August 5, 1864, and Franklin Buchanan of the "Tennessee."* (Birmingham, Ala.: Prester Meridian Press, 1993), 18; James P. Kushlan, ed., "Torpedoes," *Civil War Times Illustrated* 36 (August 1997): 47–49.

8. Browne and Browne, *From the Fresh Water Navy,* 125; ORN 1:23, 544–50.

9. *Civil War Naval Chronology* 2:105.

10. John C. Kinney, "Farragut at Mobile Bay," in *Battles and Leaders of the Civil War,* ed. Robert Underwood Johnson and Clarence Clough Buel (1887–88; reprint, New York: Castle Books, 1956) 4:391.

11. ORN 1:21, 492.

12. O. B. Curtis, *History of the Twenty-Fourth Michigan Regiment of the Iron Brigade* (Detroit: Winn and Hammond, 1891), 180; George C. Underwood, *History of the Twenty-Sixth Regiment of the North Carolina Troops in the Great War, 1861–1865* (Goldsboro, N.C.: Nash Brothers, Book and Job Printers, n.d.; reprint, Wendell, N.C.: Bradfoot's Bookmark, 1978), 54–66.

13. SECNAV Report, December 1865, 313–15; Edgar K. Thompson, "The U.S. *Patapsco,*" U.S. Naval Institute *Proceedings* 94 (December 1968): 148–49.

14. SECNAV Report, December 1865, 379–83.

15. E. B. Potter, ed., *Sea Power: A Naval History,* 2nd ed. (Annapolis, Md.: Naval Institute Press, 1981), 159.

16. Keeler, *USS "Monitor,"* 100.

17. Hunter, *A Year on a "Monitor,"* 34.

18. Knapp Journal, 2 June 1862, in Myron K. Knapp Papers, BHL.

19. Bartholomew Diggins Recollections, p. 78, New York Public Library, Manuscript and Archives Division.

20. Dana Greene, "In the *Monitor* Turret," in *Battles and Leaders of the Civil War,* ed. Robert Underwood Johnson and Clarence Clough Buel (reprint, New York: Castle Books, 1956) 1:723.

21. ORN 1:7, 26–27.

22. Robert J. Schneller Jr., "A Littorial Frustration: The Union Navy and the Siege of Charleston, 1863–1865," *Naval War College Review* 49 (Winter 1996): 38–43.

23. Harris Webster, "An August Morning with Farragut at Mobile Bay," reprinted in *Civil War Naval Chronology* 6:93, 95.

24. Keeler, *USS "Monitor,"* 35.

25. Bartholomew Diggins Recollections, pp. 85–86, New York Public Library, Manuscript and Archives Division.

26. W. M. C. Philbrick Journal, vol. 3, 19 April 1863, RG 45, NA.

27. Kirkland, *Anecdotes and Incidents,* 365.

28. Gerald Simons, ed., *The Blockade: Runners and Raiders* (Alexandria, Va.: Time-Life Books, 1983), 55.

29. W. F. Boyer and O. F. Keydel, *Acts of Bravery: Deeds of Extraordinary American Heroism, from the Personal Records and Reminiscences of Courageous Americans Who Risked Everything for Their Comrades and Country* (1903; reprint, Stanford, Conn.: Longmeadow Press, 1994), 21–22.

30. Silverstone, *Warships of the Civil War Navies,* 16.

31. Boyer and Keydel, *Acts of Bravery,* 25–28.

32. Ibid., 28–30.

33. E. Latch Diary, 14 March 1863, RG 45, NA.

34. Charles Lee Lewis, *David Glasgow Farragut: Our First Admiral* (Annapolis, Md.: Naval Institute Press, 1943), 280.

35. SECNAV Report, December 1864, xx–xxi.

36. Max Guerout, "C.S.S. *Alabama,*" *Journal of the National Geographic Society* 186 (December 1994): 73. The stern post with the shell embedded in the wood is currently on display at the Washington Naval Yard Museum.

37. John M. Browne, "The Duel between the *Alabama* and the *Kearsarge*," in *Battles and Leaders of the Civil War,* ed. Robert Underwood Johnson and Clarence Clough Buel (reprint, New York: Castle Books, 1956) 4:622.
38. Ibid., 623; J. N. O. Robertson, ed., *Michigan in the War* (Lansing: W. S. George and Company, State Printers and Binders, 1882), 988.
39. Kinney, "Farragut at Mobile Bay," 4:389–90.
40. Walter, *Naval Battle of Mobile Bay*, 37, 40.
41. Kinney, "Farragut at Mobile Bay," 4:395.
42. SECNAV Report, December 1864, 462.
43. Lewis, *Farragut: Our First Admiral*, 280.
44. SECNAV Report, December 1864, 464.
45. Stevens survived his wounds and the war and later followed in his father's footsteps by graduating from Harvard's medical school. He died on 14 March 1939, at the ripe old age of ninety-three, one of the last naval veterans of the Battle of Mobile Bay. George Cornelius, "What Did Farragut See?" *Naval History* 8 (August 1994): 17. Interestingly, Surgeon Atkins bathed the sailor's back with alcohol to treat the splinter wounds. Although today's medical profession understands the antiseptic properties of alcohol, at the time of the Civil War, doctors did not know what caused infections. Since the application of alcohol would slightly increase the bleeding and cause an open wound to sting painfully, it is unclear why the surgeon would have used alcohol. Asa Morton, M.D., USN; Penny Pierce, R.N., Ph.D; and Diane Potts, R.N.C., M.S.N., interview with author, 14 May 1996, believed that through observation, Surgeon Atkins may have noticed a decrease in postoperative infection when alcohol had been applied to the wound.
46. SECNAV Report, December 1864, 466.
47. Edgar Holden, "The *Albemarle* and the *Sassacus*," in *Battles and Leaders of the Civil War,* ed. Robert Underwood Johnson and Clarence Clough Buel (reprint, New York: Castle Books, 1956) 4:630–32.
48. Boyer, *Naval Surgeon*, 290–91.
49. Navy reports estimate that during the preinvasion naval support of troop movements, the navy fired almost fifty thousand rounds at the Confederate stronghold. SECNAV Report, December 1865, 81; Thomas O. Selfridge, "The Navy at Fort Fisher," in *Battles and Leaders of the Civil War,* ed. Robert Underwood Johnson and Clarence Clough Buel (reprint, New York: Castle Books, 1956) 4:658.
50. Selfridge, "The Navy at Fort Fisher," 659–60.
51. Evans, *A Sailor's Log*, 95.
52. Ibid.
53. SECNAV Report, December 1865, 74–80; Fox, *Regimental Losses*, 539.
54. Keeler, *USS "Florida,"* 206.
55. Engineering term that means the boiler safety valves were secured in such a manner that they would not lift, even if the pressure in the boiler became so great that the boiler could explode if the pressure were not released.
56. Keeler, *USS "Florida,"* 46.
57. Edward S. Miller, *Civil War Sea Battles, Seafights and Shipwrecks in the War between the States* (Conshohocken, Pa.: Combined Books, 1995), 13, 17–21.
58. ORN 1:12, 820–22; Samual Francis Du Pont, *A Selection from His Civil War Letters*, vol. 2, *The Blockade*, ed. John D. Hayes (Ithaca, N.Y.: Cornell University

Press, 1969), 50–51; Edward A. Miller Jr., *Gullah Statesman: Robert Small from Slavery to Congress, 1839–1915* (Columbia: University of South Carolina Press, 1995), 1–7.

59. Beyer and Keydel, *Acts of Bravery*, 13–14.
60. SECNAV Report, December 1864, 689–90.
61. Ibid., 691.
62. Ovid L. Futch, *History of Andersonville Prison* (Gainesville: University of Florida Press, 1968), 63–73.
63. Futch, *History of Andersonville Prison*, 69–73; and William Marvel, *Andersonville: The Last Depot* (Chapel Hill: University of North Carolina Press, 1994), 94, 95, 100, 143.
64. ORN 1:13, 561–62.
65. John McElroy, *Andersonville: A Story of Rebel Military Prisons* (Toledo, Ohio: D. B. Locke, 1879), 162.
66. ORN 1:19, 560. Of the 102 enlisted men captured on 21 January 1863, 10 died in captivity within two and one-half months. Ibid., xix, 557.
67. Valuska, "The Negro in the Union Navy," 114–15.
68. Ibid., 115–16.
69. E. G. Parrott, Commanding Officer, USS *Augusta* Journal, 27 August 1862, RG 45, NA.

Chapter 11. Legacy

1. SECNAV Report, December 1865, xiii.
2. SECNAV Report, December 1865, xxix–xxx.
3. ORN 1:16, 57.
4. *Times* (London), 27 March 1862, 9.
5. *Detroit Free Press*, 19 March 1862, 1.
6. Fred T. Jane, *All the World's Fighting Ships* (Boston: Little, Brown, 1899), 246.
7. White and White, *Tin Can on a Shingle*, 153.
8. Morris J. MacGregor, *Integration of the Armed Forces, 1940–1965* (Washington, D.C.: U.S. Army, Center of Military History, 1980), 4–5; Harrod, *Manning the New Navy*, 10.
9. Harrod, *Manning the New Navy*, 57–60.
10. John M. Browne, "The Duel between *Alabama* and *Kearsarge*," 4:622.

Bibliography

Primary Sources

Manuscripts

Burton Historical Library, Detroit, Mich.
    Myron H. Knapp Papers
Duke University, William Perkins Library, Special Collections, Durham, N.C.
    D. Baker Documents
    James L. B. Blauvelt Papers
    Edward Kershner Papers and Case Book
    John O'Neil Letters
    John E. Patterson Papers
Historical Society of Pennsylvania, Philadelphia, Pa.
    William J. Clark Papers
    John C. Huntly Diary
    Samuel C. Perkins, Judge Advocate, Private Docket
Mariners Museum Research Library and Archives, Newport News, Va.
    Samuel D. Greene, Letters
    J. Tyler Jobson, Personal Recollections
    Thomas F. Rowland Jr. Collections
    USS *Flag,* Ship's Diary
    USS *Macedonian* Log Book
    John L. Worden Papers
National Archives, Washington, D.C.
    Record Group 24, Bureau of Navigation

A. Muster Roles
   USS *Hartford*
   USS *Kearsarge*
   USS *Louisiana*
B. Log Books of U.S. Vessels
   USS *Florida*
   USS *Hartford*
   USS *Kearsarge*
   USS *Lexington*
   USS *Minnesota*
   USS *Niagara*
   USS *Portsmouth*
   USS *Wabash*
C. Prize Lists
   USS *Huron*
   USS *Mackinaw*
Record Group 45, Naval Records Collection of the Office of Naval Records
   and Library
   Isaac DeGraff Journal
   E. Latch Diary
   E. G. Parrott Journal
   W. M. C. Philbrick Journal
Naval Records Collection, Area File 1798–1910
   Subject File
   A. Naval Ships
   B. Ordnance
   E. Engineering
   L. Instructions
   M. Medical
   N. Personnel
   X. Supplies
   Y. Pension
   Z. History
Naval Historical Center, Washington, D.C.
   Charles Flusser Papers, ZB Collection
   Frank W. Hackett Papers, ZO Collection
New York Public Library, Manuscript and Archives Division
   Bartholomew Diggins Papers
   Captain Percival Drayton Letters
   John T. Hawkins Memorandum Book
   Levi Hayden Diary
William L. Clements Library, University of Michigan, Ann Arbor, Mich.
   Schoff Civil War Collection (includes the following journals and accounts of
       naval personnel: McCleery Letters, Ransom Journal, Henry A. Simmons
       Journal, Robert Talbot Letters)
   Rear Admiral Thomas O. Selfridge Papers
   James Aldrich Whipple Papers

Government Documents

Defense Mapping Agency, Hydrographic and Topographic Center, *Distances between Ports* Publication 151. 5th ed., 1985.

Official Records of the Union and Confederate Navies in the War of the Rebellion. 31 vols. Washington, D.C.: Government Printing Office, 1894–1927.

Public Statutes at Large of the United States of America. Vol. 1, *1789–1799.* Edited by Richard Peters. Boston: Little, Brown, 1854.

Public Statutes at Large of the United States of America. Vol. 2, *1800–1813.* Edited by Richard Peters. Boston: Little and Brown, 1848.

Public Statutes at Large of the United States of America. Vol. 5. Edited by Richard Peters. Boston: Little, Brown, 1860.

Sanderson, James M. *Camp Fires and Camp Cooking or Culinary Hints for the Soldier.* Washington, D.C.: Government Printing Office, 1862. Reprinted as *1862 Manual for Army Cooking.* Norristown, Pa.: Norristown Press, 1993.

Secretary of the Interior. *Population of the United States in 1860: The Eighth Census.* Washington, D.C.: Government Printing Office, 1864.

———. *Manufactures of the United States in 1860: The Eighth Census.* Washington, D.C.: Government Printing Office, 1865.

———. *Statistics of the United States in 1860: The Eighth Census.* Washington, D.C.: Government Printing Office, 1866.

Secretary of the Navy. *Report of the Secretary of the Navy with an Appendix Containing Reports from Officers. December, 1861.* Washington, D.C.: Government Printing Office, 1861.

———. *Report of the Secretary of the Navy with an Appendix Containing Reports from Officers. December, 1862.* Washington, D.C.: Government Printing Office, 1863.

———. *Report of the Secretary of the Navy with an Appendix Containing Reports from Officers. December, 1863.* Washington, D.C.: Government Printing Office, 1863.

———. *Report of the Secretary of the Navy with an Appendix Containing Reports from Officers. December, 1864.* Washington, D.C.: Government Printing Office, 1864.

———. *Report of the Secretary of the Navy with an Appendix Containing Reports from Officers. December, 1865.* Washington, D.C.: Government Printing Office, 1865.

Statutes at Large and Treaties of the United States of America. Vol. 9, *December 1, 1845, to March 3, 1851.* Edited by George Minot. Boston: Little, Brown, 1851.

Statutes at Large and Treaties of the United States of America. Vol. 10, *December 1, 1851, to March 3, 1855.* Edited by George Minot. Boston: Little, Brown, 1855.

Statutes at Large. 37th Cong., 1st sess., 1861. Edited by George P. Sanger. Boston: Little, Brown, 1861.

Statutes at Large, 37th Cong., 2nd sess., 1861–1862. Edited by George P. Sanger. Boston: Little, Brown, 1862.

Statutes at Large, 37th Cong., 3rd sess., 1862–1863. Edited by George P. Sanger. Boston: Little, Brown, 1863.

Statutes at Large, 38th Cong., 1st sess., 1863–1864. Edited by George P. Sanger. Boston: Little, Brown, 1864.

Statutes at Large, 38th Cong., 2nd sess., 1864–1865. Edited by George P. Sanger. Boston: Little, Brown, 1865.

Statutes at Large, 51st Cong., 1st sess., 1889–1890. Washington, D.C.: Government Printing Office, 1890.

U.S. Army Center of Military History. *American Military History.* Rev. ed. Washington, D.C.: Government Printing Office, 1988.

U.S. Congress. *Congressional Globe.* 1st sess. Vol. 21, part 2, *1850.* Edited by John C. Rives. Washington, D.C.: John C. Rives, 1850.

——. House. *Number of Vessels in the Navy.* H. Ex. Doc. 159, 40th Cong., 2nd sess., *1868.*

U.S. Department of Commerce. *Historical Statistics of the United States, Colonial Times to 1970.* Part 1. Washington, D.C.: Government Printing Office, 1976.

U.S. Department of Navy. Bureau of Medicine and Surgery. *The Dental Corps of the United States Navy.* Washington, D.C.: Government Printing Office, 1962.

——. *Medal of Honor, 1861–1949.* Washington, D.C.: U.S. Navy, 1952.

——. *Naval Education and Training Program, Management Support Activity: Principles of Naval Engineering.* Washington, D.C.: Government Printing Office, 1992.

——. *Ordnance Instructions of the United States Navy.* Washington, D.C.: Government Printing Office, 1864.

——. "Physiological Heat Exposure Limits (PHEL)." *OPNAVINST 5100.20C.* Washington, D.C.: Government Printing Office, 5 March 1985.

——. *Register of the Commissioned and Warrant Officers of the Navy of the United States Including Officers of the Marine Corps.* Washington, D.C.: Government Printing Office, 1861–65.

——. *Regulations for the Government of the United States Navy, 1865.* Washington, D.C.: Government Printing Office, 1865.

——. *Regulations for the Uniform and Dress of the Navy and Marine Corps of the United States.* Philadelphia: Lippincott, Grambo and Company, 1852.

——. "Regulations for the Uniform of the Navy of the United States, 28 January 1864." In *Illustrated Catalog of Civil War Military Goods: Union Weapons, Insignia, Uniform Accessories and Other Equipment,* edited by Schuyler, Hartley & Graham. 1864. Reprint with slight alterations, New York: Dover, 1985.

——. *Uniforms for the United States Navy, Prepared under the Direction of the Secretary of the Navy.* Washington, D.C.: Government Printing Office, 1869.

——. *Uniform Regulations.* New York: Tome, Melvain and Company, 1864.

——. Naval History Division. *Civil War Naval Chronology, 1861–1865.* Washington, D.C.: Government Printing Office, 1971.

——. *Dictionary of American Naval Fighting Ships.* Vols. 1–8. Washington, D.C.: Government Printing Office, 1959–81.

——. *Uniforms of the United States Navy, 1776–1898.* Washington, D.C.: Naval History Division, Office of the Chief of Naval Operations, 1966.

U.S. Postal Service. *We Deliver: The Story of the U.S. Postal Service.* Washington, D.C.: Government Printing Office, 1986.

U.S. Surgeon General's Office. *The Medical and Surgical History of the War of the Rebellion.* Washington, D.C.: Government Printing Office, 1870–88.

U.S. War Department. *The Medical and Surgical History of the War of the Rebellion.* 6 vols. Washington, D.C.: Government Printing Office, 1870–83.

——. *Revised Regulations for the Army of the United States, 1861.* Philadelphia: J. G. L. Brown, Printer. Reprinted by the National Historical Society, Harrisburg, Pa., 1980.

——. *The War of the Rebellion: A Compilation of the Official Records of the War of the Union and Confederate Armies.* 128 vols. Washington, D.C.: Government Printing Office, 1880–1901.

Newspapers and Periodicals

American Heritage
Boston Daily Journal
Century Illustrated Monthly
Civil War History, A Journal of the Middle Period
Continental Monthly
Detroit Free Press
Harper's Weekly
Journal of Military History
Journal of Negro History
Journal of the National Geographic Society
Naval War College Review
New York Times
Nursing History Review
Sailor's Magazine
Times (London)
U.S. Naval Institute *Proceedings*

Printed Primary Sources

Anonymous, "Life on a Blockader," *Continental Monthly* 6 (August 1864): 46–55.

Badlam, William H. *Kearsarge and Alabama.* Providence: Providence Press, Snow and Farnkam Printers, 1884.

Beyer, W. F., and O. F. Keydel. *Acts of Bravery: Deeds of Extraordinary American Heroism, from the Personal Records and Reminiscences of the Courageous Americans Who Risked Everything for Their Comrades and Country.* 1903. Reprint, Stanford, Conn.: Longmeadow Press, 1994.

Billings, John D. *Hardtack and Coffee or the Unwritten Story of Army Life.* 1887. Reprint, Williamstown, Ma.: Corner House, 1987.

Blanding, Stephan F. *Recollections of a Sailor Boy on the Cruise of the Gunboat "Louisiana."* Providence, R.I.: E. A. Johnson., 1886.

Boyer, Samuel Pellem. *Naval Surgeon: Blockading the South, 1862–1866.* Edited by Elinor Barnes and James A. Barnes. Bloomington: Indiana University Press, 1963.

Browne, Henry R., and Symmes E. Browne. *From the Fresh Water Navy, 1861–1864: The Letters of Acting Master's Mate Henry R. Browne and Acting Ensign Symmes E. Browne.* Edited by John D. Milligan. Annapolis, Md.: Naval Institute Press, 1970.

Browne, John M. "The Duel between the *Alabama* and the *Kearsarge.*" In *Battles and Leaders of the Civil War,* ed. Robert Underwood Johnson and Clarence Clough Buel, vol. 4, pp. 615–25. New York: Castle Books, 1956.

Cornelius, George, ed. "What Did Farragut See?" Edmund Horace Stevens Letter to Family Members. *Naval History* (August 1994): 11–17.

Curtis, O. B. *History of the Twenty-Fourth Michigan Regiment of the Iron Brigade.* Detroit: Winn and Hammond, 1891.

Dewey, George. *Autobiography of George Dewey, Admiral of the Navy.* New York: Charles Scribner's Sons, 1913.

Dunglison, Robley. *Medical Lexicon: A Dictionary of Medical Science.* Philadelphia: Blanchard and Lea, 1865.

Du Pont, Samuel Francis. *Samuel Francis Du Pont: Selections from His Civil War Letters.* 3 vols. Edited by John D. Hays. Ithaca, N.Y.: Cornell University Press, 1969.

Evans, Robert D. *A Sailor's Log: Recollections of Forty Years of Naval Life.* London: Smith, Elder, 1901.

Greene, Dana. "In the *Monitor* Turret." In *Battles and Leaders of the Civil War,* ed. Robert Underwood Johnson and Clarence Clough Buel, vol. 1, pp. 722–27. New York: Castle Books, 1956.

Gross, Samuel D. *A Manual of Military Surgery.* 2nd ed. Philadelphia: J. B. Lippincott, 1862.

Guernsey, Thomas. *Homeopathic Domestic Practice.* London: Turnee, 1861.

Hamilton, Frank Hastings. *A Practical Treatise on Military Surgery.* New York: Bailliere Brothers, 1861.

————. *A Treatise on Military Surgery and Hygiene.* New York: Bailliere Brothers, 1865.

Hanford, Franklin. "How I Entered the Navy." U.S. Naval Institute *Proceedings* 91 (June 1965): 75–87.

Haughton, Phyllis H., ed. *Dearest Carrie: Civil War Letters Home.* Lawrenceville, Ohio: Brunswick, 1995.

Holden, Edgar. "The *Albemarle* and the *Sassacus.*" In *Battles and Leaders of the Civil War,* ed. Robert Underwood Johnson and Clarence Clough Buel, vol. 4, pp. 630–32. New York: Castle Books, 1956.

Hudgins, Robert S. *Reflections of an Old Dominion Dragoon: The Civil War Experiences of Sgt. Robert S. Hudgins II, Company B, 3rd Virginia Cavalry.* Orange, Va.: Publisher's Press, 1993.

Hunter, Alvah Folsom. *A Year on a "Monitor" and the Destruction of Fort Sumter.* Edited by Craig Symonds. Columbia: University of South Carolina Press, 1987.

Isherwood, B. F. *Experimental Research in Steam Engineering.* Vol. 1. Philadelphia: William Hamilton, Hall of the Franklin Institute, 1863.

Keeler, William Frederick. *Aboard the USS "Florida," 1863–1864: The Letters of Acting Paymaster William Frederick Keeler, U.S. Navy, to His Wife, Anna.* Edited by Robert W. Daly. Annapolis, Md.: Naval Institute Press, 1968.

————. *Aboard the USS "Monitor," 1862: The Letters of Acting Paymaster William Frederick Keeler, U.S. Navy, to His Wife, Anna.* Edited by Robert W. Daly. Annapolis, Md.: Naval Institute Press, 1964.

Kinney, John Coddington. "Farragut at Mobile Bay." In *Battles and Leaders of the Civil War,* ed. Robert Underwood Johnson and Clarence Clough Buel, vol. 4, pp. 379–400. New York: Castle Books, 1956.

Kirkland, Frazer. *Anecdotes and Incidents of the War of the Rebellion.* Hartford, Conn.: Hartford Publishing, 1866.

Lauderdale, John Vance. *The Wounded River: The Civil War Letters of John Vance Lauderdale, M.D.* Edited by Peter Joseph. East Lansing: Michigan State University Press, 1993.

Levy, Uriah Phillips. *Manual of Rules for Men-of-War.* New York: D. Van Nostrand, 1862.

Lloyd, Christopher, ed. *The Health of Seamen: Selections from the Works of Dr. James Lind, Sir Gilbert Blane and Dr. Thomas Trotter.* London: Navy Records Society, 1965.

Luce, Stephan B. *Life and Letters of Rear Admiral Stephan B. Luce, U.S. Navy.* Edited by Albert Gleaves. New York: G. P. Putnam's Sons, 1925.

Marchand, John B. *Charleston Blockade: The Journals of John B. Marchand, U.S. Navy 1861–1862.* Edited by Craig L. Symonds. Newport, R.I.: Naval War College Press, 1976.

Plumb, Robert J., ed. "'Yankee Paymaster': Journal of Richard French Goodman." U.S. Naval Institute *Proceedings* 103 (October 1977): 51–57.

Robertson, J., ed. *Michigan in the War.* Lansing, Mich.: W. S. George, 1882.

Roe, F. A. *Naval Duties and Discipline with the Policy and Principles of Naval Organization.* New York: D. Van Nostrand, 1865.

Schley, Winfield Scott. *Forty-Five Years under the Flag.* New York: D. Appleton, 1904.

Schuyler, Hartley & Graham. *Illustrated Catalog of Civil War Military Goods: Union Weapons, Insignia, Uniform Accessories and Other Equipment.* 1864. Reprint with slight alterations, New York: Dover, 1985.

Selfridge, Thomas O. *What Finer Tradition: The Memoirs of Thomas O. Selfridge, Jr., Rear Admiral, U.S.N.* Columbia: University of South Carolina Press, 1987.

———. "The Navy at Fort Fisher." In *Battles and Leaders of the Civil War,* ed. Robert Underwood Johnson and Clarence Clough Buel, vol. 4, pp. 658–60. New York: Castle Books, 1956.

Stedman, Charles Ellery. *The Civil War Sketchbook of Charles Ellery Stedman, Surgeon, United States Navy.* Edited by Jim Dan Hill. San Rafael, Calif.: Presidio Press, 1976.

Underwood, George C. *History of the Twenty-Sixth Regiment of the North Carolina Troops in the Great War 1861–1865.* Reprint, Wendell, N.C.: Bradfoot's Bookmark, 1978.

Walke, Henry. "The Western Flotilla at Fort Donelson, Island Number Ten, Fort Pillow and Memphis." In *Battles and Leaders of the Civil War,* ed. Robert Underwood Johnson and Clarence Clough Buel, vol. 1, pp. 430–51. New York: Castle Books, 1956.

Welles, Gideon. *Diary of Gideon Welles.* 3 vols. Edited by Howard K. Beale. New York: W. W. Norton, 1960.

Wilkes, Charles. *Autobiography of Rear Admiral Charles Wilkes, U.S. Navy, 1798–1877.* Edited by William James Morgan et al. Washington, D.C.: U.S. Department of Navy, Naval History Division, 1978.

Secondary Sources

Books—General Accounts

Adams, George W. *Doctors in Blue: The Medical History of the Union Army in the Civil War.* 1952. Reprint, Dayton, Ohio: Morningside Press, 1985.

Allston, Frank J. *Ready for Sea.* Annapolis, Md.: Naval Institute Press, 1995.

Almanac of Naval Facts. Menasha, Wash.: George Bants, 1964.

Anderson, Bern. *By Sea and River: The Naval History of the Civil War.* New York: Alfred A. Knopf, 1962.

Aptheker, Herbert. *Negro Casualties in the Civil War.* Washington, D.C.: Association for the Study of Negro Life and History, 1945.

Beach, Edward L. *The United States Navy: Two Hundred Years.* New York: Holt, 1986.

Bearss, Edwin C. *River of Lost Opportunities: The Civil War on the James River, 1861–1862.* Lynchburg, Va: H. E. Howard, 1995.

———. *Hardluck Ironclad: The Sinking and Salvage of the "Cairo."* Rev. ed. Baton Rouge: Louisiana State University, 1980.

Beller, Susan P. *Medical Practices in the Civil War.* Cincinnati: Betterway Books, 1992.

Beringer, Richard E., Herman Hattaway, Archer Jones, and William N. Still Jr. *Why the South Lost the Civil War.* Athens, Ga.: University of Georgia Press, 1986.

Besse, Summer B. *C.S. Ironclad "Virginia" and U.S. Ironclad "Monitor."* 1937. Reprint, New Port News, Va.: Mariners Museum, 1978.

Billings-Yun, Melanie, et al., eds. *Above and Beyond: A History of Honor from the Civil War to Vietnam.* Boston: Boston Publishing, 1985.

Blank, David A., Arthur E. Bock, and David J. Richardson, eds. *Introduction to Naval Engineering.* 2nd ed. Annapolis, Md.: Naval Institute Press, 1985.

Boatner, Mark M., III. *The Civil War Dictionary.* New York: Vintage Books, 1991.

Bolster, W. Jeffrey. *Black Jacks: African American Seamen in the Age of Sail.* Cambridge: Harvard University Press, 1997.

Bradford, Gershom. *A Glossary of Sea Terms.* New York: Dodd, Mead, 1946.

Browning, Robert M. *From Cape Charles to Cape Fear: The North Atlantic Blockading Squadron during the Civil War.* Tuscaloosa: University of Alabama Press, 1993.

Byrne, Edward M. *Military Law.* 3d ed. Annapolis, Md.: Naval Institute Press, 1981.

Cartwright, Frederick F., and Michael D. Biddiss. *Disease and History.* New York: Dorset Press, 1972.

Collins, Johnny. *Shanties and Songs of the Sea.* London: Patterdale Music, 1996.

Coggins, Jack. *Arms and Equipment of the Civil War.* New York: Fairfax Press, 1983.

Coombe, Jack D. *Thunder Along the Mississippi: The River Battles That Split the Confederacy.* New York: Sarpedon, 1996.

Cushing, Marshall H. *The Story of Our Post Office: The Greatest Government Department in All Its Phases.* Boston: A. M. Thayer, 1893.

Dammann, Gordon. *Pictorial Encyclopedia of Civil War Medical Instruments and Equipment.* 2 vols. Missoula, Mont.: Pictorial Histories Publishing, 1987.

Davis, William C. *Duel between the First Ironclads.* Baton Rouge: Louisiana State Press, 1975.

Dickson, Paul. *War Slang, Fighting Words and Phrases of Americans, from the Civil War to the Gulf War.* New York: Pocket Books, 1994.

Dodge, Ernest Stanley, ed. *Thirty Years of the "American Neptune."* Cambridge: Harvard University Press, 1972.

Dyer, Frederick H. *A Compendium of the War of the Rebellion.* New York: Thomas Yoseloff, 1959.

Faust, Patricia L. *Historical Times Illustrated Encyclopedia of the Civil War.* New York: Harper and Row, 1986.

Fox, William F. *Regimental Losses in the American Civil War.* Albany: Albany Publishing, 1889.

Futch, Ovid L. *History of Andersonville Prison.* Gainesville: University of Florida Press, 1968.

Gabriel, Richard A. *A History of Military Medicine.* New York: Greenwood Press, 1992.

Gardiner, Robert. *The Advent of Steam: The Merchant Steamship before 1900.* London: Conway Maritime Press, 1993.

Gibson, Charles D., and E. Kay Gibson. *Assault and Logistics: Union Army Coastal and River Operations, 1861–1866.* Camden, Maine: Ensign Press, 1995.

Gihon, Albert Leary. *Practical Suggestions in Naval Hygiene.* Washington, D.C.: Government Printing Office, 1871.

Giscard d' Estaing, Valerie-Anne. *The World Almanac Book of Inventions.* New York: World Almanac Publications, 1985.

Gordon, Maurice Bear. *Naval and Maritime Medicine during the American Revolution.* Ventnor, N.J.: Ventnor Publishers, 1970.

Gosnell, H. Allen. *Guns on the Western Waters: The Story of the River Gunboats in the Civil War.* Baton Rouge: Louisiana State University Press, 1949.

Gragg, Rod. *Confederate Goliath: The Battle of Fort Fisher.* New York: Harper Perennial, 1991.

Haeger, Knut. *The History of Surgery.* New York: Bell Publishing, 1988.

Harrod, Frederick S. *Manning the New Navy: The Development of a Modern Naval Enlisted Force, 1899–1940.* Westport, Conn.: Greenwood Press, 1978.

Hattaway, Herman, and Archer Jones. *How the North Won.* Urbana and Chicago: University of Illinois Press, 1983.

Hearn, Chester G. *The Capture of New Orleans, 1862.* Baton Rouge: Louisiana State University Press, 1995.

Hoehling, A. A. *Thunder at Hampton Roads.* Englewood Cliffs, N.J., 1976. Reprint, New York: Da Capo Press, 1993.

Hutson, John A. *The Sinews of War: Logistics, 1775–1956.* Washington, D.C.: Office of the Chief of Military History, 1966.

Jackson, Donald Dale. *Twenty Million Yankees: The Northern Home Front.* Alexandria, Va.: Time-Life Books, 1985.

Jane, Fred T. *All the World's Fighting Ships.* Boston: Little, Brown, 1889.

Karsten, Peter. *The Naval Aristocracy: The Golden Age of Annapolis and the Emergence of Modern Navalism.* New York: Free Press, 1972.

Keenan, Joseph H., and Frederick G. Keyes. *Thermodynamic Properties of Steam.* New York: John Wiley and Sons, 1936.

Keevil, John J. *Medicine and the Navy, 1200–1900.* Edinburgh: E. and S. Livingstone, 1957–63.

Lambert, Andrew. *Warrior: The World's First Ironclad Then and Now.* Annapolis, Md.: Naval Institute Press, 1987.

———, ed. *Steam, Steel and Shellfire: The Warships, 1840–1905.* Conway's History of the Ship Series. Annapolis, Md.: Naval Institute Press, 1992.

Langley, Harold D. *Social Reform in the United States Navy, 1798–1862.* Chicago: University of Illinois Press, 1967.

———. *A History of Medicine in the Early U.S. Navy.* Baltimore: Johns Hopkins University Press, 1995.

Lewis, Charles Lee. *David Glasgow Farragut, Our First Admiral.* Annapolis, Md.: Naval Institute Press, 1943.

Long, E. B., and Barbara Long. *The Civil War Day by Day: An Almanac, 1861–1865.* New York: Doubleday, 1971.

Lonn, Ella. *Foreigners in the Union Army and Navy.* Baton Rouge: Louisiana State University Press, 1951.

Lord, Francis A. *They Fought for the Union*. New York: Bonanza Books, 1960.

———. *Civil War Collector's Encyclopedia*. 1963. Reprint, Secaucus, N.J.: Castle, 1982.

———. *Civil War Collector's Encyclopedia*. Vols. 3, 4, and 5. 1963. Reprint, Edison, N.J.: Blue and Gray Press, 1995.

Lott, Arnold, Joseph D. Harrington, John L. Greene, and Betty Winspear. *Almanac of Naval Facts*. Annapolis, Md.: Naval Institute Press, 1964.

MacGregor, Morris J., Jr. *Integration of the Armed Forces, 1940–1965*. Washington, D.C.: U.S. Army, Center of Military History, 1981.

Mack, William P., and Connell, Royal W. *Naval Ceremonies, Customs, and Traditions*. 5th ed. Annapolis, Md.: Naval Institute Press, 1980.

Martin, Christopher. *Damn the Torpedoes! The Story of America's First Admiral, David Glasgow Farragut*. New York: Abelard-Schuman, 1970.

Marvel, William. *The "Alabama" and "Kearsarge."* Chapel Hill: University of North Carolina Press, 1996.

———. *Andersonville: The Last Depot*. Chapel Hill: University of North Carolina Press, 1994.

McElroy, John. *Andersonville: A Story of a Rebel Military Prison*. Toledo, Ohio: D. R. Locke, 1879.

McPherson, James M. *Battle Cry of Freedom: The Civil War Era*. Oxford: Oxford University Press, 1988.

Mescher, Virginia. *Dates of Selected Inventions and Occurrences during the Latter Part of the Eighteenth Century and during the Nineteenth Century*. Burke, Va.: Virginia Mescher and Nature's Finest, 1994.

Miller, Edward A., Jr. *Gullah Statesman: Robert Smalls from Slavery to Congress, 1839–1915*. Columbia: University of South Carolina Press, 1995.

Miller, Edward M. *U.S.S. "Monitor": The Ship That Launched a Modern Navy*. Annapolis, Md.: Leeward Publications, 1978.

Miller, Edward S. *Civil War Sea Battles, Seafights and Shipwrecks in the War between the States*. Conshohocken, Pa.: Combined Books, 1995.

Miller, Francis T. *Photographic History of the Civil War: The Navies*. 1911. Reprint, New York: Castle Books, 1957.

Milligan, John D. *Gunboats Down the Mississippi*. Annapolis, Md.: Naval Institute Press, 1963.

Mitchell, Joseph B. *The Badge of Gallantry*. New York: Macmillan, 1966.

Mitchell, Wesley C. *A History of the Greenbacks*. Chicago: University of Chicago Press, 1903.

Mosby's Medical, Nursing, and Allied Health Dictionary. 4th ed. St. Louis: Mosby Year Book, 1994.

Murdock, Eugene C. *One Million Men: The Civil War Draft in the North*. Madison: State Historical Society of Wisconsin, 1971.

Musicant, Ivan. *Divided Water: The Naval History of the Civil War*. New York: Harper Collins, 1995.

Noel, John V., Jr. *Naval Terms Dictionary*. Princeton: Van Nostrand, 1957.

O'Brien, Patrick. *The Economic Effects of the American Civil War*. Atlantic Highlands, N.J.: Humanities Press International, 1989.

Owsley, Frank L. *The C.S.S. "Florida": Her Building and Operation*. Tuscaloosa: University of Alabama Press, 1965.

Peake, Nigel, ed. *The Warrior.* Portsmouth, England: Portsmouth Publishing and Printing, 1987.

Pratt, Fletcher. *Civil War on the Western Waters.* New York: Holt, 1956.

Pryor, James C. *Naval Hygiene.* Philadelphia: P. Blakiston's Son, 1918.

Quarles, Benjamin. *The Negro in the Civil War.* Boston: Little Brown, 1953.

———. *The Negro in the American Revolution.* New York: W. W. Norton, 1961.

Randall, J. G., and David Donald. *The Civil War and Reconstruction.* Lexington, Mass.: D. C. Heath and Company, 1969.

Rankin, Robert H. *Uniforms of the Sea Service.* Annapolis, Md.: Naval Institute Press, 1962.

———. *Small Arms of the Sea Service.* New Milford, Conn.: N. Flayderman, 1972.

Rasor, Eugene L. *Reform in the Royal Navy: A Social History of the Lower Deck, 1850–1880.* Hamden, Conn.: Archer Books, 1976.

Reilly, John C., Jr. *The Iron Guns of Willard Park, Washington Navy Yard.* Washington, D.C.: National Historical Center, 1991.

Robertson, James I., Jr. *Soldiers Blue and Gray.* Columbia: University of South Carolina Press, 1988.

Roddis, Louis H. *A Short History of Nautical Medicine.* New York: P. B. Hoeber, 1941.

Rothman, David J. *The Discovery of the Asylum: Social Order and Disorder in the New Republic.* Boston: Little, Brown, 1990.

Salecker, Gene E. *Disaster on the Mississippi: The "Sultana" Explosion, April 27, 1865.* Annapolis, Md.: Naval Institute Press, 1996.

Scherer, Jeanne C., ed. *Lippincott's Nurses' Drug Manual.* Philadelphia: J. B. Lippincott, 1985.

Silverstone, Paul H. *Warships of the Civil War Navies.* Annapolis, Md.: Naval Institute Press, 1989.

Simons, Gerald, ed. *The Blockade: Runners and Raiders.* Alexandria, Va.: Time-Life Books, 1983.

Sloan, Edward William, III. *Benjamin Franklin Isherwood, Naval Engineer: The Years as Engineer in Chief, 1861–1869.* Annapolis, Md.: Naval Institute Press, 1965.

Still, William N., Jr. *Ironclad Captains: The Commanding Officers of the USS "Monitor."* Washington, D.C.: U.S. Department of Commerce, National Oceanic and Atmospheric Administration, Marine and Estuarine Management Division, 1988.

Stiner, Paul E. *Disease in the Civil War: Natural Biological Warfare in 1861–1865.* Springfield, Ill.: C. C. Thomas, 1968.

Stivers, Reuben Elmore. *Privates and Privateers: The Men and Women of Our Reserve Naval Forces, 1766 to 1866.* Annapolis, Md.: Naval Institute Press, 1975.

Straus, Robert. *Medical Care for Seamen: The Origin of Public Health Service in the United States.* New Haven: Yale University Press, 1950.

Sweetman, Jack. *American Naval History: An Illustrated Chronology of the U.S. Navy and Marine Corps, 1775–Present.* 2nd ed. Annapolis, Md.: Naval Institute Press, 1991.

Tannahill, Reay. *Food in History.* New York: Crown Publishers, 1988.

Thomas, Clayton L., ed. *Taber's Cyclopedic Medical Dictionary.* 15th ed. Philadelphia: F. A. Davis, 1985.

Todd, Frederick P. *American Military Equipage, 1851–1872.* New York: Charles Scribner's Sons, 1980.

Trotter, William R. *Ironclads and Columbiads: The Civil War in North Carolina—The Coast.* Winston-Salem, N.C.: John F. Blair, 1989.

Tucker, Spencer. *Arming the Fleet: U.S. Navy Ordnance in the Muzzle Loading-Era.* Annapolis, Md.: Naval Institute Press, 1989.

U.S. Naval Academy. Department of Law and Leadership. *Naval Law.* Dubuque, Iowa: Kendall/Hunt Publishing , 1995.

U.S. Naval Institute. *The Book of Navy Songs.* Annapolis, Md.: Naval Institute Press, 1955.

Valle, James E. *Rocks and Shoals: Naval Discipline in the Age of Fighting Sail.* Annapolis, Md.: Naval Institute Press, 1996.

Valuska, David Lawrence. "The Negro in the Union Navy, 1861–1865." Ph.D. diss., Lehigh University, 1973.

Victory Music. *Victory Sings at Sea.* Bonney Lake, Wa.: Victory Music, 1989.

————. *Victory Sings at Sea: The Curse of the Somers.* Bonney Lake, WA: Victory Music, 1995.

Vinovskis, Maris A., ed. *Toward a Social History of the American Civil War: Exploratory Essays.* Cambridge: Cambridge University Press, 1991.

Vlahos, Michael E. "The Making of an American Style." In *Naval Engineering and American Seapower,* ed. Randolph W. King, pp. 3–19. Baltimore: Nautical and Aviation, 1989.

Walter, Francis X. *The Naval Battle of Mobile Bay, August 5, 1864, and Franklin Buchanan of the "Tennessee."* Birmingham, Ala.: Prester Meridian Press, 1993.

Walters, Ronald G. *American Reformers, 1815–1860.* New York: Hill and Wang, 1978.

White, William C., and Ruth White. *Tin Can on a Shingle.* New York: Dutton, 1957.

Wilbur, Keith C. *Pirates and Patriots of the Revolution: An Illustrated Encyclopedia of Colonial Seamanship.* Old Saybrook, Conn.: Globe Pequot Press, 1984.

Wiley, Bell, I. *The Life of Billy Yank: The Common Soldier of the Union.* New York: Doubleday, 1971.

Woodhead, Henry. *Echoes of Glory: Arms and Equipment of the Union.* Alexandria, Va.: Time-Life Books,1991.

Journal Articles

Apt, Benjamin L. "Mahan's Forebears: The Debate over Maritime Strategy, 1868–1883." *Naval War College Review* 5 (summer 1997): 86–111.

Boeger, Palmer H. "Hardtack and Burnt Beans." *Civil War History* 4 (1958): 73–92.

Daly, Robert W. "Pay and Prize Money in the Old Navy, 1776–1899." U.S. Naval Institute *Proceedings* 74 (August 1948): 967–72.

Guerout, Max. "C.S.S. *Alabama.*" *Journal of the National Geographic Society* 186 (December 1994): 67–83.

Hyde, Nina. "Fabric of History: Wool." *Journal of the National Geographic Society* 173 (May 1988): 552–91.

Kaeuper, Richard W. "The Forgotten Triumph of the Paw Paw." *American Heritage* 46 (October 1995): 86–94.

Kushlan, James P., ed. "Torpedoes." *Civil War Times Illustrated* 36 (August 1997): 47–49.

Lathrop, Constance. "Grog: Its Origin and Use in the United States Navy." U.S. Naval Institute *Proceedings* 61 (March 1935): 377–380.

Margreiter, John L. "Anesthesia in the Civil War," *Civil War Times Illustrated* 6 (May 1967): 22–27.

Mayers, Adam. "Stolen Soldiers." *Civil War Times Illustrated* 34 (June 1995): 56–59.

Merrill, James M. "Men, Monotony, and Mouldy Beans: Life on Board Civil War Blockaders." In *Thirty Years of the "American Neptune,"* pp. 195–205. Cambridge: Harvard University Press, 1972.

Riggs, David F. "Sailors of the U.S.S. *Cairo:* Anatomy of a Gunboat Crew." *Civil War History* 28 (September 1982): 266–73.

Schneller, Robert J., Jr. "A Littoral Frustration: The Union Navy and the Siege of Charleston, 1863–1865." *Naval War College Review* 49 (winter 1996): 38–60.

Swift, Lester L. "Letters From a Sailor on a Tinclad." *Civil War History* (March 1961): 48–62.

Still, William N., Jr. "Technology Afloat." *Civil War Times Illustrated* 14 (November 1975): 4–10, 40–47.

————. "The Common Sailor." Part 1, "The Yankee Blue Jackets." *Civil War Times Illustrated* 23 (February 1985): 24–39.

Stokesberry, James. "USS *Tecumseh:* Treasure in Mobile Bay." U.S. Naval Institute *Proceedings* 94 (August 1968): 147–49.

Thompson, Edgar K. "The U.S. Monitor *Patapsco."* U.S. Naval Institute *Proceedings* 94 (December 1968): 148–49.

Thompson, Jon. "Cotton: King of Fibers." *Journal of the National Geographic Society* 185 (June 1994): 60–87.

Wall, Barbara Mann. "Grace Under Pressure: The Nursing Sisters of the Holy Cross, 1861–1865." *Nursing History Review* 1 (1993): 71–88.

Newspaper Articles

Allen, Kurt. "Navy Uniforms." *Dolphin,* 2 February 1995, 16–18.

"Military Turkeys Do Tasty Duty Overseas." *Detroit Free Press,* 24 November 1996, F7.

"Yellow Fever Is on Rise Again in Africa." *Detroit Free Press,* 9 October 1996, 5A.

Index

Princeton, USS, 8; overpowering stench on, 50

prisoners of war, 142–44; black sailors and white officers as, 143; Confederate, 23

prize money: for enemy vessels, 97–98; enlistment, 10, 15; hazards associated with earning, 98–99

promotion to next rating, 94, 96; standardizing, 96

Property, CSS, 98

quarter bill, 33–34

quartermaster of the watch, 54

Queen of the East, 100

quinine, malaria and, 117

quota system, black enlistment, 12

racial integration, practicality of, 148

racism, ship-board, 14–15

Radford, William, 23

rammers, 61

Ransom, George M., 43

rats, 39

receiving ships, 26–27; daily activity aboard, 27–28; thievery on, 28

recruitment, Union naval, 10–25; army bonuses and, 21; army transfers, 22–23; civilian agencies, 14, 16–17, 19–20; competition with army and, 13, 18; Confederate prisoners, 23; demographics of, 24–25; engineers, skilled, 8; foreign soldiers, 16–17; merchant marine transfers, 10–11; National Forces Act and, 20–22; newspaper advertising for, 18, 19; posters, 18–19, photo section; prize money, 10

Red Rover, USS, 111

reform, naval, 2–3; religious, 3–4

religious services, on-board, 42, 43, 88–91, photo 7; daily, 89; funerals, 89–91; Sunday, 88–89

Remington navy revolver, 60

rendezvous stations, 18; North Street (New York City), 20; shipping article signing, 26

revolvers, 60

Rhode Island, USS, 19

Richards, Lewis, 137

rifled cannon, 59

rifled muskets, 58

rifles, breech-loading, 58

riots during liberty, 87–88

river boats, 37, photo 15

roaches, 39

Roanoke, 8

Rocks and Shoals, 101

Roebuck, USS, 116

Ronckendorf, William, 57–58

Rosencrans, William, 114

roving security, 54

rowing regatta, 85

Rules for the Regulation of the Navy of the United Colonies, 101

runaway slaves: competition with Army over, 13; liberty entertainment and, 86–87; policy on, 13; recruitment of, 11, 12–14; supplying provisions to Union navy, 75–76; trading supplies with river squadrons, 66; wage limits on, 12–13

running aground, 140

Rush, Benjamin, 5

Sabina, USS, 90

sail- and steam-powered warship, 7

sailor's collar, 30

Sailor's Magazine and Naval Journal, 3; library on *Hartford* and, 82; temperance articles in, 5

San Jacinto, 8

Saranac, 8

Sassacus, USS, 138

Saugus, USS, 125

scalding, boiler, 138

schedules: crew, 42; free time, 80; monthly officers', 42; weekly-at-sea, 41–42

scurvy, 109–10; army and, 114; factors for navy cases of, 113–14

seaman: rating, 41; wages of, 92

sea pie, 69

seasickness, 112–13

second-class firemen, 47; wages of, 92

security, roving, 54

Sefridge, Thomas O., 139

Seymour, Charles B., 137

shark attacks on swimmers, 85

Sharps and Hankins breech-loading rifles, 60

shell loaders, 61
Sherman, William T., 146
shipboard routine, 40–56; hazards of, 46–50; holystoning, 45; maintenance, 45–46; ratings, 40–41; Standing Orders, 43–44; weekly-at-sea schedules for, 41–42
shipbuilding program, 7–8
ship design and layout: hammocks, 34; lighting, 37; *Monitors*, 34–37; outhouses, 37; river ironclads, 37; temperature extremes on, 35; toilets, 36–37; torpedo effectiveness and, 129; ventilation in, 35
shipping article signing, 26
ship's purser wages, 6
side tacklemen, 61
Silver Lake, USS, 14
small-caliber weapons, 58–61; inadequate supply of, 59
smallpox, 117–18
Smalls, Robert, 141
Smith, George, 134
Smith, John, 137
Smith, Q. M. William, 94
Smith, William, 137
smooth muskets, 58
Sonoma, USS: pushing boiler limits on, 48–49
Sophronia, USS: laundry lost overboard, 33
sore throats, 122
sound, of large-caliber shell, 133
South Atlantic Blockading Squadron: Charleston Harbor campaign, 130–31; increase in wages on ironclads in, 94; liberty for, 86–87; mail delivery to, 83; manpower shortage, 11; mascots of, 84–85; meals aboard, 74; Sherman's march and, 146; supplies shortages, 68
specialized training, 57
Spencer repeating rifle, 60
"spirit" ration, 3, 4–5. *See also* alcohol; abolishment of, 70–73; racial disharmony and, 14
splinters, battle, 135, 136, 137–38
spongers, 61
St. Mary's Convent (South Bend, Ind.), 111

St. Thomas, West Indies riots, 87–88
Standing Orders, Commanding Officer's, 43–44
station bill, 33–34
steam frigate, wooden, 146–47. *See also* splinters, battle; brig on, 105; coaling of, 51–52; fire room on, 47–48; health of crews on, 125; stench retained in timber of, 50
stenciling clothing for identification, 31
sterilizing agents, naval use of, 110
Stevens, Edmund H., 137
Stringham, Silas, 12
Summer, D. H., 98
Sunday routine, shipboard, 42, 43, 88–89
Supplementary Pension Act of 1864, 99–100
supply distribution system, 65–68; fresh provisions, 64, 66–68; mail processing/delivery, 83; ship tours, 65; shortages, 68; sutler schooners, 72, 86
Susquehanna, 8
sutler schooners, 72, 86
swimming off ships, 85
syphilis, 121–22

tailoring, 32, photo 3
Tecumseh, USS, 128
temperature extremes aboard ship, 35, 37, 48, 50–51
Tennessee, CSS, 136, 137
theatrical groups on board, 82
30th U.S. Colored Regiment, 22
Tibbets (sailor), shark attack on, 85
toilets on ships, 36–37
torpedo. *See* mines, waterborne
training, shipboard, 57–63; cutlasses, 59–60; large-caliber cannon, 61–63; Levy's manual of, 57; marksmanship, 61; small-arms weapons, 58–59, 63
train tacklemen, 61
Treatise of the Scurvy, A, 109
24th Michigan Volunteer Regiment, 128
26th North Carolina Infantry Regiment, 128
Tyler, USS, 39, photo 4; man overboard, 46; mascots on, 85; meals aboard, 74–75

typhoid fever, 118–19
typhus, 118; hygiene and, 110

Uniform Code of Military Justice, 101
uniforms: descriptions of, 29–31; issue,
27; paying for, 28, 29; regulation,
28–29

vaccination, smallpox, 117–18
Vallejo, Jose M., Jr., 66
Valley City, USS, 141
ventilation on board, 35; coal dust and,
123; communicable disease prevention and, 110; excess steam, 48;
mechanical failures and, 49; sailors'
health benefits from, 109
Vernon, Edward, 4
Vicksburg, Miss., 146
Virginia, CSS, 22, 58, 70, 79, 146; *vs.*
design of USS *Monitor,* 130; song written about sinking *Cumberland,* 82
voting at sea, 83

Wabash, USS, 8; increase in pay rating
for engineers on, 94; mascot on,
84–85
Wachusetts, USS, 48–49; engineering
performance of, 53–54; extreme
temperatures on, 50; liberty *vs.* operational commitments for, 88; seasickness on, 113
wages: advances on, 93; allotment system of, 93; *vs.* civilian labor force, 92;
increases in lieu of "spirit" ration, 5,
94; low, enlistments and, 6; monthly
pay for enlisted men (1864), 95;
raises in, 93–94, 101; ship's purser, 6
Wamsutta, USS, 119
war, engagement in, 126–44. *See also*
Mobile Bay; Peninsula Campaign;
ammunition size and, 131–32; boiler
ruptures, 138; casualties, ratio to
wounded, 126–27; deafening noise
of, 132; design of ironclads, 130;
engineers and, 138; Fort Fisher invasion, 138–40; *Galena* at Fort Darling,
133–34; *Kearsarge* and, 135–36; large-
caliber shell sounds and, 133; nighttime, 129–30; prisoners of war, 23,

142–44; sailors' dedication to,
148–49; sinking of *Cumberland,* 132;
slow firing of ironclads, 130–31;
waterborne mines, 127–29; wooden
splinters and, 135
watches, difficulty of, 54–56
water. *See* drinking water
Waverly Magazine, 83
Webster, Harris, 131
Weehawken, USS: capture of CSS *Atlanta*
and, 98; slow firing of, 131
Welles, Gideon, 9; on Conway's heroism, 141; on fresh provisions, 65;
MacDonald Company and, 16–17; on
National Forces Act, 21–22, 23; on
navy omitted from Supplemental
Pension Act of 1864, 100; recruiting
efforts, 11, 12–14; requests for dis-
charge, 77; Sherman's March and,
146; on "torpedoes," 128; on whiskey
consumption during combat, 72–73;
yellow fever report to president, 116
Wertz, Henry, 142–43
Western Gulf Blockading Squadron, 89
Western Waters Naval Forces: man-
power shortage, 11; minesweeping,
127–28; shallow rivers and intestinal
disorders of, 121; supply system and,
66
Whelna, William, 72–73
Whitney navy rifles, 60
Wilder, CSS, 98
Wilkes, Charles, 22
Williams, Peter, 96
Williams, Thomas, 137
William Underwood Company of
Boston, 68
Wilson, Woodrow, 148
Winslow, John, 17, 58; as disciplinarian,
106; on Gouin's death, 136; promo-
tion of Q. M. W. Smith, 94
Wood, William Maxwell, 117, 120
wooden ships. *See* steam frigate, wooden
Worden, John, 70; injured during battle
with CSS *Virginia,* 96

yellow fever, 114–16

Zeta, SS, photo 10

About the Author

Cdr. Dennis J. Ringle, USN (Ret.), is a native of Detroit, Michigan. He graduated from Wayne State University in 1976 with a degree in biology before entering the navy through officers candidate school that September. Ringle also holds masters degrees in business management and history. The navy awarded him a proven specialty in mechanical engineering as a result of his multiple assignments in marine engineering.

Ringle has served at sea as a damage control assistant, main propulsion assistant, chief engineering officer, and executive officer. His career has also included many interesting shore billets: instructor, United States Naval Academy; staff officer for the commander, Surface Forces, Pacific; and executive officer, University of Michigan, NROTC Unit.

Ringle retired from the Navy 1 December 1997, and he is the naval science instructor for Monroe High School NJROTC. He currently resides in Newport, Michigan.